Twenty
TWENTY

Twenty TWENTY

JEWISH VISIONARIES THROUGH
TWO THOUSAND YEARS

Morris B. Margolies

JASON ARONSON INC.
Northvale, New Jersey
Jerusalem

This book was set in 10 pt. Carmina Light by Alpha Graphics of Pittsfield, NH and printed and bound by Book-mart Press, Inc. of North Bergen, NJ.

Library of Congress Cataloging-in-Publication Data
Margolies, Morris B.
    Twenty/twenty : Jewish visionaries through two thousand years / by
  Morris B. Margolies.
       p. cm.
    Includes index.
    ISBN 0–7657–6057–6 (alk. paper)
    1. Jews—Biography. 2. Rabbis—Biography. I. Title. II. Title:
  20/20.
  DS115.M25 2000
  296'.092'2—dc21
  [b]   98–40644

Printed in the United States of America on acid-free paper. For information and catalog write to Jason Aronson Inc., 230 Livingston Street, Northvale, NJ 07647-1726, or visit our website: www.aronson.com

To my beloved friend
Hy Vile
May his memory be ever blessed

CONTENTS

Contents

INTRODUCTION

This book is intended to spark an interest in the history of the Jews. It highlights people, events, ideas, and currents that animated Jewish life over the past twenty centuries. It features one significant person for each of these centuries, the tale of whose life is intertwined with the dynamics of the Jewish society of his time.

The book had its genesis in a series of twenty lectures I delivered some thirty years ago as part of the Institute of Adult Jewish Studies of my congregation in Kansas City. I spoke extemporaneously from carefully prepared notes. The talks were recorded on tape. They were then typed by my secretary and, after some editing by me, were printed locally at the personal expense of the man to whom the present work is dedicated. Several thousand copies came off his presses. Without advertisement of any kind, the supply was exhausted a good many years ago.

Late last year, with the encouragement of Arthur Kurzweil, the moving force of Jason Aronson, Inc., I undertook some necessary editing and revision of the book, whose title then was *The Jew of the Century*. The reader will sense at once the tones and nuances of a book originally presented to listening ears, rather than for reading eyes. It was my decision to retain those tones and nuances because they reflect my attitude toward my subject matter—the Jews and their history. I confess to the role of both partisan and advocate. I am passionate about my subject and, therefore, the present work is not cool or detached. This is not to say, however, that I have been careless with the historical record. Considerable research has gone into every chapter, and I have taken pains not to mislead or mispeak, even while frankly intending to raise the level of interest and excitement in the minds and hearts of the readers.

I learned a long time ago that I cannot write dispassionately. My late and revered mentor, Salo W. Baron, pointed that out to me after he had approved my doctoral dissertation on Samuel David Luzzatto. He thought that my passion for the man and his work was laudable, but that it might have been better had I toned it down. Because of the book's tone, I would surmise, one of its reviewers labeled it "middlebrow." He did not intend it as a compliment, but I was quite pleased to be called "middlebrow," rather than lowbrow, or, even worse, highbrow.

This book, then, is intended for the general reader, not for the professional scholar. If it stimulates some minds and touches some hearts, I shall have achieved my objective, which is to demonstrate how a tiny folk that experienced massive afflictions throughout its history nevertheless managed to survive, and, moreover, to bestow a priceless legacy upon the human race.

The tireless work of Diane Margolies in reading, typing, and computerizing this work has earned my deepest gratitude and admiration.

It is a pleasure to acknowledge the dedicated help and encouragement of my editor, Hope Breeman, as well as the other good people at Jason Aronson.

THE FIRST CENTURY

GAMALIEL OF YAVNEH

The year 70 marked the disastrous end of the four-year battle waged by tiny Judea against mighty Rome. It was a struggle for independence doomed to failure from the outset. Its outcome was the destruction of the Holy Temple in Jerusalem, the loss of hundreds of thousands of Jewish lives, the devastation of the land, and the elimination of the vassal Jewish state as a semi-autonomous political unit within the Roman Empire.

The Jewish people were at a critical crossroads. The question was: Could that people survive with neither political nor military power nor a land to call its own? There was no precedent in the history of the world preceding the year 70 of a demolished nation whose people managed nevertheless to retain its identity, its vitality, and its creative life force.

Indeed, Judea ceased to be the most populous habitat of the Jewish world. The massive dispersion of Jews—diaspora—had begun as far back as 586 B.C.E. with the destruction of Jerusalem's first Holy Temple by the Chaldeans of Babylon. With the destruction of the second, the numbers of Jews in the diaspora swelled to the point of overwhelming the ever-shrinking community of Jews in their ancestral homeland.

Certainly, one of the miraculous feats of the Jewish people was its ability to overcome the formidable odds of wide dispersal and to retain both its religion and its peoplehood down to the present day.

How did they do it? They did it by substituting Torah-craft for statecraft, by building a new foundation for survival, one that was bound to neither physical territory nor political power. It entailed the assumption of a way of life governed by religious law. That law, whose headwaters were the Mosaic teaching of the Pentateuch and whose interpretation was in the hand of the acknowledged sages, flowed like a mighty stream through every conceivable area of human life.

The reconstruction of a landless and powerless people had begun even before the war against Rome had ended. In a little town called Yavneh off the Mediterranean coast, a modest academy of learning had been established. It was to become the rallying point for the survival of Judaism and its adherents. Yavneh retained the essence of the Judaic spirit even as the magnificent Temple built by Herod was going up in flames. Torah was the new flame that was to lead the Jewish people out of the darkness of physical ruination and psychological despair. Yavneh and its sages were the keepers of that flame.

A new course for Jewish survival had been inaugurated in Yavneh. Torah became the highest ideal of Jewry, the bond that compensated for physical frustrations and military debacles, for persecutions and expulsions, for hatred and murder, for homelessness and national impotence.

Yavneh established the rule of Torah-law as the main vehicle for the organization and preservation of the Judaic ethos: Torah-law was henceforth to be co-extensive with life itself. The law embraced Jewish activity from dawn to dusk and from the cradle to the grave. The law was to govern every facet of Jewish life: ethical, ritual, economic, marital, mortuary, organizational, and social. No area of doing, no space for living, no fantasy for dreaming was devoid of the law. Torah-law was to become ubiquitous and for some seventeen centuries all-pervasive.

The instruments for all of this were either forged or revitalized at Yavneh. It was there that the Sanhedrin—the seventy-one-member body vested with legislative, executive, and judicial powers—was given the authority to guide the Jewish people through its post-Temple transition. That so wide-ranging an authority could be voluntarily embraced by the Jewish people was due among other reasons to the most remarkable dynasty of spiritual leadership ever to grace the annals of any people in history. From father to son, generation after generation, and over a period of 400 years, the dynasty of Hillel headed the Sanhedrin. Hillel, a contemporary of Jesus, had been born in Babylonia and had migrated to Judea when quite young to study Torah at the feet of the great rabbis. In due course he had become the greatest of them all and had been chosen to head the Sanhedrin. His title was Nasi, or "the one raised above the people." His son Simon succeeded him after his death. Gamaliel I, Hillel's grandson (the Gamaliel mentioned in the New Testament), reigned as Nasi and was probably killed during the war against Rome. As soon as the dust settled after the disaster of 70, Simon ben Gamaliel I followed as Nasi of the Sanhedrin. He, in turn, was succeeded by Hillel's great-grandson Gamaliel II, who headed the Sanhedrin (which had been relocated from Jerusalem to Yavneh) during the years 96–115. By any historical yardstick, Gamaliel II must be rated as one of the most influential Jews of the twenty centuries with which this book deals.

It is useful to outline briefly at this point the functions of the Sanhedrin. The full body of seventy-one, the Nasi included, served as the Supreme Court of world Jewry. It alone was called *Sanhedrin Gedolah*, or the Great Sanhedrin. Lower courts of twenty-three judges were distributed throughout the land of Israel, which included both Judea and the Galilee. They were vested with broad powers, but the Great Sanhedrin was the ultimate court of appeals that decided issues that were contested or shrouded in doubt. When conflicting opinions emerged among the lower courts, the issue was submitted to the Great Sanhedrin for resolution.

It was also within the Great Sanhedrin's authority to pronounce the verdict of heresy upon beliefs that it regarded as counter to Judaic faith. Besides serving as the paramount judicial body, the Great Sanhedrin was also the source of new legislation. Among its most important functions was affixing the Jewish calendar, thereby assuring that every Sabbath and festival occurred on its designated day, not sooner or later. All Temple rituals (before it was destroyed) were subject to the supervision of the Great Sanhedrin. Before the year 70, the Sanhedrin also judged all capital cases which carried a possible death penalty. Finally, during Hasmonean rule (c. 140 B.C.E. to 4 B.C.E.), the Sanhedrin was theoretically involved in the business of foreign diplomacy.

With the loss of national sovereignty in the year 70, most of the political, military, and criminal jurisdiction was taken away from the Great Sanhedrin by the Roman power, though Rome did continue all of the Sanhedrin's prerogatives in the spheres of religious belief and

practice as well as in matters of civil law. However, it is highly doubtful that the body could have functioned effectively were it not for the
vigorous and imaginative leadership exercised by Rabbi Gamaliel II.

Gamaliel was tough and imperious, even to the point of occasional
tyranny, but through most of his career as Nasi, the other seventy
deferred to him. This was for two reasons: he was a legitimate heir of
the dynasty begun by Hillel, and he was a man of superior learning.
Moreover, they saw in Gamaliel the qualities required of a leader during a tremulous time in Jewish history, with the aftershocks of the 70
earthquake and faint rumblings of restiveness and rebellion in circles
that refused to accept subjugation and national humiliation as the final word in Jewish destiny.

Gamaliel was a traveling Nasi. He realized the importance of solidi-
fying and consolidating Judaism in the lands of the diaspora. His travels
took him to Rome and Greece, to Babylonia and Egypt, as well as other
places where Jews dwelt in the Mediterranean world. He brought encour-
aging words and the inspiration of his imposing personality to fellow
Jews and thereby strengthened their bonds with the homeland.

The Torah went with Rabbi Gamaliel wherever he went. Even *in
extremis* he would not flout its rules. One day, so the Talmud tells us,
he was aboard his ship on the high seas when Succot, the Feast of Tabernacles, was about to occur. Gamaliel ordered some planks removed
from the boat, and out of them the Torah-mandated *succah* was built
and set up. The Jew of the Century floating on the undulating Mediterranean waters nevertheless had a *succah* in place.

The achievements of Rabbi Gamaliel taken all in all may justifiably
be seen as having saved the foundering ship of Judaism and its people
from going under. It was he who established the hegemony of the Palestinian Jewish center over the rest of the Jewish world. By his zealous
guardianship of the pre-eminence of the Jewish leadership in the Holy
Land, he averted the schism and splintering that the impact of Rome's
devastating blow might have forced upon world Jewry. Yet he was
always mindful of the special needs of the Jews in the diaspora. To cite
one example, he so arranged the calendar as to avert the occurrence of
Yom Kippur on a Friday or a Sunday. This was because of his concern
for the livelihood of the huge Jewish population in Babylonia (present-
day Iraq). Many of them were growers of vegetable crops that if not
picked almost daily at harvest time would wither under the searing
Babylonian sun. It was necessary, then, to avert a situation in which

the crops could go two days without being picked. A Friday or a Sunday Yom Kippur would indeed have prevented crop-picking for two consecutive days.

Gamaliel may be seen as the founder of a philanthropy that foreshadowed our modern-day United Jewish Appeal. During the six centuries of the life of the Second Temple, Jews from all over the world regularly sent fixed contributions to the Temple treasury to maintain its ramified religious, social, and economic services. With the destruction of the Temple, it seemed for a time that this immense diaspora assistance was in jeopardy. Rabbi Gamaliel averted such a potential calamity by establishing what came to be called the *aurum coronarium*, or crown tax. The monies from abroad were now directed to the treasury of the Sanhedrin, which supervised ramified networks of learning and philanthropy through an impoverished Jewry in Eretz Israel. We have the testimony of several Church fathers who accord grudging admiration to the fact that a people with no government, no military capabilities, no tax collecting bureaucracy was nevertheless able to raise the monies necessary to maintain its vital institutional life.

In the sphere of Jewish ritual, Rabbi Gamaliel II was responsible for beginning the process of organizing and systematizing the core of Jewish liturgy—the *Shmoneh Esrai* or the *Amida*—which stands to this day as the heart of every synagogue (or privately recited) service. We learn from the Talmud that Gamaliel assigned the arrangement of the sequence of the eighteen benedictions (the *Shmoneh Esrai*) to Shimon ha-Fakuli. Those benedictions had been in existence for at least three hundred years and were apparently recited by Jews in synagogues even during the days in which the Holy Temple was flourishing. The apocryphal work called the Wisdom of Ben Sira, or Ecclesiasticus (not to be confused with the biblical book of Ecclesiastes), which had been composed about 200 B.C.E., already contained a series of benedictions that correspond closely to the content of Gamaliel's *Shmoneh Esrai*.

With the destruction of the Temple, the rabbinic leadership realized that liturgy—the *Avoda she'balev*, or the service of the heart—was a powerful unifying element for world Jewry, the only possible substitute for the magnetizing force of the now defunct Temple ritual. To serve this crucial role, it was imperative that Jews recite the *Shmoneh Esrai* in precisely the same way and in the same order wherever and whenever it was employed. The measure of Gamaliel's achievement in this area is virtually incalculable. To this day, traditional synagogues have retained the Gamaliel version of the *Shmoneh Esrai* almost word for word. It is possible for an American Jew, for example, to visit any synagogue on earth and feel immediately at home. The *Shmoneh Esrai* has accomplished that.

To the standard Eighteen Benedictions, Gamaliel added one more: the *Birkat ha'minim*, a denunciation of the heretics within the Jewish community. Specifically, he had the Jewish Christians in mind. They attended the synagogues and attempted there to persuade the people that Jesus, dead some eighty years, was the Messiah for whom the Jewish people yearned, that he was literally the son of God, and that he was to be worshiped as part of the Deity itself. This indeed was heresy. Gamaliel wished to discourage the presence of such Jews in the synagogue. The original *Birkat ha'minim* read approximately as follows: "May there be no hope for the Nazarene heretics. May all who blaspheme the unity of God's name be written out of His book. Blessed are you, O Lord, who subdues heretics." When the Christian Church rose to political power some 200 years after Gamaliel, the direct reference to Christians was eliminated. The general sense of animosity toward those both without and within the Jewish community who hate God's people and persecute them has been retained in the "nineteenth benediction" down to our own time. It may truly be said that its inclusion in the *Amida* marked the final rupture between Judaism and the followers of Jesus. One may add that the phrase "Jews for Jesus" is oxymoronic.

The forceful, often dictatorial, leadership of Rabbi Gamaliel II led toward the end of his career to a memorable confrontation with Rabbi Joshua Ben Hananiah, a formidable contemporary who had had the audacity to dispute the Nasi. In his computations for the annual calendar, Rabbi Joshua arrived at a date for Yom Kippur that was at odds with the day Gamaliel was about to proclaim. Angered by what he considered insubordination, Gamaliel ordered Rabbi Joshua to appear before him on the day Joshua reckoned to be Yom Kippur with his walking cane and with purse and coins (a blatant violation of Yom Kippur).

The humiliation of so distinguished and beloved a peer as Rabbi Joshua led the Sanhedrin to depose Gamaliel from the office of Nasi. Despite his own humiliation, Gamaliel sat at the feet of a newly elected Nasi along with the colleagues who had impeached him. In due course Rabbi Gamaliel made his way to the humble abode of Rabbi Joshua in order to seek his forgiveness. He noticed upon entering the house that its walls were blackened. He said: "From the evidence of your walls, it would appear that your calling is that of a blacksmith." Joshua responded: "Woe to the generation whose leader you are. Woe to the ship of which you are the pilot. For you have no idea of the pain of scholars, of what they must do for their living, and by what they are fed." Said Gamaliel: "Forgive me!" He was ignored. Said Gamaliel: "Forgive me for the sake of the honor of my father's house." At that, he was forgiven and was ultimately restored to his post as the head of the Sanhedrin.

Rabbi Gamaliel of Yavneh was a man of intense national pride. Two narratives from the Talmud are illustrative of the love he had for his people and the contempt he bore toward its Roman enemy. One day he immersed himself in the waters of a bathhouse dedicated to the pagan goddess Aphrodite. When asked how he could even enter a place so alien to the spirit of the Jewish people as Aphrodite's bathhouse, he responded: "I did not invade her territory; she invaded mine." To better understand the tenor of these words, we must know that on his constant trips abroad he was taunted by Roman pagans as a phantom leader of a phantom people—a people that was yet to realize it was hopelessly dead. What the taunters failed to see was that the "dead" leader of a "dead" people was doing the work that would ultimately be a stunning refutation of their arguments.

We read in the sources that Gamaliel was once asked by a Roman philosopher how God remained occupied after His six days of creation when His work had been fully accomplished according to the Hebrew scriptures. We may with good reason read into this question the position of Hellenistic philosophy that God is to be seen as the Creator of the world, not the ubiquitous Providence who continues to care for His creatures forever and ever, a Providence that Judaism insistently affirmed. Gamaliel's answer was: "God is busy stoking the fires of hell for people like you."

Gamaliel had gone to the heart of the issue. He was surely implying that the pillage and destruction Rome had wrought in Jerusalem was not the end of God's people. It was, on the contrary, a new beginning. In the end, the fires of Gehenna would consume the Roman Empire. It would fall prey to savages who would render unto Rome what Rome had rendered unto Jerusalem.

Gamaliel's life had been dedicated to the central idea that Jerusalem would triumph over Rome because *it*, not the other, was the Eternal City.

THE SECOND CENTURY

Simon Bar Kokhba

Gamaliel, as events were to demonstrate, was certainly right. The war between Rome and Jerusalem did not end with the year 70. Even as the flames set to the Holy Temple were flickering to extinction, the flames of rebellion within the hearts of many Jews were leaping ever higher— and not only in Judea. Many Jewish refugees had fled their homeland to join already considerable Jewish communities in the diaspora. It is reasonable to assume that they were a factor in the outbreak of widespread hostilities between Jews and their Hellenic neighbors. Jews rebelled against the challenges to their way of life, both religious and societal.

Violent fighting exploded in Cyrenaica in the year 115 where, led by one Loukuas-Andreas, Jews engaged the local population in a battle so fierce, the Roman overlords were forced to intervene. At about the same time, Jews were embroiled in battle with their perceived Hellenic enemies in Egypt, Cyprus, and Mesopotamia. These revolts lasted for the three years 115-17, and there is some evidence that their spirit was reflected in the mood and actions of the Jews in Palestine as well. The Roman general who had been sent to crush the uprisings in Mesopotamia was

Lucius Quietus, later to become governor of Palestine. Jewish sources of the period, mainly the Talmud and Midrashim, speak of the "Troubles (or wars) of Kitus (Quietus)." No fully documented citations of the causes of these diaspora outbreaks are now available. But there is hardly any question that they were manifestations of a collision course between the hellenized Roman superpower and the Judaism that remained intensely monotheistic, passionately national, and bitterly hateful toward the enemy who had destroyed its Temple and subjugated its worshipers to the environment of cults and practices radically alien to its ethos.

A close reading of the history of the Jews for the nearly seventy years following the destruction of the Second Temple renders the unmistakable impression that many, if not most, of the Jewish people were expecting an imminent restoration of their sovereignty in Palestine, along with the rebuilding of the Temple in Jerusalem. Their Messianic hopes were not deferred to some dim and distant future. Many expected their redemption to arrive within their own lifetimes.

They recited the Gamaliel-edited *Shmoneh Esrai*—the core of their daily prayers. Of the nineteen benedictions it embraced (see the previous chapter), no less than six express the aspirations for imminent national redemption:

> "Look upon our affliction and champion our cause; redeem us speedily for your name's sake. . . . Blessed are you, O Lord, redeemer of Israel."

> "Sound the great Shofar (ram's horn) for our freedom; lift up the banner for the ingathering of our exiles. . . . Blessed are you, O Lord, who gathers the dispersed of your people Israel."

> "Restore our judges as at first. . . . May you alone reign over us in kindness and mercy. . . . Blessed are you, O Lord, who loves righteousness and justice."

> "Return in mercy to your city Jerusalem and dwell in it as you have promised. Rebuild it *soon, in our days* (italics added), as an everlasting structure and speedily establish in it the throne of David. Blessed are you, O Lord, Builder of Jerusalem."

> "Speedily advance the advent of your servant David's offspring and let his glory be exalted by your help. For we look for your deliverance every day. Blessed are you, O Lord, who causes salvation to sprout."

> "May our eyes see your return in Mercy to Zion. Blessed are you, O Lord, who restores His divine presence to Zion."

The Jewish passion for Zion and its redemption burst into a conflagration in the year 132. Seemingly out of nowhere there emerged one Simon Bar-Kosiba to head a full-scale war of Judea against Rome. The war lasted almost four years, during almost three of which the Jewish forces under Bar-Kosiba managed to wrest Jerusalem from the occupying enemy and even to strike coins marking Jewish sovereignty. It proved to be the final battle between Judea and Rome. It ended in Betar, a fortified town southwest of Jerusalem, with the triumph of Rome under its leading general, Julius Severus, and with the reported loss of 580,000 Jewish lives as well as thousands of dead Roman soldiers.

The main source for our knowledge of the Bar-Kosiba Revolt comes from a passage in the multi-volume *Roman History* by the early third-century historian Dio Cassius. It deserves to be quoted nearly in full:

At Jerusalem he (the Emperor Hadrian) founded a city in place of the one which had been razed to the ground, naming it Aelia Capitolina, and on the site of the god (The Jewish Temple) he raised a new temple to Jupiter. This brought on a war of no slight importance nor of brief duration, for the Jews deemed it intolerable that foreign races should be settled in their city and foreign religious rites practiced there. So long, indeed, as Hadrian was close by in Egypt and again in Syria, they remained quiet, save insofar as they purposely made of poor quality such weapons as they were called upon to furnish, in order that the Romans might reject them and they themselves might thus have the use of them; but when he went further away, they openly revolted. To be sure, they did not dare to try conclusions with the Romans in the open field, but they occupied the advantageous positions in the country and strengthened them with mines and walls, in order that they might have places of refuge whenever they should be hard pressed. . . .

At first the Romans took no account of them. Soon, however all Judea had been stirred up. . . . Then, indeed, Hadrian sent against them his best generals. First of these was Julius Severus, who was dispatched from Britain. . . . By depriving them of their food and shutting them in, he was able . . . with comparatively little danger, to crush, exhaust, and exterminate them. Very few of them in fact survived. Fifty of their most important outposts and 985 of their most famous villages were razed to the ground. Five hundred and eighty thousand men were slain. . . . Many Romans, moreover, perished in this war. Therefore Hadrian, in writing to the senate, did not employ the opening phrase commonly effected by the emperors, "If you and the children are in health; it is well; I and the legions are in health."

From Dio's account we learn several important facts. First, the Jews in Judea rebelled against Rome because the Emperor Hadrian desecrated their holy city by erecting a temple to the pagan god Jupiter on the site of their Holy Temple, which had been demolished by Rome in the year 70. Second, that Hadrian had renamed Jerusalem Aelia Capitolina (after himself). Third, that the rebel Jews prepared themselves for open war by using guile in amassing military weapons. Fourth, that the Jewish forces were successful enough to induce Hadrian to send in his top general from remote Britain to tiny Judea in order to put down the uprising. Fifth, that the Jews sustained the staggering loss of 580,000 people. Sixth—and very significantly—that the Roman "body count" as a result of the war was considerable.

All of this is very helpful to the contemporary historian. It is also very vexing because of what Dio does *not* tell. Where is the name of the leader, born Bar-Cosiba and adulated as Bar Kokhba (or vice versa) in the stories about the rebellion that have come down to us from the Talmud and Midrashim? Dio does not even mention him. What about the locales of the war? What about the progress of its battles, the disposition of military forces, logistics for both sides, Hadrian's motivations? Most importantly, Dio maintains total silence about the stunning achievement of Bar Kokhba and his fighting forces to wrest Jerusalem from Roman hands and to occupy the city for some three and a half years.

This last information is established fact. Thousands of coins struck by Bar Kokhba are extant bearing the dates of the Jewish occupation of Jerusalem in the years 132,133, and, possibly, 134. Despite the lacunae in Dio's account, we must be grateful to him for the picture of the revolt he has transmitted. After all, he was writing a history of Rome through the eyes of a Roman and not of Jerusalem through the eyes of a Jew.

Dio Cassius likely put his finger on the chief cause of what has come to be called the Second Jewish Revolt against Rome, which was bitterness over Hadrian's policy to adulterate and idolatrate their holy city of Jerusalem and to substitute Jupiter for Israel's unseen and unseeable God, sole Creator and Sovereign of the universe. Spartanius, the third-century biographer of Hadrian, attributes the revolt to Hadrian's order prohibiting the practice of circumcision, the sign of the covenant that

Jews believe God to have established with Abraham, their first ancestor. According to modern historians of the era, what Hadrian did was to extend the ban on castration issued by his predecessors Domitian and Nerva so as to include circumcision as well. This, along with other and later anti-Judaic edicts of Hadrian, was totally unacceptable to a beleaguered Jewish people whose very survival was posited upon its observance of the Torah commandments along with the rules and regulations that the rabbis had promulgated and elaborated and that some three hundred years later formed the core of both the Jerusalem and the Babylonian Talmud.

The Talmud does contain material, largely legendary, about the Bar Kokhba revolt. Some of it will be discussed presently. The Church Father Eusebius was the author, early in the fourth century, of Ecclesiastical history. For the first time we find mention of Bar Kokhba (in somewhat altered form) in his narrative about the history of the church in Jerusalem. Despite the tendentious anti-Judaism of Eusebius, which he had in common with virtually all patristic writers, his account of the revolt is important both because of the information conveyed and because it tells us much about the early stages of anti-Jewish prejudice that saturated the teaching of the Church about Jews and Judaism. Says Eusebius:

> The rebellion of the Jews once more progressed in character and extent, and Rufus the governor of Judea, when military aid had been sent to him by the Emperor, moved out against them, treating their madness without mercy. He destroyed in heaps thousands of men, women, and children, and under the law of war enslaved their land. The Jews were at that time led by a certain Bar Chochebas; which means "star," a man who was murderous and a bandit. . . . The war reached its height in the eighteenth year of the reign of Hadrian in Beththera [Betar], which was a strong citadel not very far from Jerusalem; the siege lasted a long time before the rebels were driven to final destruction by famine and thirst and the instigator of their madness paid the penalty he deserved.

Eusebius goes on to cite one Ariston of Pella: "Thus when the city (Jerusalem) came to be bereft of the nation of the Jews . . . it was colonized by foreigners and the Roman city which afterwards arose changed its name, and in honor of the reigning emperor, Aelius Hadrian, was called Aelia. The church, too, in it was composed of Gentiles, and after the Jewish bishops the first who was appointed to minister to those was Marcus."

Elsewhere Eusebius gleefully adds: "From that time (on), the permission was denied them even to enter Jerusalem first and foremost because of the commandment of God, as the prophets had prophesied; and secondly by authority of the interdiction of the Romans." Other Church fathers, Epiphanius and Jerome, both of the fourth century, are notable promoters of the theme that the end of Jewish statehood spelled by the outcome of the Bar Kokhba Revolt had been predicted by the prophets of Israel as punishment for the willful rejection of Christianity's Christ, by the Jews of his time and Jews ever since.

In Jewish sources, Bar-Cosiba is portrayed as a leader of heroic dimensions. Although it is difficult to separate the historic facts from their legendary embellishments, the prudent historian can write with confidence about the following elements in the Bar Kokhba revolt:

One, the revolt was an uprising of the great majority of the Jews in Palestine, united as never before, by a larger-than-life persona, a man of indomitable courage and determination, an organizing genius, and a brilliant military strategist.

Two, he marshaled tens of thousands of volunteers from all segments of Jewish society throughout Palestine, having industriously amassed an imposing arsenal of weapons in preparation for what we would now term a guerrilla war against the occupying Roman power.

Three, one of his ardent champions was none other than the most respected rabbi of his age, Rabbi Akiba ben Yosef. It was, according to the Talmud, that Rabbi Akiba, in a play on words, changed the name Bar-Cosiba to Bar Kokhba, which means "son of the Star." Akiba applied the biblical verse "A star shall go forth out of Jacob" to Bar Kokhba. He even added blatantly: "This is the King Messiah." While not all of Akiba's colleagues concurred, there can be little question that a great many of them did. It was the war of a people, not the madness of a sect.

Four, while the disastrous end of the Bar Kokhba revolt led to the deep demoralization of the Jews who survived, the impact of his hugely charismatic essence continued to be felt for many centuries after his death and, as we shall presently see, achieved its most dramatic effect only yesterday, as it were.

In the year 132, Bar Kokhba's troops attacked simultaneously throughout Judea. Under his personal leadership, troops stormed Jerusalem at night, completely surprising the Tenth Legion of the Romans stationed in that city. The Legion was driven out, and Bar Kokhba proclaimed an independent Jewish government with Jerusalem as its seat. Thousands of Bar Kokhba coins have survived with such inscriptions as: "Year one of the redemption of Israel," "Shimeon (Bar Kokhba's given name) President of Israel," "Eliezer the Priest," "year two of the freedom of Israel," and "of the freedom of Jerusalem"—all of these on bronze. Silver coins issued include beautifully wrought objects such as the *lulav* (palm branch used on Succot, the Feast of Tabernacles), the holy trumpets of the Temple, and the facade of the Holy Temple. It is perhaps symbolic that these coins were not freshly minted. They were superimposed on Roman coins. Glimpses of parts of the originals sometimes can be caught, especially on coins particularly ravaged by time and the elements.

For two or perhaps three years, the Jews occupied Jerusalem. The Romans had sent the forces in Syria under Publius Marcellus, along with batallions from Egypt and Arabia. They were soundly routed by Bar Kokhba's ever-growing army. Finally the Emperor Hadrian called on his illustrious general Julius Severus, who arrived from far-off Britain with parts of some thirteen legions no less. The die was cast. The ultimate outcome could no longer remain in doubt. Goliath was upon the scene, and all of David's slingshots were to no avail.

Valiantly the Jews held out for almost a year. In the end the surviving army, including Bar Kokhba, retreated to the nearby fortress of Betar. In the summer of 135 that last bastion went down in a sea of blood, its leader dead by a Roman sword.

The man was a legend in his own lifetime and remained a legend shrouded in mist for exactly 1,885 years. In 1960, a group of archaeologists led by Yigael Yadin explored the caves near the canyon of Nahal Hever on the Israeli side of the Dead Sea in search of artifacts that might shed light on the Bar Kokhba period in Jewish history. The jacket cover of Yadin's book on what they found tells the simple truth:

"Out of a crevice in a canyon near the Dead Sea, where it had lain for almost two thousand years, came a woman's bag. Out of the bag came a fragile batch of papyrus inside which were wrapped four wooden slats. And as the excited archaeologists stared incredulously at the strips of wood, one name blazed at them. It was the name of Bar Kokhba. . . . The batch of papyrus contained letters from Bar Kokhba. . . . This was a find to excite the whole archaeological world."

The letters are written to subordinate officers in Bar Kokhba's army, either in Hebrew or Aramaic, the spoken language at the time of the Jews in Palestine. Most of them begin with the words: "From Shimeon ben/bar Kosiba" and are addressed to Yehonatan son of Be'aya and Masabala son of Shimeon, who were stationed in En-gedi. They are abrupt and to the point. Their sender is clearly not a person to be fooled with. He orders specified provisions to be sent to him without delay, on pain of punishment. He orders the confiscation of wheat held by a prosperous farmer. He commands the incarceration of "all men from Tekoa" to be sent to him under guard. He orders the arrest of one Eleazar bar Hitta, a wealthy landowner of En-gedi who failed to comply with previous orders of the supreme commander.

Perhaps the most captivating letter is the one sent from "Shimeon to Yehudah bar Menashe" in which Bar Kokhba writes:

"I have sent to you two donkeys that you shall send with them two men to Yehonatan bar Be'ayan and to Masabala in order that they shall pack and send to the camp . . . palm branches and citrons. And you, from your place, send others who will bring you myrtles and willows. See that they are tithed and send them to the camp. . . . Be well."

A war is going on. Jews are being killed by the tens of thousands. Jerusalem is already back in the hands of the Romans. Fragments of an otherwise illegible Bar Kokhba letter read: "till the end/they have no hope/my brothers in the south/of these were lost by the sword/these my brothers. . . ."

And Bar Kokhba is ordering "the four kinds: *lulav*, *etrog*, *hadas*, and *Arava*" because his battle is for the Jewish way of life.

But what Hadrian dealt out was blood and desolation and death. The Hadrianic edicts for Judea following the war were designed to eradicate Judaism. His fury at the insolence of a tiny people who dared defy his glorious empire was so vented as to destroy the lives of scholars and saints; of poets and peasants; of man, woman, and child who bore the name Jew.

The land of Israel was decimated. Thousands left for safer shores, making sure to carry their Torah with them.

Some of the great masters of Judaic teaching, including the incomparable Rabbi Akiba, had been savagely slaughtered because they had defied the Hadrianic *ukase* prohibiting both the study and the teaching of Torah. Stories had begun to circulate about the martyrdom of ten giants of Jewish learning. The story told about one of them—whether literally true or not—might well be the epitome of what is meant by snatching victory from the jaws of defeat. It relates the circumstances of the death of Rabbi Hananiah ben Tradyon, who is said to have written out 400 Scrolls of the Law (The Torah or Pentateuch). This had been banned on pain of death by the edicts of Hadrian. R. Hananiah was apprehended, stripped naked, swathed in cotton cloth that had been saturated with oil, and wrapped in the last scroll that he had written. To all of this his executioner set the torch. His death was slow and excruciatingly painful. Nevertheless, his disciples who were forced to look upon this gruesome sight, discerned an expression of exultation on his countenance, even as his burning body was writhing in anguish. One of the disciples could not refrain from asking his rabbi: "How can you exult at a time like this?" Said Rabbi Hananiah ben Tradyon: "I am joyous because even as the parchment of the Torah is being consumed, I see all of the letters rising into the air."

The spirit of Hananiah's dying words reverberated in the whole of the Jewish world. It was carried by those of his disciples who left Judea to the lands of their destination.

It helps explain the extraordinary story of the Jewish community in Babylonia for an uninterrupted millennium following the bitter end of Bar Kokhba, the fallen star.

THE THIRD CENTURY

ABBA ARIKHA

With the end of the Bar Kokhba revolt, the Palestinian center of Jewish life literally burned itself out in a blaze of costly glory considering the 580,000 victims of the Jewish people who died because of the Bar Kokhba revolt. But there is a Yiddish folk-saying: "God summons the cure even before He summons the disease." The cure was already available in the form of a new center of Jewish life that was to develop in what we today call Iraq, which was then still known as Babylonia. The Greeks tell the tale of the marathon runner bringing the good news of the victory. The heralds of victory ran from the battlefield with torch aloft and collapsed before reaching their destination. They died, but not before handing over the torch to another marathon runner, who continued at full speed until *he* fell. But, falling, he yet succeeded in passing the torch to the hand of another.

The Jewish people have been the true marathon runners of the generations. They have had an uncanny ability to vault over disaster. This is reflected in a Talmudic statement that on the day that Rabbi Akiba died, Rabbi Judah the Prince was born. This, historically speaking, is not accurate, but symbolically it is. Rabbi Akiba was a great leader of the Jewish people who was one of the many victims of Hadrianic persecution. Rabbi Judah the Prince was a scion of the house of Hillel, that dynasty of glory described in the first chapter, who raised the prestige of the Sanhedrin to its zenith. Judah the Prince lived through the first decade of the third century. He was a man who was a rare combination of elements. He was wealthy, of noble spirit and distinguished ancestry. He exercised authority in the same affirmative manner as did his grandfather, Rabbi Gamaliel of Yavneh. He consorted with some Roman rulers. The Talmud tells of his association with the Emperor Antoninus. Who this "Antoninus" was we don't know. Some say it was the famous king-philosopher Marcus Aurelius Antonius; some say it was Caracella, the ruins of whose baths now form the stage for operatic settings in Italy. We don't know exactly with whom Rabbi Judah the Prince consorted, but it is quite obvious that he must have been a man of very high station to be received in the presence of monarchs. The Talmud has a whole series of stories, legends perhaps, but they reflect the spirit of the age, of conversations between Rabbi Judah the Prince and the emperor, whoever that emperor may have been.

According to one story, the emperor had been invited to the home of Rabbi Judah the Prince for Sabbath. He enjoyed the meal immensely, so he asked the rabbi for the recipe which, of course, was gladly given. The following week, the emperor returned and said to Rabbi Judah: "You didn't give me the right ingredients. My cook followed your recipe but the meal was far from being as tasty as was yours." Said Rabbi Judah: "That is because the basic ingredient was missing." "But that's impossible!" cried the emperor, "My cook followed the recipe carefully." Rabbi Judah said: "All the ingredients except one." "And what was that?" asked the emperor. Rabbi Judah replied: "The flavoring called the spirit of the Sabbath."

WORK OF JUDAH, THE PRINCE

Rabbi Judah was the architect of the most important code of Jewish law in the history of the Jewish people since the original classic codes of the Torah. Rabbi Judah the Prince saw to the assembling of all of the accumulated laws of the Jewish people over the hundreds of years since the Torah had been canonized. He edited them into what we know now as the Mishnah. The Mishnah is the foundation of the Talmud. It was divided into six categories: Plants, Festivals, Women, Damages, Holiness, and Purity. Into these six categories, Rabbi Judah the Prince and his academy of scholars managed to gather an updated collection of Jewish law, which to the present day serves as the basic fountainhead of traditional Jewish life.

At this time, the Jews of Babylonia were increasing in number, in station, and in wealth. It was already a venerable community. In the year 586, the First Temple had been destroyed by Nebuchadnezzar, king of Babylon, and many Jews had been exiled there. The Jewish community dated from that year, 586, and continued for 1,500 uninterrupted years as a solid, well-entrenched body of Jews in the world. Babylonia was ruled by Babylonians and then by Persians and then by Parthians and then by neo-Persians, but the Jewish people continued strong, confident, and relatively secure. They had a self-governing body over which presided the Exilarch, the head of the exile, who was deemed to be a descendant of the house of David. This exilarchate actually constituted a government within a government for the Jewish people of Babylonia. It had control over everything internal—religion, taxes, civil law, and social life. The economy was diversified. They were farmers, artisans, tradesmen, and common laborers, but chiefly they were farmers. Some ninety percent of the Jewish population of Babylonia derived its livelihood from agriculture. The main towns of Jewish settlement were called Nehardea, Pumbedita, Mechoza, and a suburb of Baghdad called Sura. The history of the Jews in Babylonia up until the end of the second century is wrapped in obscurity. Seven hundred years of it are relatively blank pages, so far as our knowledge is concerned. There were no established Jewish schools in Babylonia of any distinction during this long period, and in order to train their scholars, Babylonian Jews sent them to Palestine to study. Many students were sent to Palestine, especially during the second half of the second century. The greatest of these were Samuel, who was a physician; Nathan; and a very tall Jew named Abba Arikha (Abba, the Long), who is the outstanding Jew of the third century.

ABBA ARIKHA

Abba Arikha was a brilliant student and a protégé of Rabbi Judah the Prince. His uncle was Rabbi Hiyya, who was one of the most respected members of the academy of Rabbi Judah. Immediately it became evident that this tall young man from Babylonia was destined for greatness. In no time at all, he outshone all of the rest of the established scholars in the school of Judah the Prince. As a matter of fact, he was regarded as so brilliant that only five short years after his arrival, he stood alongside of the master when the master lectured, frequently repeating and explaining the master's words.

Abba Arikha had come to Palestine for the specific purpose of qualifying himself to become a teacher of the Jewish community of Babylonia. In the year 219, a significant date in Jewish history, Abba Arikha returned to Babylonia, and there inaugurated a career that lasted for three decades and that was both to transform the spiritual image of Babylonian Jewry and to leave a permanent imprint upon the entire history of the Jews down to the present day. The most brilliant scholar in the academy of Rabbi Judah the Prince, Abba Arikha was spiritually as great as he was physically tall. Before he left, he asked to receive formal rabbinical ordination—*semicha*. Rabbi Judah the Prince refused. He was deeply concerned that, equipped with *semicha*, the luminous Abba Arikha would achieve independent religious authority, thereby reducing or even eliminating any recourse to Palestinian leadership by the huge Jewish community of Babylonia. So Abba Arikha returned home without *semicha*. And he did his job—without *semicha*. So magnificently did he do it that his given name was almost forgotten. They called him "Rav," which means simply "*The* Rabbi."

A MAN OF MANY PARTS

Rav was a diplomat. When he returned to Babylonia, he did not usurp the prerogatives of Rabbi Shaila, who was then the head of the academy in Nehardea, his hometown. Rabbi Shaila was a good man, but not a great scholar. When Rav sat among his pupils and listened to Rabbi Shaila's lectures, he resisted constantly the urge to rise and correct Shaila's errors. It was the title "rabbi" that Abba Arikha or Rav was destined to magnify manyfold, not by words but through action. He established a lifelong friendship with his colleague Samuel, the physician, who had returned from Palestine to Babylonia earlier. Samuel sponsored him before the Exilarch. A rabbi was not allowed to take one *shekel* for any service that he rendered to his people by way of teaching them. Rav needed a source of livelihood. He was appointed by the

Exilarch as inspector of weights and measures in the Jewish markets. It was a well-paying position, enabling Rav to do the great work of his calling as the teacher of his generation.

BIRTH OF THE SURA ACADEMY

When Rabbi Judah the Prince died, Rav went back to Palestine once more in hope of getting his rabbinic ordination—his *semicha*—but again he was denied. This time he came back to Babylonia with the determination to lift the level of Jewish learning and practice of Babylonian Jewry. He decided to build his own academy on virgin soil. He selected Sura, a suburb of Baghdad, and there, in about the year 227, established his center of Jewish learning. Sura became the Yavneh of the diaspora, the fortress of the spirit for world Jewry, for almost a thousand years. In a short time the reputation of Rav grew so rapidly that he had 1,200 pupils in his academy at Sura. How does one provide for 1,200 pupils? There were no millionaires to help support them. Rav had a remarkable idea. He said: Sura has good, fertile land. We are going to spend half of our day in studying Torah and the other half in cultivating the soil around our academy. Thus was built the most remarkable Jewish university in the history of the Jewish people, and perhaps in the history of any people. For the academy was self-supporting. It lived from the agricultural production of its own students. The young men who studied Torah in the mornings tilled the soil, plowed it, seeded it, harvested it, and marketed its produce in the afternoon.

Thus Rav developed scholars as well as agrarians. These agrarians would never condescend for the rest of their lives to receive any compensation for their spiritual teaching. To cite an example: One of Rav's pupils in later years became an outstanding rabbi. He was out plowing his field when a woman came to him with a practical question involving *halakha* (Jewish law). Said the rabbi: "You bring your husband here to take over my plow during the time that I will be searching for the answer to your question."

ADULT STUDY: GRAND STYLE

Rav understood that the basic problem of Babylonian Jewry was not only the training of rabbis. There were some two million Jews in

Babylonia by that time. Rav understood that a Jewish community can- not prosper unless it sponsors an intensive adult program of studies designed for the masses of people. Large numbers of people must be educated in order to combat titanic ignorance. Rav found such titanic ignorance in Babylonia. The Jews there were not greater scholars than the average Jews today in the United States. They were loyal Jews, but scholars they were not. Rav decided that while training rabbis was very important, he had to undertake a massive adult studies program. He inaugurated what was by all odds the vastest adult studies program in the history of the Jewish people.

The month before Pesach, which is Adar, and the month before Rosh Hashanah, which is Elul, were slack agricultural months that Rav dedi- cated for the purpose of imparting to masses of Jews a knowledge of their laws and traditions. Thousands of Jews assembled in Sura during the months of Adar and Elul for the purpose of being instructed by the 1,200 pupils of the academy. They held classes over vast outdoor areas of Sura. It was a massive spiritual picnic at which thousands of Baby- lonian Jews nourished their souls from Judaism's opulent Torah table. This institution was called "the Kallah," or the plenary session. It was a feature of Babylonian Jewish life for centuries. Rav began it all. The effect was total banishment of ignorance for wide segments of Baby- lonian Jewry. Babylonian Jewry, under the inspiration and determi- nation of Rav on this issue, became the most scholarly Jewish com- munity in history.

Rav was a rigid interpreter of Jewish law. When he came to Baby- lonia, he found a looseness in Jewish observance that appalled him. In the course of traveling from town to town as the inspector of weights and measures, he learned a great deal. He had his ears attuned to the people. The Talmud records that he overheard one lady saying to an- other: "Give me the recipe for this." Rav would not have paid any at- tention, except for the next remark. She said: "How much milk do I use with this roast?" She was not even aware that milk may not be used with meat, such was the ignorance of Babylonian Jewry prior to the arrival of Abba Arikha. Another example: One of the laws of the Mishnah in the section called "Women" reads as follows: A woman might be married in three ways, providing there are witnesses. All three ways are valid. A woman might be married through a monetary gift, as an example, a ring of some value. A woman might be acquired as a wife through the writing of a contract of marriage in the presence of witnesses. Or a woman may be wedded through intercourse in the presence of witnesses, providing that such intercourse is effected for the specific purpose of marriage. This latter procedure was never really practiced in Jewish life. Perhaps it was a vestige of some primitive custom. But in Babylonia, it was occasionally practiced. Rav, of course, didn't like this at all, and we hear in the Talmud that he abolished this custom with ruthlessness.

RAV'S BEAUTIFUL PRAYERS

Rav's work in the field of education did not extend merely to adults. He set standards of curricula for school teachers of little children, and he ruled that any Jew who lives too far away from any academy for the training of his children is to be excommunicated. It had the desired result. Education for the young became mandatory and effectively enforced throughout the career of Rav and for centuries thereafter. Rav's talents extended to other areas as well. He was one of the most prolific contributors to the liturgy. Every morning as Rav awakened he prayed: "I want to thank you, my God and God of my fathers, for each tiny drop of rain that You see fit to bestow upon us." Rav felt that religion implied gratitude to God for every little drop that He sees fit to direct our way. He did not make great demands upon God in his prayers.

It was Rav who developed the concept of the Day of Judgment for Yom Kippur. Yom Kippur in the Torah is not clearly defined as the Day of Judgment. It was Rav who introduced this prayer that Jews recite to this day, that on Yom Kippur humankind is judged as to who shall live and who shall die, who shall perish by the sword and who shall live in peace, who shall have life and who shall have death. Perhaps the most magnificent of all of the prayers introduced by Rav is the Oleynu, the Adoration. Its second section reads: "We therefore hope in Thee, O Lord our God, that we may speedily behold the arrival of Thy glory, when Thou wilt eliminate idolatry from the earth, and all idols shall be cut off, when Thou wilt turn unto Thyself all the evildoers, when all the people of the world shall perceive and know that unto Thee every knee must bend, every tongue must pay fealty. Let them all accept the yoke of Thy Kingdom, and mayest Thou reign over them forever. For the kingdom is Thine, and for all eternity Thou wilt reign in glory, as it is written in Thy Torah, the Lord shall reign forever and ever. It has been foretold, the Lord shall be King over all of the earth. On that day the Lord will be One, and His name One." There is not a more universal prayer to be found anywhere in any liturgy. It is a prayer for the universal kingdom of God, a prayer for an age in which all hostility and all malice, all strife and all hatred, all pettiness and all selfishness, all misunderstanding and all misgivings will have been eliminated because all mankind will have been united under the concept of one God as the Father of all.

TEACHER BY EXAMPLE

Rav called God "the King of the King of Kings." In his day Ardashir, the mighty emperor of the Parthians, called himself the "King of Kings" and Rav's very sardonic comment was that "there is a King who is the King of the Kings," and this is why he included it in his Aleynu. The prayer that Jews recite for the new month was also composed by Rav. "May it be your will, O Lord our God, that you will give us a life of good, a life of plenty, a life of peace, a life of satisfaction, a life of love, a life of study, a life in which all of the desires of our hearts shall be fulfilled for good. Amen." This blessing is recited on the Sabbath preceding the New Moon.

Rav was a man who was a teacher by example and by aphorism. He said: "It is better to have black bread every day than to dream of pie in the sky." He was a man whose ideas were noble but not so exalted as to remove them from the sphere of reality. You cannot dream of the impossible, because the impossible will make you a laughing stock. Dream of the improbable, yes, but not of the impossible. The improbable Rav dreamed of and carried out. The impossible he never dreamed of. He had a practical word of advice on polygamy. (Polygamy was not officially banned in Judaism until the tenth century.) Rav's advice was as follows: If you must be a bigamist, don't marry two women, marry three. His meaning is worth pondering.

A *ketubah* is a marriage contract in which is written the built-in guarantee of alimony. If a husband divorces his wife, he has to pay her a certain amount of money. Usually it is a minimum of 200 Zuzim. Now, the husband could put in any sum above that in the *ketubah*. This is called "the increase" over the minimum. Rav said there is nothing more tragic for a human being than to have a miserable wife with a fat *ketubah*. He knew whereof he spoke. He had just such a wife! The Talmud relates that this man, the greatest scholar of his generation, was afflicted with a wife who was deliberately contradictory. Rav was the one who pronounced the following dictum: "Whoever would deprive his pupil the opportunity to hear the knowledge he, his teacher, has, it is as though he is robbing that pupil of the inheritance of the generations." In other words, every rabbi and anyone who has some knowledge is duty-bound to make sure that others know about it, too. Knowledge has only one validation: its dissemination and communication to others. Among Jewish prayers is the *Ahava Rabbah*, in which we read: "Lord, give us wisdom that we may learn so that we may teach." The real purpose of scholarship is to teach other people.

KADDISH FOR ABBA ARIKHA

When Rav died in the year 247, the whole Jewish community of Babylonia recited Kaddish for him for a whole year. He established Babylonia as the foremost land of world Jewry, the spiritual center and the inspirational fortress, the fountainhead of Jewish teaching and instruction for centuries to come. Had there been no Babylonian Jewry as Rav Abba Arikha established it, it would be hard to conceive of Jewry existing today.

A Rav story: He was on good terms with the Persian king Artaban IV. One day on his birthday, Artaban IV sent Rav a gift studded with jewels. Rav felt that he had to reciprocate; he sent the king a mezuzah. When he received it, he called Rav into his presence and said: "O, distinguished Rabbi, I didn't mean for you to reciprocate. I didn't expect you to send me back anything at all. But as long as you did, how can you compare what I sent you with this little piece of wood in which is enclosed a bit of parchment? How can you compare the two?" Said Rav: "You sent me a gift, and gave me problems. One of the problems is that it is so expensive. I'm going to have to set four guards to protecting it. I sent you the kind of gift that is infinitely better. This gift not only does not have to be watched, but it will watch over you. On the inside of this mezuzah, which you may affix to your door, is written: 'You shalt love the Lord your God with all your heart, with all your soul, and with all your might.' Anyone whose doorstep breathes this spirit is immune and invulnerable to damage of any kind. As far as I am concerned," said Rav to Artaban the King, "you short-changed me."

THE FOURTH CENTURY

ABBAYE AND RAVA

The arrival of Abba Arikha, our Jew of the third century, to Babylonia marked the beginning of the vast transfer of cultural force from the Palestinian Jewish community to the Babylonian Jewish community. The spiritual hegemony of the Babylonian community was to last fully a thousand years. In the meantime, the Palestinian center was deteriorating rapidly. One of the primary physical reasons was the emigration of so many thousands of Jews from Palestine because they found it very difficult to earn a livelihood there, and the Promised Land at that time was Babylonia. Thither they betook themselves. Secondly, the caliber of leadership of Palestinian Jewry was rapidly deteriorating. One virtue of a dynasty is continuity, but on the other hand, there is no guarantee that successive generations will match the caliber of their predecessors. There were not too many Hillels or Gamaliels of Yavneh or Judah the Princes in the great dynasty established by Hillel. Indeed, after the death of Judah the Prince, there was a decline in the quality of spiritual leadership of the Jewish community of Palestine. Correspondingly, with the arrival of Abba Arikha—Rav—to the community of Sura, where he established his great academy and where shortly thereafter the outstanding Academy of Pumbedita was established, Babylonia progressively eclipsed Palestine.

PALESTINIAN PROBLEMS

Moreover, anti-Semitism of a new kind was developing in Palestine. The Greek population in Palestine, which was increasing as the Jewish population was decreasing, just could not comprehend the ways of the Jews. They could not understand circumcision, for example. They regarded it as barbarian, and we find criticism of circumcision in the most derisive terms in the literature of the historians of that time, one of whom was Tacitus. All of the Jewish customs pertaining to the dietary laws and to the observance of the Sabbath were regarded by the Greeks with contempt. They thought that they were dealing with a people who were not civilized at all. These Jewish people who observed the Sabbath were wasting a potentially fruitful economic day. The dietary laws struck them as rank superstition or arrant nonsense. We have records of theatrical performances staged by Palestinian Greeks of the time. They give us an inkling as to how the rest of the population looked upon the original inhabitants, the Jews. For example, here is the script of one such skit:

> A clown comes out on the stage, Momus by name. He is unshaven, covered with dirt, and foul smelling. But he has no oil with which to cleanse his body. Someone asks him—the straight man—why are you crying, Momus? Momus answers: "Because oil is very expensive." Then the straight man says: "Why is oil so expensive?" Momus responds: "Oil is expensive for this reason. Jews use up all of their earnings on the Sabbath. They work all week long, six days a week, in order to accumulate enough money to prepare a sumptuous table for their meal on the Sabbath, in order to garb themselves with the proper expensive attire. Therefore they have no money left over for fuel. Therefore, the Jews have to burn their beds for fuel and they must sleep on the dusty ground. Hence they become afflicted with vermin, and so require deodorization. In order to deodorize, they buy huge quantities of oil, thereby driving the price up beyond Momus' means. Since I can buy no oil, I am foul smelling. That is why I weep." This skit comes down to us from the third and fourth centuries of cultural interaction between the dwindling Jewish population in Palestine and the ever-increasing Greek population.

CONSTANTINE ADOPTS CHRISTIANITY

During the first quarter of the fourth century, one of the must crucial events in history took place. The emperor Constantine of Rome undertook to adopt Christianity as the official religion of the Roman Empire. When that happened, the result was that this religion, whose presumed founder once declared, "My kingdom is not of this world," became precisely of this world. Once Constantine declared Christianity the official faith of the Roman Empire, the church became involved in the politics of the Roman Empire. The result was intense suffering for the Jewish population of Palestine. Christianity wished to adopt Palestine as its land, as it had already adopted the Jewish Bible. In order to achieve this purpose, anti-Jewish persecution became state policy. The first ecumenical council was held in Nicea in the year 325. This was the first officially organized church council that enunciated a clear-cut anti-Jewish policy.

One of the acts of that council was to change its calendar. Pesach and Easter coincided from the very beginning, because, as you will recall, Jesus had arrived in Jerusalem when Pesach was about to begin. The Last Supper was the Seder feast. Naturally, Easter coincided with Pesach. The Council of Nicea decided that this was not desirable. Therefore, Easter was moved away from Pesach, and so it is very rare that Easter and Pesach coincide. This was indicative of the spirit of the Council of Nicea. The council also passed a law that any Jew who had a pagan or a Christian slave and who converted that slave to Judaism would be put to death. Ultimately, the church legislated, with the aid of the political arm, that a Jew may not hold a Christian slave in his service at all. The church was ever fearful of Jewish proselytizing.

The situation in Palestine deteriorated to such an extent that finally, in 359, Hillel the Second, one of the last members of the great dynasty founded by Hillel the First, formalized what we today call the *Luach*. Prior to that time the only way of setting the calendar was through testimony each month regarding the birth of the New Moon. Witnesses before the Sanhedrin testified to the exact time at which they saw the moon rise. Based upon the acceptance of this testimony, the entire calendar was set. Thereby the world Jewish community was made dependent upon the Jewish leadership of Palestine for setting of the time for all Festivals. But once the calendar was established with mechanical precision, it was another nail in the coffin of the spiritual leadership of Palestinian Jewry. Hillel saw the handwriting on the wall. He saw the Palestinian Jewish center coming to an end. He felt it crucial to assure that the Jewish community all over the world would not become fragmentized sects with each celebrating its own date for the particular Festivals.

RISE OF BABYLONIAN JEWRY

These were all negatives of the situation in Palestine contributing to the ascendancy of the Babylonian center. But negative factors alone do not build a center. There were affirmative elements in the growth of the Babylonian Jewry. The first one was the titanic work of Abba Arikha. But Abba Arikha had his successors. From two great academies in Babylonia, Jewish teaching radiated for many generations. As mentioned above, Abba Arikha had founded Sura. The other great academy was Pumbedita. We hear of Sura and Pumbedita constantly for almost 700 years. In both places, outstanding rabbis held the helm of spiritual leadership, not only for Babylonian Jewry, but for Jews all over the world. Abba Arikha's successor in Sura was a rabbi named Huna. He was wealthy, noble, and humane. He did not have his predecessor's learning, but he had something that very few spiritual leaders are in a position to exercise. He had an enormous sense of philanthropy and the wherewithal with which to implement it. He was one of the richest Jews in Babylonia. Now an oddity of ancient Babylonian history as demonstrated in the case of Rabbi Huna is this: Nowadays, the rabbi depends upon his congregation for his livelihood. In Rabbi Huna's case, *he* supported hundreds of members of his congregation who could not earn a livelihood. This in itself is an inspiring phenomenon that is almost inconceivable these days.

Rabbi Huna was buried in Judea, in Palestine, even though he died in Babylonia, thereby setting a precedent. He had willed that his body be taken to Palestine for burial. For many hundreds of years thereafter, almost to our own time, it was one of the most pious and fondest wishes of a good Jew, wherever he might have died, to be buried in the Holy Land. In a way, this was tragic. For hundreds of years there was an influx of dead Jewish bodies into Palestine while the living Jewish bodies remained in the comfort of their homes in the diaspora. It was only when the procedure was reversed, and living Jews started to arrive in Palestine and began to outnumber the people who were buried there, that Zion was reborn in our own time.

RABBA

After the death of Rabbi Huna, outstanding rabbis headed both academies in Sura and in Pumbedita. Shortly after the death of Rabbi Huna of Sura, two candidates were considered for the rabbinate of the Pumbedita academy. One was Rabbi Joseph and the other was Rabba. Each one of them had fine qualifications. Rabbi Joseph had a fantastic memory and an encyclopedic knowledge of the whole realm of Jewish law. Rabba was the more brilliant and incisive. Pumbedita Jewry sent a question to Palestine at that time: Who should be elected? Shall we elect the man whom we call the "Sinai," because his knowledge is as that of Sinai, embracing the whole realm of Jewish law? Or shall we elect the man whom we have described as the "mountain grinder," because he can pulverize the arguments of any adversary? The answer came back: Elect "Sinai," the man whose knowledge is broader. They were about to elect Rabbi Joseph, when Rabbi Joseph asked the following question: "Is Rabba going to remain a member of my congregation? Let me know." Rabba said: "Why, yes, I am remaining right here. This is where I was brought up, this is where I stay." Rabbi Joseph said: "You take the job. I am not going to deliver lectures and have you 'grind' them for me. What respect would I then receive?" So Rabba was elected. Rabbi Joseph remained in Pumbedita, but never did he offer any opposition to the teaching and the preaching of Rabba, never criticized him, and never evinced any jealousy of him.

There was an intensified thirst for Torah on the part of the Babylonian Jewish community. Earlier mention has been made of the institution of the Kallah, that mammoth adult study project that had been first organized by Abba Arikha. Rabba was so brilliant and dynamic that he was able before long to attract as many as 12,000 adult Jews who left their farms and came during the month of Elul and during the month of Adar (the month before Rosh Hashanah and the month before Pesach) to listen to his lectures. This created a very severe problem, as a matter of fact, because the Babylonian authorities were at that time in the habit of coming to each household and farm to collect taxes. Whenever they came and knocked on the door, they were told: The owner is not here. Where is he? He is studying Torah. This became a severe problem for the revenue men, and Rabba was persecuted for this reason. His adult education project was interfering with the internal revenue department of the Babylonian state. The result was that for a number of years, Rabba was exiled from Pumbedita.

41

We cannot leave Rabbi Joseph without speaking briefly of his latter years. He grew old, but still had a host of pupils. The discerning pupils preferred Rabbi Joseph to Rabba, because Rabbi Joseph's knowledge was encyclopedic, as already noted. One could always learn something from him. Rabbi Joseph himself was a very humble man, and he taught his pupils quietly but persistently. One day he was smitten with a severe stroke and suffered blindness and loss of memory. One of the pathetic situations described in the Talmud is how Rabbi Joseph was about to deliver a lecture on a particular phase of Jewish law and suddenly was arrested in the middle. He just could not remember: His mind went blank. His pupils would try their very best to help him out. One of those pupils was Abbaye. Abbaye was a man cut from the same moral fiber as his master, and when his master forgot a law, or when his master found himself halting in quest of a point that he wanted to make, Abbaye would say to him: "My Master, if I may be so bold, I want to tell you what you taught us only two years ago. Is this what you were searching for?" The way he put it made it very palatable for Rabbi Joseph. But not all were Abbayes. There were other pupils who became impatient with the teacher, who was now a shred of his former self. They made comments that sometimes hurt the old man deeply. He bore them with patience. But on one occasion he could not control himself. He delivered himself of the following homily: "When Moses brought down the first tablets of the Ten Commandments, he saw the children of Israel worshiping the Golden Calf. In chagrin, he shattered the tablets. Did it ever occur to you to ask yourself what he did with the fragments? They were, after all, supremely holy. If you will look into the rabbinic tradition you will find that the fragments of the broken tablets were placed in the Holy Ark alongside of the new, whole tablets and that throughout the forty years of the wilderness the broken fragments were carried forward by the people. So," concluded Rabbi Joseph, "we learn that even fragments of a once solid whole should be accorded honor."

"SINAI" AND "MOUNTAIN GRINDER"

Abbaye, Rabbi Joseph's star disciple, was twice an orphan. The word "abbaye" would approximate "Tatenyu" in colloquial Yiddish. He had lost both his father and his mother when he had been a mere child. His given name was Nachmani. He was born in the year 280, and he died in the year 338. When Rabbi Joseph died and when Rabba departed from the scene, there was a question as to who would become the rabbi of Pumbedita. It was a contest among four: Abbaye's great colleague Rava; Abbaye himself; a rabbi name Zeira; and Rabba bar Matna. The electors decided that each one of the candidates should give a lecture and let the others ask questions designed as critiques of that lecture. Whoever would succeed in fending off the opposition of the other three would be elected. Rava talked first, and was solidly rebutted by the other three. Then Rabbi Zeira spoke and was met by the same treatment. Rabba bar Matna had the same experience. Finally, Abbaye spoke. His intellectual assailants could not daunt him or weaken his thesis in the least, so brilliant and scholarly was he. He combined the encyclopedic knowledge of his master, Rabbi Joseph, with the brilliant insight of Rabba. "Sinai" and "Mountain Grinder" both, Abbaye was elected to be the head of the academy. Abbaye was so incisive in his thinking that he was later characterized in Talmudic lore as a man who was able with his talent to push an elephant through the eye of a needle.

Abbaye and his colleague Rava veritably dominate the Babylonian Talmud. You can hardly study a page of the Talmud (and there are thousands of them) without coming across the discussions of Abbaye and Rava. In Jewish tradition, they are known as the *Havayot*—the dialogues, as it were, of Abbaye and Rava. It is no more conceivable to study the Talmud without the constant company of the personalities and the teachings of these two, than it is conceivable to study the constitutional history of the United States without encountering the opinions of Justices Marshall, Holmes, and Brandeis. Abbaye and Rava constituted a study in contrasts. They were as different as two people could be. There is something inspiring in the fact that these two human begins—who were so diverse in their personalities, who were so divergent in their outlook on life, whose characters were so different, whose approach to study was so different—were able to make a career of working together and thereby benefitting not only their generation, but Judaism down to the present day. They dominated the spirit of Jewish law in the fourth century and for centuries thereafter.

What about this man Abbaye? Abbaye was a sterling human being. It is worth spending some time discussing his character. Brilliant and knowledgeable as he was, he was humble and peace-loving. He said: "Always and forever a man must be diligent in his love of God, he must always be diligent in his sweetness of disposition and his conversations with men, remembering that a soft response will sometimes allay the fiercest anger. A man must be dedicated to the advocacy of peace with and within his brethren, *and* with his relatives and with every man, and even with the pagan in the street. For God will love only those men who are beloved of men."

He was both scrupulously honest and fearless. He had this to say: "When a teacher of the law is too greatly beloved by his fellow citizens, it is not generally because of his great merit but on account of his indulgence, which causes him to refrain from calling attention to their vices and from earnestly reprimanding them." This was said in the fourth century c.e., and note that times in this respect have not changed much. History does not repeat itself, but human nature does. Abbaye himself was a poor man. Whether there was any connection between what he said and the fact that he was poor is a matter for conjecture. He was so poor that his colleague Rava said that he never saw a bottle of wine on his table.

RAVA AND PUBLIC RELATIONS

Rava was born in 299 and died in 352. He was a different person altogether. Also a great scholar, also an enormous contributor to the Talmud and its lore, also indispensable to the development of the Talmudic tradition—he established a school of his own not far from Pumbedita, in the town of Mechoza. These places would never appear on the map of world history were it not for the fact that for Judaism, they were of transcending importance. Rava said of himself that when he became a rabbi, he prayed to God for three gifts: He wanted the wisdom of Rabbi Huna, and he got it; he wanted the wealth of Rabbi Hisda, and he got it; and he wanted the modesty of Rabba the son of Huna, but he failed to get it. He was honest enough to admit that he lacked modesty. He did for Mechoza what Rav did for Sura, and what Rabbi Joseph, Abbaye, and Rabba had done for Pumbedita. But unlike Abbaye, he catered to his people's whims. He was a successful rabbi in the modern sense of the word. To give an example: Mechoza had a very small Jewish population and there were many proselytes in it, pagans who had become Jews. As in small towns on the Jewish map of America today, it was a problem: Where does a Jewish girl meet a Jewish boy? And where does the Jewish boy meet a Jewish girl? The problem is so severe that inter-marriage is the frequent result. This was a problem that came up in the Mechoza of Rava's day. Now, the question came up whether Jewish law could be liberalized so as to permit a Jewish woman to marry a bastard—a bastard in the Jewish legal sense. In the Jewish legal sense, a bastard is not one who is born out of wedlock, but a child who is a product of adultery. Now there is a law in the Torah that a bastard may not be accepted into the congregation of Israel. In Mechoza it happened that there was no shortage of bastards, but there was a shortage of pedigreed Jewish families. The people came to Rabbi Zeira, one of the rabbis in Mechoza, and asked the question whether the law could be waived and whether it would be permissible for nice Jewish daughters to marry Jewish sons who were, technically speaking, bastards. Zeira consulted with Rava, and they agreed that the law could be waived under these circumstances in order to prevent intermarriage, on the theory that a technical Jewish bastard would be better suited than a pagan for the continuity of Judaism, since his status was not his fault. Rava and Zeira agreed on this decision. Rava said to Zeira: "You tell them." Zeira took to the pulpit to say: "I am in a position to say that it is perfectly all right for your daughters (speaking to the members of the Jewish community) to marry bastards." The people, not knowing what was involved, became incensed. They regarded it as an insult. It happened to be Succoth, and the men had *etrogim* (citrons) in their hands. They pelted Zeira with them. When Rava saw what was happening, he jumped up like a demagogue (be it said to his discredit) and said to the people: "Oh, I disagree. By no means should your daughters be reduced to the condition where they have to marry 'mamzerim.' Why, your daughters are fit to marry the children of the High Priest himself!" He had himself agreed with Zeira, but when he saw which way the wind was blowing, he changed his mind quickly, because with him popularity was apparently more important than courage.

Rava had a run-in with the king of Babylonia at that time, Shapur II. The circumstance was as follows: One time, Rava punished a Jew for a public display of immorality. The punishment was in the form of the traditional flogging. Thirty-nine lashes are prescribed by the law. The flogging was administered to a man who happened to have a weak heart. In the midst of the beating, he died of a heart attack. Rava in thus doing had violated the basic law of the land, which was that no

Jewish court is to handle any criminal cases of any kind. He was ordered arrested for trial, which would carry a possible death sentence. He fled for his life, was saved in due course through the intervention of the Queen Mother, whose name was Ifra. She had intervened because she had the highest regard for the scholarship of the Jews and for Rava, a man with friends at court. When he was returned and pardoned, Queen Ifra made him a gift of 400 dinarim. She gave him that gift in order to mollify his hurt feelings. His colleagues said to him: "Don't accept the gift of this pagan woman. It is an undignified thing to do. Be thankful that you are back home and a free man." He said: "No, I am accepting it." "You don't need it," they said to him. "And how I need it!" They thought that he was going to pocket the money, and for a while there was consternation on the part of the people. But Rava took the money, went out to the marketplace, and distributed it among the pagan poor, making sure in the process that the act was well advertised. Now this, too, is illuminating and indicative of Rava's instinctive talent for good public relations.

Abbaye and Rava conducted a lifelong dialogue on Jewish law and lore, which fill the pages of the Talmud, and which helped make the Talmud a fascinating work, a work of teaching and preaching, sermonics and psychology, folklore and history, in sum, of Jewish hopes and dreams and aspirations, of the Jewish quest for survival, of the Jewish passion for the preservation of even the minutiae of its tradition. Abbaye and Rava were, in a sense, the middle architects of the Talmud. The original architect was Rabbi Judah the Prince, who was the editor of the Mishnah, and his colleagues. It was he who had completed the work of Akiba and Rabbi Maier and the great Hillel and Gamaliel of Yavneh and of Yochanan ben Zaccai. We might call the first stage in the development of the Talmud the work of Rabbi Judah the Prince, who had died about the year 220. The middle stage of the development falls squarely upon the shoulders of Abbaye and Rava. The final stage belongs to the two men to be discussed in the chapter that follows, Ashi and Rabina.

But Abbaye and Rava represent the Alpha and Omega of the Talmudic spirit. Incidentally, Abbaye was the expert in monetary law, in civil law. Rava was the expert in ritual law. Wherever there is a difference in opinion between Abbaye and Rava in the area of the competence of Abbaye, he is ruled as the authority whose opinion is accepted. In the area of Rava's competence, he is ruled the authority with whom the decision rests. These two Jews, Abbaye and Rava, cannot possibly be given too much credit for the development of the Talmud, which lies at the heart of Jewish survival with and through the law.

JULIAN AND THE JEWS

An epilogue. Those of you who light Sabbath candles will notice that when the candle is about to go out, there is a flaring up, a kind of last gasp attempt on the part of the little candle to live a little longer. In that respect, candles are so much like human beings. Palestine was such a candle. One of the intriguing might-have-beens of history is concerned with the activity of the Roman Emperor of the fourth century, a contemporary of Abbaye and Rava, who ruled for too short a time. He was Julian, later dubbed the Apostate. Julian had wanted to turn the clock back. He did not believe in Christianity. Julian, as a matter of fact, was an agnostic, a philosopher-king, and a man with very strong character and convictions. When he became emperor in November 361, he decided to undo the work of Constantine and to eliminate Christianity as the official church of the Roman Empire. He began to work in that direction. One of his acts was to write the Jews a letter (and this letter is on record) in which he gave them permission to rebuild their Temple and in which he said he would supply the necessary help for it. He would, said Julian, restore the glory to that people that had been so unjustly deprived of it. He began to implement his promise by sending workers to the scene of the ruins of the Temple to clear away the debris. When rocks cover an area for a long space of time, highly combustible gasses accumulate. There was an explosion while the rocks were being cleared away. The explosion killed most of the workers. The finger was pointed by the Christian leadership saying: "There, we told you. This proves that God has rejected the Jews, that God does not want the Jews to restore their Temple, that they are a despised and a rejected people. This is the punishment of God, and Julian, too, will soon suffer death." And indeed, Julian did. He went to war against the Persians, about the beginning of the year 363. His initial efforts were promising, but then an enemy arrow caught him between the shoulder blades. It had been shot by one of his own Christian soldiers. Julian died. Tradition has it that as he died, his last words were: "Thou hast conquered me, O Galilean!" (Jesus).

He had been quite right. The Galilean did conquer. The Roman Empire was to stay Christian. The subsequent history of European civilization was to be Christian civilization, and therefore, the subsequent history of Western civilization was to be basically Christian civilization. And the Christians, those who had advocated peace by means of the sword, who had accepted the Pax Romana idea, were beginning to boast that the death of Judea was at hand. They were wrong. Because Judaism did not depend upon Julian. Kindly as was his disposition toward them, Judaism depended upon Abbaye and Rava. Abbaye and Rava helped erect a structure that no explosion could rend asunder. That building stands to this present day. The architects of the Talmud are many, but two of the grandest were Abbaye and Rava.

The Fifth Century

RAV ASHI

The Talmud is that gigantic work of Jewish law and lore whose chief architect in its final form was Rabbi Ashi, aided by his pupil Rabina. The Talmud is so vast, so comprehensive in breadth and in depth, that it would take the mind of a person of intelligence who is willing to spend a lifetime in its study to reach a point at which he might say that he knows something of the Talmud.

Ashi, the Jew of the fifth century, was the most important architect of the Talmud as we know it today. He was born in Babylonia in the year 352, and died there in the year 427. Our rabbis so appreciated in later years the astounding achievement of Rav Ashi that they declared that since Rabbi Judah the Prince there had never been a man who combined such great learning and immense prestige until Ashi's advent. To compare Rav Ashi to Rabbi Judah the Prince was to pay him the highest tribute possible. He validated the aphorism that the apple doesn't fall far from the tree. His father was a man named Shimi, an endearing contraction of Shimon. So brilliant was Shimi that Rab Pappa, his illustrious contemporary, had said in public: "I don't like to lecture when he is present. God protect me from him." Shimi was the kind of man who kept his rabbi honest. For to lecture with Shimi in the audience, intensive and conscientious preparation becomes mandatory.

Rav Ashi became the head of the academy at Sura, which had been founded, as you will recall, by our Jew of the third century, Abba Arikha. Ashi became the head of that academy at the age of nineteen. This, of course, would give an idea of the mind that he must have owned. He, too, was very wealthy. His father had bought up considerable forest acreage in Babylonia. Its value increased greatly over the years. An interesting sidelight about Rav Ashi was that he was hard-headed as a business man. Although he was scrupulously honest in his dealings, he had no hesitation selling his lumber to the Persian priests who were to use it in their cult of fire-worship.

ASHI'S ACHIEVEMENT

Let us now consider the work and achievement of Rav Ashi. In the first place, Ashi paid the cost of an entire new Sura Academy building. The Talmud informs us that he set up a cot outside the building and slept there nights for the full time that it took to construct it, so conscientiously did he superintend every detail.

The second achievement of Ashi was to bring the Academy of Sura to the peak of its fame. A very healthy competition had developed between the two great Babylonian institutions of Jewish learning, the one in Sura and the one in Pumbedita. For awhile it seemed as though Pumbedita was forging ahead to become *the* spiritual center of Babylonia, and therefore of world Jewry. This trend continued until Ashi arrived upon the scene. As a result of his enormous energies, great capacity for leadership, and phenomenal scholarship, Sura's preeminence was firmly established. So much so, indeed, that the installation ceremonies for the Exilarch, which had always been held at Pumbedita, were—during Rav Ashi's incumbency—held instead at Sura.

Rav Ashi fought for sanity amongst the Jewish people at a time when they were threatened with collective mania. The circumstances may be summarized as follows: The fifth century, as you may know, constituted a turning point in the history of the world. The barbarian hordes invaded Rome and its provinces. The Vandals, Visgoths, Ostrogoths, Lombards, and Huns all took their turn at devastation of the once-invincible Roman Empire. The Jewish people hated Rome with unparalleled bitterness. They had suffered through two wars with Rome, in the years 66–70 and during the Bar Kokhba rebellion, which was cruelly subdued in 135. The Jews now began to envisage with glee the collapse of the Roman Empire. When the barbarian invasions of Rome took place at the beginning of the fifth century precisely during the career of Rabbi Ashi, many Jews began to believe that the Messiah was at hand. Messianic pretenders emerged upon the scene and led many Jewish people astray. A collective psychosis threatened to grip the Jewish people. To cite a specific instance: One Moses of Crete succeeded in persuading practically the entire population of Crete that he was the Messiah, that he would lead them to the shores of the Mediterranean, that they would then plunge into the water, and that, like the Moses of old, he would smite the waters, they would part, and the Jews would cross the Mediterranean dryshod on their way to Palestine. So strong was the delusion that hundreds of people followed this mad man and were drowned. This is a historically recorded instance of insanity that struck Jewry at the beginning of the fifth century. Ashi, who was above all a rationalist, spoke out constantly in trying to reassure the Jewish people that the Messiah is not around the corner, that the Messiah is not about to change the order of nature, and that Jews had better concentrate on the cultivation of their own spiritual fortress. *"That* is the Messiah," said Rav Ashi. His sobering influence was a vital factor in maintaining the balance of his core ligionists during a critical period.

THE EDITING OF THE TALMUD

But the greatest achievement of Rabbi Ashi and of his pupil, Rabina, was a project in which he invested decades. It was the monumental task of editing of the Talmud. It was a far more difficult job than the Mishnah itself. It was a formidable undertaking, but Rabbi Ashi was equipped for it, if anybody at all was. Ashi was both "Sinai" and "mountain-grinder." Everyone recognized Ashi's authority, including such veterans as Amaymar and Rabbi Zutra, who were outstanding rabbinic stalwarts of the time. Because Rav Ashi's authority was unchallenged, he was able to accomplish the staggering challenge that the editing of the Talmud entailed.

The Babylonian Talmud is an elaboration and a discussion of the Mishnah of Rabbi Judah the Prince. To refresh memory, toward the end of the second century, Rabbi Judah the Prince had collected all of the Jewish laws that were extant at that time and had edited them into a code of Jewish law that he had divided into six different sections, known as "The Six Orders of the Mishnah." The Mishnah thereupon served as a text for the discussion of the law in the academies of Babylonia, namely Sura and Pumbedita. These discussions of the Mishnah were not reduced to writing nor formalized in any way. It was a very loosely connected type of discussion. Students here and there took down notes. These notes were accumulated over a period of two or three hundred years, and it was Ashi who decided that it was time to take the best of these notes and call upon the most distinguished scholarship of the time for the compilation of all this discussion into a coherent form.

At the core of the Talmud is the Law itself. The Law of the Talmud meant the regulation of every step, every move, every breath, every act of the Jew. There is virtually *nothing* that man could do about which the Talmud does not speak out. The Talmud speaks about everything. St. Jerome, the eminent church father who translated the Bible into Latin, the translation known as the Vulgate, had said somewhere: "Behold these miserable Jews, how they live mid the nations and tremblingly adhere to their own customs, always saying to one another: 'Do not touch this, do not eat this, don't come near that.'" He saw the Talmud as a series of strictures. You can't move, you can't sit, you can't walk, you can't talk, you can't sleep, you can't breathe, you can't sing, you can't chant, you can't jump, you can't have children, you can't sit down to the table, without following specific regulations set down in the Talmud. Now, of course, Jerome was right. His description of the Talmud was correct, but his implied contempt was misbegotten. For the Jews the Law was the substitute for the State, which they no longer had. It was the Law that preserved them as Jewish people, when all of the winds of assimilation were directed with full force against them. Were it not for the Law, the Jew could never have survived.

HALAKHA AND AGGADA

The Talmud consists basically of two types of matter: one is known as *halakha*, and the other as *aggada*. *Halakha* is drawn from the Hebrew root "haloch," which means "to go." *Halakha* means "the way in which to go," or the course of action or the manner of living. This is the *halakha*, and it is the Law. The *aggada* consists of lore and encompasses legends, maxims, aphorisms, superstitions, old wives' tales, historical fragments, biographical sketches, and even some bagatelle. It is inevitable that there should be in an immense work of such all-encompassing scope, material that is less than excellent. Indeed, some material is quite inferior. In one sense *aggada* stands to *halakha* as poetry stands to prose. Again *halakha* may be described as the words and *aggada* as the music. Where *aggada* sometimes soars in the celestial spheres, *halakha* trods the road of the mundane. *Halakha* teaches living with reality; *aggada* cultivates the meaningful dream.

The Talmud is a most unusual book. We could open to any actual page of the Talmud, translate sections of it, to get some of its style. Perhaps improvisation upon its method might achieve the purpose. Let us take something from Civil Law. The Mishnah says: If a man walks in a public street, stumbles on a pitcher and smashes it—he is not responsible for damages, because the owner of the pitcher had no right to place it in a public thoroughfare. This is actually the Law of the Mishnah. The rabbi (let us say Ashi) begins a discourse upon the law. There is an open discussion. Someone asks a question. "When you say 'pitcher' (here is where we are beginning to improvise), what do you mean? Do you mean pitcher and nothing else? Or can it mean any object?" The answer would be: "Well, obviously any object." Then the next question: "If any object, why do you say 'pitcher'? Why don't you say 'any object lying in the street'? Why do you have to say 'pitcher'?" A possible retort to that by another student might be: "Obviously, the word 'pitcher' is put there because it is a commonly used item, it is the most common thing that could be thought of." The next student might say: "Incidentally, that is true. In the marketplace, I know that the fastest-selling commodity is the pitcher. And by the way, last night, I walked through the streets of Sura and I saw a thin-handled pitcher selling for a half a shekel." And another young student would say: "Half a shekel? Why, that is an exorbitant price!" Then a discussion would begin about fair prices for pitchers. As a result of this, they might begin to discuss the necessity for regulating prices because there are some who take advantage of the laws of supply and demand and charge exorbitant prices. Then the question might come up, if that is the case, to what extent may the authorities interfere in private enterprise? After all, it's a man's own business. A discussion might then ensue as to the conflict between the principle of a free market and morality. Is it possible to interweave morality and private enterprise? Then someone might begin to quote from the Ethics of the Fathers, which is another tractate of the Mishnah, in which we are told that the moral person conducts himself in such manner as to meet with approval both of his fellow man and of his God. So you have got to meet with the approval of your fellow man, and then God will approve of you. Here a student might interrupt the discussion to say: "I do not like this reduction of God to the role of a secondary element, because God is what we must begin with. It is written: 'Hear, O Israel, the Lord our God, the Lord is One.'" Then a long discussion on theology might begin—which would in the final analysis be traceable to a little pitcher upon which someone stepped while walking a public thoroughfare.

THE TALMUDIC METHOD

Now if this seems too far-fetched, be assured that it is not. It is not as far-fetched as some of the actual discussions to be found in the Talmud. Why are these discussions so loosely connected? Because they are discussions as they actually took place, often recorded word for word. To be sure, Talmudic give and take is often of the hair-splitting variety. "Pilpul" has found its way into Webster's Dictionary in the form of the adjective "pilpulistic." Now, the word "pilpul" derives from the Hebrew word for pepper. Pilpul means "peppering the discussion," spicing it with fine and complicated arguments. A Jew who has a pilpulistic mind doesn't want to take surface value: he desires to go beneath and beyond the surface. Here is an example from the Talmud itself. The laws of *t'fillin* are discussed involving the proper manner of wearing these accessories of traditional prayer. A bit put out with the excess of improbable hypotheses offered at this particular session, a scholar named Plimu interjected the query: "Does a two-headed man require two sets of *t'fillin*?" On another occasion, they were discussing the following: Supposing a little chick is seen wandering about in a public thoroughfare. Now, how far does this chick have to be away from some private backyard in order to be regarded as *"hefker,"* that is, belonging to nobody. The conclusion is fifty yards. At this point some hair-splitting commences. Why not twenty-five yards? Why not seventy-five yards? Why exactly fifty yards? Reasons are adduced and everything is satisfactory. At this point Rabbi Jeremiah facetiously poses the question:

"What if the little chick had one foot inside and the other outside the aforementioned 'fifty-yard' line? What then?" The answer he received was eviction from the lecture hall. His sarcasm was apparently not appreciated. What has been said here is not by any means designed to ridicule the Talmud, which is a Book of Books among the Jewish people, without which it is inconceivable that Jews would be here at all. The Talmud has sustained the Jewish people through the ages. The Talmud has been the very backbone of the life of the Jew. It has been the way in which he has walked, and the way in which he has thought, and the basis upon which all Jewish law later on was to be developed. The intent here was to supply some of these *outre* examples in order to demonstrate how wide and deep the scope, and sometimes how far-fetched the rambling discussions could become.

BELIEFS IN THE TALMUD

What are some of the basic theological creeds in this Talmud that Ashi, the Jew of the fifth century, edited? The Talmud contains much theology without any claim to thoroughness. Seven basic elements on Jewish belief drawn from the Talmud and accepted by most of the Jewish people might serve as illustrations of Talmudic tenets. The Talmud holds that the soul survives the body. It believes in heaven and in hell as actualities of the world beyond our earthly state. It affirms the coming of the Messiah, a personal Messiah, a descendant of the House of David, who would emerge as the great leader of the Jewish people, who would lead them from slavery unto freedom, from darkness unto light, from misery unto glory. The Talmud affirms the revival of the dead; that someday those who deserve it, in some miraculous fashion, would be restored to bodily life. This belief had been formalized in the second blessing of the *Shmoneh Esrai*: "Blessed are Thou, O Lord, Who brings the dead back to life." The Talmudic sages believe in a final judgment day. They believe also that God created the world out of nothing—*Creatio ex nihilo*—that the world was not created out of pre-existent matter, but that God created it out of nothing. The Lord said: "Let there be," and there was. Before the Lord had said: "Let there be," there was nothing. But most important from the point of view of human morality, the Talmud believes emphatically in the doctrine of Free Will, which means that every one of us is the master of his own behavior, that we aren't forced by circumstances to behave in a certain way, that God did not predetermine for us to be either righteous or evil. The evil one does not have God to blame; only himself. The righteous has not God to thank, but only himself. The rabbis insisted on Free Will as the essence of all morality. Protestant theology in the sixteenth century, particularly that which was advanced by John Calvin, believed in precisely the opposite, in predestination, that whatever a human being does has been decreed by God from time immemorial. As a result the whole system of Calvinist morality had to undergo change. Free Will has remained the basis of the Jewish concept of morality down through the ages. Every human being makes up his own mind as to what he is going to be. If he is going to be Brother Rat, *he* made the choice. If he is going to be Brother, he made the choice too. It has not thus been decreed from time immemorial. This business of blaming circumstances and heredity and everything else but the human being himself for being errant is something that Judaism has never been able to accept, not only from the time of the Talmud, but going back to biblical times. Moses is quoted as saying to the children of Israel in emphatic terms: "Behold I put before you this day the choice between the blessing and the curse, between good and evil. I advise you to choose good." But it is up to you. Everyone makes his own bed, and everyone therefore must sleep in it.

FOLKLORE IN THE TALMUD

But the Talmud is not only law; it also contains folklore. There are superstitions in the Talmud. There are stories about the horoscopes. What does the world *mazel* mean? *Mazel* originally did not mean luck; it meant a sign of the Zodiac. In Talmudic days many a Jew believed in the horoscope, believed in devils, and believed in Lillith, who was the wife of Satan. The Angel of Death is pictured in the Talmud as being all eyes. It is hard to think of anything more monstrous than an Angel of Death who has neither arm nor leg nor anything else save eyes. The Talmud contains quack remedies, old wives' tales, and other superstitions. The rabbis did not necessarily hold to these superstitions, but in the course of the discussions they were often thrown into the conversational pot. They were not necessarily eaten, much less digested.

There are also some whimsical and humorous and homey tales in the Talmud. There is the story, a true story, of a Jewish scholar who had left Palestine and gone to Babylonia because he could not earn a livelihood in Palestine. He waxed rich. On his deathbed he wished to transmit all of his accumulated wealth to a son he had left behind in Palestine. He had with him one faithful slave. His first thought was to send the title to all his property by the hand of his slave to his son. But then he bethought himself: "This slave may decide not to deliver the deed at all but rather to keep everything for himself." So he decided on another method: He wrote out something like the following contract: "All of my property I bequeath to my slave on one condition: that he go back and give my son the opportunity to select just one item out of all my property. Besides that item, everything else will belong to my slave." Now Talmudic Law says that anyone who owns a slave, owns everything that the slave owns. In other words, a slave in those days didn't have powers of acquisition for himself. The father knew that his son was a Talmudic scholar. The servant was delighted with this piece of paper. Thought he: "Let the son take any item he desires. The bulk of the property would still remain to me." The servant quickly and eagerly delivered this document. Without hesitation the son declared to the servant, "I choose you," and the result was, of course, that the court of law awarded all of the property to the son in consequence of the fact that having come into possession of the slave, he had come into the possession of everything else.

RELIGIOUS POLEMICS

A running polemic between Christians and Jews coincided with the Talmudic era, and we find instances of it in the Talmud. Employing a New Testament metaphor attributed to Jesus, a Christian once asked a Jew: "Tell me, what is to be done with salt that has rotted? How is it cured?" The implication was that the children of Israel had been the salt of the earth but had turned rancid when they allegedly slew the Christ and that, therefore, they had ceased to be God's chosen people. To this question the Jew responded: "When the salt becomes putrid there is a cure for it. The water bag of a mule. Apply a mule's water bag to the salt and it will be cured." The puzzled Christian looked at him and retorted: "For heaven's sake, since when does the mule have a water bag?" The Jew replied: "Since when did the salt of the earth turn rancid?" He was denying the basic premise, denying that Judaism's validity had been superseded by that of Christianity. There is one passage in the Talmud that is both raw and vital. Amongst those who argued polemically with the Jewish people about the validity of their faith were not only the Christians, but also the Persians who believed in two gods, the god of Good who was Ahura-Mazda, and the god of Evil, who was Ahariman. One of the magi, the religious teachers of the Persians, addressed himself to a rabbi named Amaymar: "Since your upper part belongs to Ahura-Mazda, the god of Light, and since your lower belongs to Ahariman, the god of Darkness, you must recognize that you are a personality divided between two gods, not one." Rabbi Amaymar replied: "If Ahariman did indeed control the nether regions of my anatomy, would he ever permit the passage of my water through his domain?" This was his way of reducing Parsee dualism to absurdity.

PARABLES AND ETHICS

The Talmud very often spoke in parables. Very instructive, and amusing, is one about a middle-aged man who married two women (in those days it was permissible). One of them was very young and the other was quite old. This man—being middle-aged—had both gray and black hair on his head. The young woman plucked all of his gray hair so that he should appear youthful like herself, while the old woman plucked all of his black hair, so that he should appear aged like her. The result was that he became totally bald! The Talmud meant to say: You cannot please everybody. If you wish to please all sides, you can have no point of view at all. You will be nothing at all.

Ethical teaching is a Talmudic constant. The tractate *Aboth* is exclusively concerned with ethical conduct. Indeed, the sages comprehended fully that ritual is the handmaid of morals, not the other way around. Hillel, the great first-century rabbi who was the progenitor of a fabled dynasty, when asked what is the essence of Judaism, replied: "That which is hateful to thee, do not perpetrate upon your fellow man." The minutiae of religious practice must never become ends in themselves or the heart of Judaism will be overwhelmed by its mechanisms.

Perhaps the most appropriate way of ending this chapter is a quotation from the Talmud that might well summarize its fundamental outlook: "The world rests on three foundations: on Torah (which is learning); on *Avodah* (which is dedication to the ideal of God); and on acts of kindness, which we perform one to another." Learning, love of God, and love of one's fellow man—these are the three pillars upon which the world must survive. In the year 499, Abina, or Rabina, the student of Ashi, put the closing touches to the final editorial work that is the monumental opus we call the Talmud. Examine any page. The big print in the middle of the page is the Talmudic text itself. Around it you see smaller print. These are the commentaries on the Talmud of Rashi and Tosefot. There are commentaries to the commentaries. And to the commentaries on the commentaries, there are also commentaries. And to the latter named there are commentaries. Commentaries, commentaries, commentaries, commentaries—and that is the greatest commentary on the nature of Judaism. Judaism is an ongoing process. Nobody ever closes the book on Judaism. Rabbi Judah the Prince closed the book on the Mishnah. Rav Ashi and Rabina closed the book on the Gemara, but they did not close the book on the development of Jewish law. There came Maimonides, and Jacob ben Asher, and Joseph Caro, and the Gaon of Vilna, and Professor Saul Lieberman, and Rav Soloveitchik—all of them following the tradition of the endless, ongoing process of Judaism, a religion that is quite incapable of the act of closing books. It is forever opening them. Rabbi Ashi stands out along with his younger colleague Rabina as the Jew of the fifth century because by closing the book on a particular phase of the development of Judaism and its lore, he opened up even wider horizons for posterity.

The pages of the Talmud pulsate with life, with vigor, with flux. Talmudism in its best sense will never be eradicated from the Jewish psyche. For it really represents nothing less than a consummate passion for relating the mundane to the heavenly.

And is not this the *raison d'etre* of religion?

THE SIXTH CENTURY

JOSE BEN JOSE

The fifth century marked a turning point in the history of the world. The barbarians had invaded the "Eternal City" of Rome toward the beginning of the fifth century. Before that century was out, the mighty Roman Empire, which had lasted for so many hundreds of years, was rent asunder. It was split into two parts—the western, whose capital was at Rome, and the eastern, whose capital was in ancient Byzantium, later known as Constantinople. The Byzantine Empire had jurisdiction over Palestine and its constantly diminishing Jewish community. The Christian–Jewish polemic intensified as time went on. The acerbity and bitterness between the two communities, the Jewish and the Christian, was especially rampant in Byzantium.

In Palestine particularly, where the Christians were rapidly becoming the majority and the Jews just as rapidly becoming the minority, the polemic arguments often reached a boiling point. The Christians, who possessed political power, exercised it without restraint against the Jewish community. We see this reflected in the writing of the church fathers. Terteulian, Jerome, and Anthony were among the most noted purveyors of anti-Judeo sentiments among many other Church fathers in their writing.

JUSTINIAN'S CODE

Centuries of such literature led to the crystallization of laws specifically designed to degrade and humiliate the Jews of Byzantium. It was
during the sixth century reign of the Emperor Justinian that the great
Code—known as the *Corpus Juris Civilis*— was compiled. This was accomplished about the year 540. It remains as one of the foundations
for the legal systems of the Western world. In this *Corpus Juris Civilis*
the Novellae, or by-laws, to the central body of the Code were added.
Novella No. 146, which was composed in the year 553, prohibited the
reading of the Torah in the synagogue in Hebrew. The Torah could
only be read in the Greek version, which was the Septuagint. That
Greek translation from Hebrew had been the very first translation into
a foreign language of the Torah. It had been done in the middle of the
third century B.C.E. This Greek translation of the Torah was the only
version the Code of Justinian permitted to be read in the synagogue.
In addition, all sermons by a rabbi were prohibited. No new synagogues were allowed to be built. But the persistence and the tenacity
of the Jew loyal to his tradition rendered him impervious to all restrictions, codified or not.

The Jews found a way to circumvent the laws of Justinian. While
technically abiding by the bans of Justinian, they brought preaching
and teaching Torah into the synagogue nonetheless. Since the Hebrew
liturgy was not prohibited, they set about to compose special prayers
that were really sermons. The sermons were thus smuggled in, as it
were, into the text of the prayer book. The prayer of the congregation
and the chanting of the cantor actually involved extensive poetic passages that were repositories of Jewish law and instructive guides to
Jewish living. Today we call a *hazzan* a man who chants the service. In
the sixth century, a *hazzan* was much more. The *hazzan* not only
chanted and led the service, but also composed new prayers that included the teaching that could not be otherwise communicated in public. Thus the *hazzan*, perforce, became both scholar and poet. Into the
poetic prayers that he composed were interwoven the laws, the lore,
the practices, the beliefs—the very essence, indeed—of the Jewish way
of life. In a very real sense the liturgy was a continuation of the Talmudic tradition. This type of liturgy, which was designed for learning
purposes, was called *piyyut*, from the Greek word for poetry. The people
who composed this *piyyut* were called *payyetanim*, of which the singu-

lar is *payyetan*. The father of all the *payyetanim* was Jose ben Jose, our Jew of the sixth century.

JOSE, THE ORPHAN

He was born fatherless. His mother died delivering him. An orphan from the beginning, he was named after his father. He was called *Kohen Gadol* either because he was a priest and therefore a member of the Kohen clan, or because most of his poetry, his *piyyutim*, was concentrated on the section of the Yom Kippur liturgy that deals with the service in the Temple during the holiest period of the year, when the High Priest entered the Holy of Holies—the service called the *Avodah*. That is all we know about his life.

He was the father of the *payyetanim*. He began a long tradition that lasted for a thousand years of continuing the process of Judaic instruction and inspiration by means of the liturgy of the *machzor*, thereby circumventing the edicts of Justinian. Fortunately some of his works have survived, and they represent the most desirable and beautiful qualities of this new genre of Jewish literature known as *piyyut*. The Jewish people in the sixth century and for centuries thereafter had few places to frequent for the purposes of relaxation or exaltation. Their joy in life was the synagogue. The synagogue was their place of recreation as well as their place of inspiration. In that synagogue the Jews heard sweet music. When it became known, for example, that a new *piyyut* was to be introduced by the *hazzan*, the synagogue was filled to capacity hours before the service began. It was much like a premiere performance, let us say, of a new opera by a world renowned composer. This was the joy of the Jew, this was the life of the Jew, this was the inspiration of the Jew. It was his substance, sustenance, and his vitality. The synagogue and its *piyyut* was not peripheral to the life of the Jew; it was indispensable.

RAPOPORT, LUZZATTO, AND ZUNZ

The field of research into *piyyut*, the religious poetry of which Jose ben Jose was the founder, was opened wide by three scholars who lived in three different parts of Europe in the nineteenth century. Their scholarly activity embraced the approximate span of 1820 to 1865. Samuel David Luzzatto lived in Padua, Italy. He taught there in the Collegio Rabbinico. Solomon Rapoport was the rabbi of Tarnapol in Galicia, and Leopold Zunz lived in Berlin. None of these three men ever got to meet each other, but they engaged in a prolific correspondence embracing a full spectrum of Jewish scholarship. Their correspondence was concerned in large measure with the origin, authorship, content, and form of the literature of *piyyutim*.

The trialogue began with a question that appeared in the form of a letter to the editor of a scholarly Jewish magazine. It was written by Rapoport, the first man in this triumvirate. He said: "I came across the name of Yannai. I know that he was a composer of *piyyutim*, but that is all I know about him." Intensive research by the three scholars yielded some solid knowledge about Yannai and other *payyatanim*. They disagreed as to the place of his birth, but they all agreed that he lived and worked during the tenth century.

Modern research was to establish that Yannai actually lived in the seventh century. The Jewish section of the famous St. Petersburg Library had been greatly enriched by a gift of Jewish manuscripts from Baron de Guenzburg. Its librarian, Alexander Harkavy, discovered a manuscript written by the Karaite scholar Kirkisani, who writes that the founder of Karaism, Anan ben David, used material from the poetry of Yannai. That means Yannai could not have lived any later than the eighth century, when Anan flourished, and in all probability Yannai lived in seventh century Palestine.

THE CAIRO GENIZA

There followed one of the most interesting dramas in the history of Jewish literature. It begins in a stuffy little study in Cambridge, England, where a bearded man of massive head, piercing eyes, and disheveled hair is disturbed by two spinster ladies. They had just come back from a trip around the world, including a stop in Cairo. They brought to this man two leaves of an old manuscript that they had bought from an Arab in Cairo. They showed them to our man in Cambridge, who examined them carefully for a moment and then jumped up to ask: "Where did this come from?" They told him that they came from the attic of a synagogue near Cairo. A few hours later, he appeared before the dean of Cambridge University (he was a professor of Judaic studies and Semitic languages at Cambridge) and said: "I beg permission for a leave of absence for six months." "What for? Aren't you feeling well?" "Oh, I'm feeling great, and I hope to feel even greater. I'm going to Cairo. Not only do I want a leave of absence, but I want a subvention of several thousand pounds. The University will not be the loser." The dean granted his request. Our man took the next ship to Cairo, and there he hunted down the dealer who had sold the pages to our spinster ladies. The information he received led him to the *geniza* of the old Cairo synagogue. A *geniza* is a place usually located under the Holy Ark or in the synagogue attic where torn fragments of holy writings are consigned. Our Cambridge professor went up to that *geniza* attic and spent seventy-two hours there without eating or sleeping, while inhaling the accumulated dust of centuries. What he found there was perhaps the greatest literary treasure-trove of Jewish history. Our man from Cambridge was Solomon Schechter, who was later to become the president of the Jewish Theological Seminary of America. In the Cairo *geniza* was found the most amazing collection of Jewish writing ever discovered. There has been a lot of sensation about the Scrolls from the Dead Sea, but compared in importance to the Cairo *geniza*, the Scrolls from the Dead Sea are not nearly as vital to Jewish scholarship. The Cairo *geniza* included selections of ages of Jewish scholarship about which the Jewish people, even the scholars in their midst, had been in ignorance for hundreds of years.

For the purposes of our present chapter, the following is of great importance. Schechter came back home. Among the items that he handed over to some of his colleagues were some Greek manuscripts. Two of his colleagues were named Burkitt and Taylor, both Greek scholars who were consulted by Schechter with regard to some Greek fragments found in the *geniza*. It turned out that these were an old Greek translation of the Bible, and Burkitt and Taylor wrote monographs on this particular discovery. Included in these monographs were photostats of the fragments themselves. Their work came into the hands of a scholar at the Jewish Theological Seminary who was occasionally interested in Greek, but whose prime interest was the work started by Luzzatto, Rapoport, and Zunz a hundred years before, namely the work of the *payyetanim*. When he looked carefully at this photo-offset, he realized that something was written under the Greek in Hebrew letters. The technical term for it is a palimpset. A palimpset is writing upon other writing. In those days, the eighth, ninth, and tenth centuries, paper was very expensive and not easily come by. If somebody wanted to write something, and he found a piece of paper upon which something was already written, he tried to erase it as best as he could and write over it. But the erasing job was in many cases sloppy. Israel Davidson (that was the name of the scholar) looked at it carefully with his magnifying glass, and he realized that he had here for the first time the poetry of that Yannai whose name only had been known to Zunz, Luzzatto, and Rapoport. On the basis of this, he pursued intensive research, which ultimately led to his publication of the *Machzor Yannai*: an entire *machzor* consisting of fragments of poetry that had been woven by this seventh-century Jewish *hazzan*-poet into the prayer book. They are magnificent. As a result of the Cairo *geniza* find, there was established the Institute for the Study of Hebraic Medieval Poetry. First it flourished in Germany and then, after the advent of Nazism, was transferred to Jerusalem. A stream of volumes on ancient and medieval Jewish poetry has since followed. Our knowledge of liturgical poetry has been enriched beyond the wildest dreams of Luzzato, Rapoport, and Zunz.

RESURRECTION OF MEDIEVAL POETRY

"Boruch ato Adonoi mechayeh hamaysim" is a blessing in our *Shmoneh Esrai*. "Blessed are Thou, O Lord, Who bringest the dead back to life." What has been told here is the actualization of that blessing. The father of this entire genre of Judaic spiritual music was Jose ben Jose, about whom we have already learned that he was an orphan from birth and that he was called the High Priest. We know that he wrote in impassioned and very clear Hebrew. His poetry was without rhyme or meter. It was in the form of acrostics. Many an outstanding *payyetan* has been identified because he was kind enough, or vain enough, to sign his name into his composition. Jose ben Jose's prayers are very touching. They were not complicated, and his language is pure and simple. Here is an example: "Oh God, listen to the plaint of an oppressed soul, and may I remind You, O Lord, that it is written in the Book of Psalms that they who sow in tears shall reap in joy." What he was saying here was that prayer had its own value. Even without its being answered, the value resides in the prayer itself if it emanates from the heart of him who offers it. In essence, a prayer is a love letter to God. Its response is in the feeling that God does respond.

YANNAI AND KALIR

Jose ben Jose *was* the father of *payyetanim*, but Yannai became known as the master. From Luzzatto's, Zunz's, and Rapoport's days, when we knew nothing but the name and some speculations about where Yannai came from, we have traveled a long way. We have scores of his *piyyutim*, most of them collected by Israel Davidson. The best known of all his prayers is the *Al-het*—"For the sins that we have sinned before You, etc." That is Yannai's composition. Only fifty years ago were we able definitely to ascribe *Al-het* to the pen of this man whom Luzzatto, Zunz, and Rapoport could only identify by name.

Yet the most famous and prolific of this entire school of composers of religious, didactic poetry was Eliezer, who was known as Kalir. What Kalir means, we do not know. It may have been his father's name. According to Luzzatto, Kalir comes from the Greek "kalyron," which is some kind of bun. Legend has it that Eliezer ate a bun dipped in honey as a child and became immediately possessed of the muse of poetry.

Eliezer Kalir wrote most of the *piyyutim* that we find today in the Jewish liturgy for Passover, for Succoth, for Shavuoth, for the High Holidays. Eliezer Kalir was the greatest master of the Hebrew language since the days of the Bible. He used words that no one used before, and he invented words that apparently never existed. He wrote abstruse, difficult poetry. He made an exercise of the Hebrew language. He bent it to every purpose, he squeezed it, he turned it right and left, he elongated it, he elaborated it, and he contracted it. He glorified it, he did everything that could possibly be done with a word. After all, Hebrew in his days had not been spoken for hundreds of years. He was able to take this language and employ it in such a pliable manner that he could express almost anything he wanted with it. He has contributed some of the most glorious passages in our liturgy. He had been inspired, as Yannai had before him, by Jose ben Jose, the pioneer in the field of liturgical poetry.

The High Holiday Prayer Book is filled with glorious *piyyutim*. "I come to implore Thee with a troubled heart. As a poor man knocking at the gate have I come to seek mercy. Dispense not stern justice but tender mercy. O Lord, do Thou teach me what to say." The most vital talent of a people's servant is to use his words properly and effectively. So wrote a *payyetan* of the eleventh century in Germany named Simon ben Isaac. *Unesaneh Tokef* is a magnificent prayer that speaks of the great shofar being sounded, of mortals passing before the God of Judgment as a flock of sheep: "As a shepherd musters the sheep causing them to pass under his staff, so dost Thou cause every living soul to pass before Thee." Although attributed by legend to Rabbi Amnon of Mayence, it was actually composed by Kalonymus ben Meshullam, an Italian Jew of the eleventh century.

We find magnificent *piyyutim* throughout the *machzor*. Take that wonderful but anonymous composition *"Veye'sayu"* in its lovely English rendition by Israel Zangwill: "All the world shall come to serve Thee and praise Thy glorious Name, and Thy righteousness triumphant the islands shall acclaim, and nations shall give Thee homage who knew Thee not before, And the ends of earth shall praise Thee, Thy name they shall adore. And the islands laugh exultant that they to God belong, and all their congregations so loud Thy praise shall sing, That far away peoples hearing, shall hail Thee crowned King."

The *payyetanim*, spiritually sired by Jose ben Jose, left their indelible imprint not merely within the pages of Jewry's book of prayers, but also upon Israel's life and destiny.

The Seventh Century

BUSTENAI

The story of the Jewish people is, of course, one of wide dispersion. There is hardly a country on the face of the civilized earth in which the Jew has not lived and whose culture he has not affected. It should come, therefore, as no surprise that the Arabian peninsula was also inhabited by Jews. The settlement of the Jews in Araby goes back a long time. Today there are no Jews in Saudi Arabia, and Jews have been virtually eliminated largely through immigration to the newborn State of Israel from almost every Arab country in the world. But once upon a time, the Jewish population of Arabia was considerable, with a long history behind it.

Jews in the Arabian peninsula claimed to have been there since the days of Joshua—a manifest absurdity. We may safely state, however, that the peninsula harbored Jews from the year 70 and onward. The likelihood is that many of the Jews who left Palestine after the disaster of that year found their way to Arabia. Over the next several centuries, the Jews there gradually came to resemble Arabs in their outer appearance. But they remained loyal, after their own fashion, to their faith. Because they were cut off from the center of the Jewish world, their religious practice in many respects differed from that of the dominant Jewish communities. The Jews in Arabia for centuries were Arabs in most respects. They were warriors, they belonged to tribes, and they were as petulant about their tribal possessions as were the non-Jewish Semites who constituted the rest of the population. The Jewish-Arabic tribes even indulged in the patented Arab tradition of feuding with each other. They had sheiks at the head of their tribes, and their tribes had distinctive identifications. There existed for example, the Nadhir tribe, the Kuraiza tribe, the Chaibar tribe, and others. Before the title of each tribe came the Arabized prefix *Benu*, which was the equivalent of *B'nai*, meaning "sons of." Thus the Benu-Nadhir, the Benu-Kuraiza, the Benu-Chaibar tribes. Most of them were located about oases of palms and streams in the area now known as Medina, but which in those days was known as Yathrib.

ARAB JEWS

The Jews lived in fortified towns and castles. Unlike most of the Arab tribes, they were not Bedouin. They preferred to live in one area that they could cultivate. The result was that Bedouin frequently attacked their strongholds, and so the Jews fortified themselves against such onslaughts. It may be of interest to know that Yemen, now *Judenrein*, once had a Jewish kingdom. This came about in the following fashion: An Arab named Abu-Kariba inherited the kingdom of Yemen and was persuaded by his Jewish friends to convert to Judaism. In those days the Arabs were not Moslems. We are talking about the fourth, fifth, and sixth centuries. They were pagans, idol-worshipers, with a variety of cults. Abu-Kariba was converted about the year 500 to Judaism. In Yiddish there is a saying: "Someone who becomes convert to a cause is more passionate in espousing that cause than one who is born to it." Converted Jews sometimes are more firmly Jewish than Jews who were born to the religion. Abu-Kariba trained his son so well in Judaism that when his son, Yussuf Dhu-Nowas (Dhu-Nowas in Arabic means "curley locks"), inherited his father's throne, he became violently anti-Christian. There were Christians in the Arab peninsula, too, and the Christians were vying with the Jews in trying to persuade the pagans of the merits of their respective faiths. In effect, a cultural rivalry raged between Jews and Christians living in the Arabian peninsula over the conversion of the majority of the natives to one or the other of the religions. Yussuf, who was the son of a pagan king converted to Judaism, actually inaugurated an anti-Christian crusade, so passionately zealous was he for his recently acquired faith. Ethiopia was then already Christian. Indeed, Ethiopia is the oldest Christian country in Africa. The Ethiopians, in resentment over the activities of Yussuf, invaded the Arabian peninsula and the result was a fierce engagement between Yussuf and the Ethiopian–Christian forces. Yussuf and his army were routed. The situation was hopeless. The Arab–Jewish king raced his horse to a high rock overlooking the Mediterranean Sea and, cornered by the enemy, he exclaimed, *"Shema Yisroel Adonoy Elohenu Adonoy Ehod,"* and with his horse plunged into the depths rather than be taken alive by the enemy.

MOHAMMED

Judaism in Arabia was to undergo a severe upheaval and ultimate extinction with the emergence of one of the most intriguing personalities in history. The man known as Mohammed arrived on the scene in the early decades of the seventh century. His battle cry was: "There is only one god, and he is Allah." Mohammed claimed that he was Allah's greatest prophet. He began to teach and to preach. Apparently he was a very forceful personality. His driving leadership succeeded in welding a large number of disparate and feuding tribes into one of the most powerful forces the world had ever seen. It was Mohammed who lent coherence to the concepts Arab and Muslim.

We do not know much about his life; it is cloaked in mystery. But we do know that he was unlettered. We know that unlike most great religious teachers like Confucius, Buddha, Jesus, and Moses, he was not a spiritual personality. For one thing, he loved women too much. At first he was much impressed by the Jews. He called them the "Ahl Ul Kitab" which means "the writing nation." To him it was a miracle that most of the people within a certain group were able to write at all. The fact is that not one in one hundred in those days could read or write. The Jews were dubbed by Mohammed "the people of the Book," a sobriqet that has survived to the present day. The Book that he referred to was the Bible. He would hear many tales from his Jewish friends from the Bible, as well as from some of the Haggadic legends of the Talmud. From the Jews he received some of the religious ideas that he was later to incorporate into the new religion known as Islam. It must also be said that he borrowed very liberally from the Christian teachers whom he encountered. The result was a remarkable amalgam of Judaism, Christianity, and paganism.

Islam is as stringent a monotheistic faith as ever existed. In that respect, Islam is closest to Judaism. Mohammed, who never graduated himself out of the rank of prophet to the rank of deity, had some fond hopes about the Jews. He had hoped that he would make them converts to his new doctrine. After all, had not the Jews told him that they and the Arabs are brothers? The Jews of Araby had disseminated the idea that Isaac, son of Abraham, was the progenitor of the Jewish people and that Ishmael, Abraham's oldest son, was the forbear of the Arabs. Whether or not the Ishmael genealogy is true is not important. What is true is that the Jews and the Arabs issue from Semitic stock.

Mohammed had hopes that the Jews would be the first to rally to his banner. He was sorely disappointed because, unlike some of the others whom he managed to influence, the Jews treated him with utmost contempt. Indeed, in their own language, Jews would often refer to him as "the deranged one."

Mohammed did not take kindly to this treatment. Although initially he had been very friendly toward the Jewish people, he subsequently turned against them in full fury. There followed vengeance. The Koran contains virulent anti-Jewish writing. When he originally started his new religion, Mohammed thought of Jerusalem as his holy city. But, when the Jews turned away from him, he turned away from Jerusalem and instead he chose Mecca, the city of his birth, as the place toward which all Arabs must turn when they offer prayer. He conducted wars of extermination against the Jews in which thousands lost their lives. For instance, the Jewish city of Chaibar was completely wiped out in the year 628. There is a legend that Zainab, one of the many wives of Mohammed, was partially Jewish. The legend has no foundation. The circumstance that she once tried to poison her husband accounts for the story.

JEHAD

But Mohammed did succeed in arousing the consciousness of nationality and peoplehood in the Arabic world. He raised the banner of *jehad*, which means holy war. Mohammed offered the assurance that all who would fight in behalf of Allah and die gloriously in his name would be assured of heaven. Amongst other heavenly emoluments, beautiful maidens would be made available to the faithful. Because the vision of heaven conjured up by Mohammed was so tempting, the Arabs fought with fierce abandon and often welcomed death in a battle for Allah. If we are to understand the almost unbelievable phenomenon that tribes of wild people could be so solidly organized as to be able to conquer half of the civilized world, to come within a whisker of becoming masters of the whole of it, to come within a hair of rendering all of Europe Arabic, we must comprehend the frenzy that animated Mohammed's followers. Their courage was absolute because death was not to be feared but rather to be welcomed. For beyond it lay immeasurable heavenly bliss.

JEWS AND ARABS AFTER MOHAMMED

Persia fell to the Arab hordes. Palestine, too. Egypt was a victim. When Mohammed died, Omar the Great succeeded him, and in 638 he entered Jerusalem. On the site once occupied by the Temple, he built a structure that still stands, the Mosque of Omar. Legend has it that Omar the Great had been anti-Jewish to begin with. The so-called Covenant of Omar (which cannot be historically substantiated) prohibited Jews from building new houses of worship, ordered them to pray silently so as not to offend Moslem ears, forced them to genuflect before the faithful, forbade their filling of administrative or judicial posts, prohibited their riding of horses (which was a mark of rank), and—this is probably true—imposed the badge of shame, which Christianity was later to adopt and to carry to great extremes. Despite all this, the fact is that the Jews actually enjoyed relative placidity in Arab lands. There was simultaneous flowering of Jewish culture and Arab culture. The partnership of the Jews and the Arabs from the ninth through the eleventh centuries was to result in a most prolific explosion of knowledge. The Arabs and the Jews formed a cultural partnership that produced some of the most important work of western civilization. They were the link between barbarism, which had resulted from the defeat of the Roman empire, to the civilization that ultimately flowered into the Renaissance.

THE EXILARCHATE

The institution with which Bustenai, the Jew of the seventh century, is closely identified was the institution of the exilarchate. It was under the Arabs that the head of the Jewish community of all Arab lands, the Exilarch, was raised to a position of power and glory that the Jews had not known since the destruction of the Temple and were not to know again until the rebirth of the State of Israel.

The exilarchate was the political leadership of the Jews of the Arab world. Alongside of it stood the gaonate—from the word "*gaon.*" The *gaon* was the successor to the great rabbis of the Talmud, who were the heads of the academies of Sura and Pumbedita. The gaonic period dates from about the middle of the seventh century through the eleventh century. The exilarchate emerged into its full glory in the seventh century through the magnificent, colorful, almost unreal personality of Bustenai. Bustenai was a compound of fact and legend. He was a remarkable person, but his life has been adorned with so much legend that today it is difficult to separate the fact from the fiction. There are eight different sources for the story of Bustenai: four gaonic sources, three exilarchic sources, and one sixteenth-century source. What follows is a synopsis of the many versions of the Bustenai story.

The *gaonim*, the heads of the academies of Sura and Pumbedita in Babylonia, received letters of inquiry from Jews the world over with respect to legal and ritual matters. Tens of thousands of questions ranging over the whole domain of Jewish law were addressed to the *gaonim*. The *gaonim* answered most of them. A very peculiar question crops up repeatedly throughout this literature of the *gaonim*. The question is as follows: Is the son of a pagan maidservant sired by her Jewish master to be regarded as a slave or as a freeman? This particular question recurs with puzzling frequency. To explain this, Bustenai must be brought into our picture.

Here is the picture that emerges. The last of the Persian kings in Babylonia who preceded Arab rule was a fierce persecutor of the Jews. He particularly persecuted the Jews who claimed to be of the House of David. He made it his special project to kill off all of the descendants of the House of David and came close to accomplishing this purpose. He hoped to root out any potential political rebellion by the Jews through the eradication of its traditional Messianic fount—the House of David. Once he had a nightmare in which he saw himself going out to his favorite garden, which in Persian is called *"bustan,"* where he assiduously had cultivated magnificent trees. He saw himself mercilessly hacking these trees down, one after another. He destroyed them all, except for one big tree left standing in the center. He had been on the point of bringing that tree down, too, when an old man appeared with a mallet in his hand, smote the king over the head shouting: "How dare you cut down this last surviving tree! Cut it down, and it will be the end of you." The king woke up from his nightmare. His pillow was full of blood. He called his wise men and asked them for an explanation. One of the wise men told the king that he knew the interpretation. The *bustan*, or garden, consists of all of the members of the House of David whom he had persecuted and destroyed. He had destroyed them all except for one female descendant of the House of David who was pregnant. She is in hiding and if the king desires to live, then he had best seek her out and see to it that she is safely delivered of a sound and healthy male child. Thus the central tree in the garden would continue to fructify the House of David, which was meant never to perish.

The story goes on to say that the king found this pregnant woman of the House of David. He took very good care of her, and a healthy boy was born. They called him Bustenai, the child of the garden. For this child the king appointed a guardian, an elderly Jewish gentleman, who was also to serve as acting Exilarch pending the maturity of this child, who would then be installed in office. When the boy was 16 years old, he demanded the title and the position. But his aged guardian, betraying his trust, refused to give up his post. Undaunted, Bustenai brought his case before Omar, who by then had become the monarch of Araby, including the conquered provinces of Babylonia. The acting Exilarch was at the point of convincing Omar that Bustenai's claim was not valid, when suddenly, Omar's eyes were fascinated by a fly that was doing a dance on Bustenai's nose with such efficacy as to draw blood. The ordinary reflex action would have been to brush it away. Bustenai would not budge. Omar was curious. He said: "Young man, why don't you swat the fly away?" Bustenai answered very simply: "Your Majesty, the Caliph, I have been instructed by my late mother that in the presence of royalty, one must stand at rigid attention no matter what." So impressed was Omar by the young man's manner that he ruled in his favor. Thus Bustenai became the head of a long dynasty of Exilarchs of the House of David that was to last for 500 years.

THE CHILDREN OF PRINCESS AZADWAD

So impressed with Bustenai was Omar that he gave him for a wife a captive princess, daughter of the Persian King Khosoroe, whom he had defeated in battle. Bustenai had children by her. He also had children by fully Jewish wives. Bustenai had wanted the children of this fair maiden, whose name was Azadwad, to succeed him as Exilarchs. But the descendants of his Jewish wives were opposed to that and for generations a rivalry existed between the descendants of Bustenai's Princess Azadwad and the descendants of his Jewish wives. Each group claimed for itself the right of succession to the exilarchate whenever a vacancy developed. Questions were addressed to the *gaonim*, century after century, to the following effect: Supposing a man had relations with a maidservant who is a pagan, and she bears a child, is that child a Jew or is he to be regarded as slave? Obviously, these questions were inspired by Busteani's Jewish progeny with a not-so-subtle reference to the origins of their rivals. They hoped to get a ruling that would declare Azadwad's descendants to be slaves and therefore unfit to be Exilarchs. But the children of Azadwad continued to serve as Exilarchs because the *gaonim* ruled steadily that Bustenai was too good a Jew not to have freed his princess and have made her a Jewess before he had any relations with her at all. Therefore, having surely freed and converted her, all of her lineage were to be regarded as legitimately entitled to serve as Exilarchs. The descendants of Bustenai from his Jewish wives, century after century, refused to give up their claim. They were persistent in pelting the successive *gaonim* with the same question, hoping that perhaps one *gaon* would finally be found who would rule that Azadwad's children were not Jews, and that therefore they had no right to be Exilarchs.

It is through this rather circumlocutory way that we get the story, after a fashion, of Bustenai and his house. The one thing that we could never understand: The seal of the House of David of the Exilarchs for 500 years was baffling to scholars. It had in it the design of a fly. No one knew why. We now know that the fly was a symbol of the dramatic appearance of Bustenai—founder of the dynasty—before Omar the Great.

The exilarchate became a mighty force in the solidification of Jewish life. Mohammed's son-in-law, Ali, succeeded Omar as the head of the Arabic world, and in the year 658 he gave official recognition to

Bustenai as the head of the exilarchate, following the tradition of Omar, and simultaneously recognized a man named Mar-Zutra as the first *gaon* of Sura. The pageantry of the Exilarch's installation is formidable evidence of the glory and the power that the Jews found in the institution of the exilarchate. An eyewitness, Nathan the Babylonian, a Jew who lived in the latter days of the first millennium, had described the installation ceremony of the Exilarch in detail. His account reads as follows:

AN EXILARCH IS INSTALLED

When the community agreed to appoint an Exilarch, the two heads of the academies with their pupils, the heads of the community, and the elders assembled in the house of a prominent man in Babylonia, one of the great men of the generation, for instance, as Netira or somebody like him. That man in whose house the meeting took place was honored thereby. It was regarded as a mark of distinction. His esteem was enhanced when the great men and the elders assembled in his house. On Thursday they assembled in the synagogue, blessed the Exilarch, and placed their hands on him. They blew the shofar that all the people, small and great, might hear. When the people heard the proclamation, every member of the community sent him a present according to his power and means. All of the heads of the community and the wealthy members sent him magnificent clothes and beautiful ornaments, vessels of silver and vessels of gold, each man according to his ability. The Exilarch prepared a banquet on Thursday and Friday, offering all kinds of food and all kinds of drinks and all kinds of dainties and different kinds of sweetmeats. When he arose on Sabbath morning to go to the synagogue, many of the prominent men of the community met him to go with him to the synagogue. At the synagogue, a wooden pulpit had been prepared for him on the previous day, the length of which was seven cubits and the breadth of which was three cubits. They spread over it magnificent coverings of silks—blue, purple, scarlet—and it was entirely covered and nothing was seen of it. Under the pulpit there entered distinguished Jews with melodious and harmonious voices who were well versed in the prayers and all that appertains thereto. The Exilarch was concealed in a certain place together with the heads of the academies, that is to say, the *gaon* of Sura and the *gaon* of Pumbedita. The youths stood under the pulpit. No man sat there.

The *hazzan* of the synagogue would begin the prayer, "Blessed be He Who spoke," and the youths who stood there would respond to every sentence of that prayer, "Blessed be He." He chanted the psalm of the Sabbath day, and they responded after him, "It is good to give thanks unto the Lord." All the people together read the verses and songs until they finished them. The *hazzan* then arose and began the prayer: "The breath of all living" and the youths responded after him: "He shall bless thy name." He uttered a phrase, and then they responded after him, until they reached the *Kedusha*, which was said by the congregation with a low voice and by the youths with a loud voice. Then the youths remained silent and the *hazzan* alone completed the prayer up to "He redeemed Israel." All the people then stood to say the *Shmoneh Esrai*. When the *hazzan*, repeating the *Shmoneh Esrai*, reached the *Kedusha*, the youths responded after him with a loud voice: "Holy, Holy, Holy is the Lord of Hosts." When they had completed the prayer, all the congregation sat down. When all the people were seated, the Exilarch came out of the place where he was concealed. Seeing him come up, all the people stood up until he sat down on the pulpit that had been made for him. Then the head of the Academy of Sura came out after him and after exchanging courtesies with the Exilarch, sat down on the pulpit. Then the head of the Academy of Pumbedita came out, and he too made a bow and sat down on his left. During all this time, the people stood upon their feet, silent, until these three were properly seated. The Exilarch sat in the middle, the head of the Academy of Sura at his right and the head of the Academy of Pumbedita at his left. Empty places were left between the heads of the academies and the Exilarch. Upon his place, over his head, above the pulpit, they spread a magnificent covering fastened with cords of linen fine. Then the *hazzan* put his head under the Exilarch's canopy in front of the pulpit, and with blessings that had been prepared for him on the preceding day, he blessed him with a low voice so that they should be heard only by those who sat around the pulpit and by the youths who were under him. When he blessed him, the youths responded after him with a loud voice: "Amen." All the people were silent until he had finished his blessings. Then the Exilarch would begin to expound on matters pertaining to the biblical portion of the day, or he would give permission to the head of the Academy of Sura to deliver the exposition.

The head of the Academy of Sura would give permission to the head of the Academy of Pumbedita, they would thus show deference to one another, until the head of the Academy of Sura would begin to expound. An interpreter stood near him, repeating his words to the people. He expounded with awe, closing his eyes and wrapping himself up in his *tallis* so that his forehead was covered. While he was expounding, there was not one in the congregation that opened his mouth or chirped or uttered a sound. When he finished his exposition, he would begin with a question, saying: "Indeed, needest thou not learn?" An old man who was wise, understanding and experienced, would stand up and make a response on the subject, then sit down. The *hazzan* stood up and recited the Kaddish. When he reached the words "During your life and in your days," he would interpolate the following: "During your life and during your days and during the life of our newly elected Prince of the Exiles, may blessings come to the entire people of Israel." When he had finished the Kaddish, he would bless the Exilarch, then the heads of the academies. Having finished the blessings, he would stand up and say: "Such and such a sum was contributed by such and such a city and its villages." He mentioned all the cities that sent contributions to the academy, and he blessed them. Afterwards, he blessed the men who busied themselves in order that contributions should reach the academy. Then he would take out the Book of the Torah and call upon a Cohen and a Levi after him, and while all of the people were standing, the *hazzan* of the synagogue would bring the Torah to the Exilarch, who took it in his hands, stood up and read from it. Afterwards, he blessed the two heads of the academies and returned the Torah to its place. They then prayed the additional prayer and left the synagogue exalted and inspired at the fact that the Tribe of Israel had been afforded continuity.

The rule of the Exilarch extended from the days of Bustenai to the end of the eleventh century. Were it not for the strong hand, the leadership, the vision, and the determination of this self-sufficient Jewish politico-religious institution that was the exilarchate on the one hand and the gaonate on the other hand, it is doubtful that Judaism would have survived.

The importance of Bustenai and the Exilarchs who followed him in office cannot be overstated. A vibrant lay leadership was mandatory for Babylonian Jewry if the spiritual and cultural leadership of the *gaonim* were to be effective. The reverse is equally true. The near one thousand years of a thriving diaspora community that was the inspiration and fountainhead of Jewry wherever it was to be found remains the symbol *par excellence* of Judaic continuity.

THE EIGHTH CENTURY

ANAN BEN DAVID

Judaism had been very fortunate in one respect: Unlike other religions, it had not been subject to cataclysmic upheavals. There have been few major schisms in the history of Judaism. As an example, in the sixteenth century the Christian world was rent asunder by the advent of Luther, Zwingli, and Calvin, and there are no less than 250 Protestant denominations in the United States today. There have been only two major schisms in the history of the Jewish people. One took place after the death of Jesus called the Christ, and the other took place in the eighth century and is associated with Anan ben David.

Anan ben David was the founder of the Karaite movement in Judaism. For a while, this movement threatened to split the Jewish people into two currents of belief and practice. Were it not for the emergence upon the scene of one of the towering giants in the history of the Jews, the *Gaon* Sa'adia, who lived during the tenth century, it is possible that the Karaite movement begun by Anan would have wrought havoc in the traditional ways of Jewish living. He was certainly not the outstanding Jew of his time, but he was one of the most important, if importance is measured in terms of one's lasting effect upon succeeding generations. Karaism was not a purely negative force in Judaism. It had some distinctive contributions to make to the history of its faith, its literature, its mode of thinking, which have lasted on to the present day. It is necessary to examine some of the background to the rise of Karaism.

The academies of Sura and Pumbedita had been ruled by the *gaonim* with an iron hand. Jewish discipline was at its strongest at that time. The academies issued edicts that they expected to be followed. Only a Jew who cared to expose himself to the scorn of, if not the outright excommunication from, his community would dare to question the authority of the *gaonim*. When the *gaonim* ruled that a certain procedure in Jewish law must be followed, the decision was final. The *gaonim* were able to enforce their decisions precisely because of the institution of the exilarchate discussed in the last chapter. The Exilarch was the president of the Jewish community of Babylonia, which was the fulcrum of Judaism throughout the world. He was a president who governed with force and vigor, one whose decisions were obeyed because he had governmental power to enforce them. Violators of gaonic decisions could be imprisoned, flogged, or subjected to a variety of other penalties. It had to be that way, for Jewish survival depended on it. On the other hand, it could not be expected that a people would react with docility to such stringent leadership. When authority is tight, there is always the potential for rebellion. In part the Karaite movement was a reaction to the authoritarian nature of Babylonian Jewish leadership. Another factor was the development of a haughty aristocracy. There were the "haves" and the "have-nots," the Jews who were rich farmers and owned much of the land and the Jews who were ordinary workers and artisans who were forced to make their living by the sweat of their brows and whose life was far from comfortable. The burden of taxation that was imposed upon the man in the street came from two sides: taxation from the Arabic governing authority and taxation from the Jewish authority, the Exilarch. After all, the exilarchate and the gaonate could not be run on spiritual inspiration alone. They needed funding. Taxation fell heavily and undemocratically upon the "have-nots." The very rich were generally able to lessen, if not completely eliminate, the burden of taxation that they should have borne. Karaism was in part the outburst of what had long been a smoldering rancor toward this economic injustice.

HERESY VS. TRADITION

Judaism does not exist in a vacuum. A Jew is always subject to influences from his general environment, and it must be said that the Moslem religion was invaded by many heresies during the eighth century. The bible of Islam is the Koran. The Koran is an inspiring work and must by all counts be reckoned as one of the most influential works in the religious history of man. But it is one of the most loosely organized works in that theological history. It is a wilderness that lends itself to a variety of interpretations. Within Islam, there developed a great many interpretations of the Koran. There were those who said we must live only by the book which is the Koran. There were others who advocated changes in Koranic interpretation so as to make their holy book applicable to the times.

It is an old problem: how are time-hallowed ideas and practices to be altered without doing violence to the explicit prescription of sacred texts? The rabbis of the Talmud realized that one cannot live by the letter of the Torah alone. Conditions change and times change. In order for religion to retain its validity, mechanisms for adapting both theory and practice to the needs of life must be ready at hand and, if necessary, used. Nothing is more dangerous to a religion than inflexibility. The rabbis fully understood that. The Talmud, the so called Oral Law, is the monumental record of that understanding.

The rabbis had developed in the Talmud thousands of laws that had never been anticipated by the Torah because they could not have been anticipated by the Torah. Because the rabbis developed these laws, and because the rabbis found ingenious means of reinterpreting the Torah in such a way to make these laws possible, Judaism was able to survive. The work of the Talmud was progressive, not reactionary. The work of the *tannaim* and the *amoraim* and the *gaonim* was designed primarily to make it possible for Judaism and life to travel along parallel lines.

Finally, the clashing of personalities also enters into the background of the Anan ben David story. He was a close relative of an Exilarch who died childless in the year 765. Because there was no one clearly in line to succeed him as Exilarch, rivalry developed between the two leading candidates, the nearest relatives. One was Anan and the other was Josiah. The matter was put to the *gaonim* of Sura and Pumbedita, and they favored Josiah over Anan. This made Anan very bitter, and he and the people who had championed his candidacy rebelled not only against the decision of the *gaonim*, but against the *gaonim* themselves and everything that the *gaonim* stood for. One day Anan proclaimed that there is only one authority for the Jewish people and that is the Torah. Anything that has been legislated since the Torah is invalid. Thus with one stroke, Anan wished to cancel out over a thousand years of pharisaic, Talmudic, and gaonic creativity in the development of Judaic laws and principles. Surely, this was heresy in its most extreme form.

When the caliph heard about this, he threw Anan into prison because rebelling against the authority of the Exilarch meant rebelling against the authority of the caliph, since the Exilarch was an extension of the power of the caliph. Anan was sentenced to die. While in prison, he met a man who changed the course of his life and almost succeeded in changing the course of Judaism. The man he met was an Arab heretic named Abu Hanifa. Anan was waiting to be executed on Friday. Abu Hanifa said to him: "I know one device by which you can save your life. You are being accused of heresy, and under Arab law that is punishable with death. But suppose you were to say that you do not even belong to the Jewish religion, that you are an exponent of another religion entirely. If you say that, they cannot put you to death because being an advocate of another religion immediately absolves you from heresy within the religion of which you were accused of being a member. Claim, then, that you are not a member of the Jewish faith."

When Anan was brought before the caliph for his final plea, he said: "I am not a Jew at all. I am the founder of an altogether new religion, not a heresy." He spoke so well and so convincingly that Caliph Al-Manzur released him. It was then that Anan began to teach the new precepts of his religion, the Karaite religion. The word in Hebrew for scripture, for the Five Books of Moses, is *Meekrah*, "that which is read." Anan was an exponent of *Meekrah*, of the Torah only. He called his followers and himself *B'nai Meekrah*, or *Karaeem* (Karaites), those who recognized only the authority of the written law. He expounded his philosophy in a book that unfortunately has come down to us only in fragmentary form, the Book of Precepts. But the most important declaration of Anan is very clear. He said it in Aramaic, which was the vernacular for the Jews of that time. He said: "Search well for the law in the Torah, and do not simply rely on my opinion." Everybody, said Anan, is an authority. Rabbis are unneeded.

THE KARAITE DILEMMA

This dictum is untenable from its very outset. For example, the Torah says: "An eye for an eye," the famous *lex talionis*. At some ancient time (perhaps the middle of the second millennium B.C.E.) this law was an integral part of the penal code. But as far back as the fifth century B.C.E., it had been realized that the law was unacceptable, that mankind had advanced beyond this savage concept of justice. The rabbis did not wish to nullify the Torah, nor did they wish to violate the sanctity of the Torah. So instead of declaring the law invalid, they reinterpreted it to mean the *value* of an eye for an eye. They substituted monetary compensation for eye-gouging. The rabbis wanted to accomplish two things simultaneously: to break the shell and to preserve the egg, as it were. So they read into the Torah a meaning that was more in consonance with their conceptions of justice.

To take another example, the Torah absolutely prohibits loaning money or goods on interest. In the days of the Torah, there was a good and sufficient reason for it. Economy was not money-based. The economy was a barter economy. The main source of people's livelihood was not finance but agriculture and sheep-herding. The typical borrower was some poor farmer who suffered a crop failure and had no seed to plant. He would come to the more prosperous farmer and say: "Let me have some seed." It was a matter of life and death for him. The Torah said: "Do not take advantage of the man's misery by asking him to return to you a bushel and a half of seed when you only lent him a bushel." Whatever was borrowed was not borrowed for the purpose of using it in order to make more money. With the development of a money-based economy, it became untenable to live under a rule that no money could be lent on interest. The institution of credit has been the lifeblood of the economic system. Even the United States Steel Corporation could get nowhere without credit. When the rabbis realized that it was no longer possible to live under laws that would have made the extension of credit impossible, they again re-interpreted the Torah rule in such a way as to enable the lender to have a return on his investment. Again the Torah was harnessed by the rabbis to the exigencies of their contemporary circumstances.

Anan ben David, on the other hand, said: "If this is what the Torah says, this is the way we have got to live." An eye for an eye? Yes!

No interest? Yes! And so with other laws. The rabbinic approach was progressive. Anan ben David's approach was really Toryistic not Toraitic. It was reactionary. It was not a forward-looking program. It was a program that, if followed through with the utmost rigor, would have sounded the death-knell of the religion that had given birth to both the rabbinites, as most of the Jews were called, and the Ananities or the Karaites, as the followers of Anan were called.

KARAITE PRACTICES

Anan's life is not in itself interesting. He lived and he died. The only dramatic incident was the rivalry over the exilarchate and his escape from the sword of the executioner through a very clever ruse. He died at the end of the eighth century. His followers say he died in Palestine, but that is historically questionable. The Karaites still exist today, but there are very few of them. It is estimated that there are not more than several thousand Karaites in the world today. But the Karaite prayer book has survived, and part of its text dating from the eighth century includes the following very touching prayer:

> May our God and God of our Fathers enfold his love about our Rabbi, Anan, the Prince, who paved the way of the Torah, opened the eyes of the Sons of Scripture, returned many from the path of sin. May the God of Israel keep him in a good and lovely resting place along with the seven groups of righteous who inherit Paradise. Amen.

Karaite practice is a deviation from the rabbinic. For example, it is written in the Book of Exodus: "Thou shalt not light any fire in thy dwelling place on the Sabbath day." Does that mean that one is required to sit in darkness on Sabbath? It does not. The procedure even in the most stringent Orthodox home is to light the fire before Sabbath and, if that fire will last through the night, well and good. The Karaites interpreted this law to mean that there must be no light in the house on Sabbath at all, whether it was lit before or not. Therefore Karaites spent their entire Sabbath in gloom, in darkness. Their food was cold. Their Sabbath was lugubrious and dank; it was virtually a day of mourning the way they celebrated it.

Every seventh of the month was for the Karaites a fast day. They refused to abide by the accepted calendar of Jewry. They clung to the old method of setting the month ahead on the basis of eyewitness testimony as to the time of the monthly birth of the moon. The Karaites insisted on using scissors or a form of scissors for circumcision because the Bible uses the plural when speaking of the instrument to be used in the rite of circumcision. To the Karaites, all fowl were *trefa* (nonkosher). They interpreted the Torah as allowing only the pigeon to be eaten. Wine and meat were absolutely taboo to the Karaites. Hanukkah was not observed by the Karaites at all because there is no reference to it in the Bible for the obvious reason that the events giving birth to it were post-biblical. Also, Karaites had no mezuzahs on their doors, and wore no *t'fillin* at prayer. They interpreted the Torah passage: "Thou shalt write them upon the doorposts of thy house and upon thy gates," to mean that the home of the Jew must bespeak the observance of Torah. The law of the *t'fillin* is derived from the words: "Thou shalt bind them for a sign upon thy hand and they shall be for frontlets between thine eyes." The Karaites regarded this, too, as metaphorical language, not meant to be understood literally.

In sum, one of the rabbinite observers of their way of life put it: "Their harp is turned to mourning; their organs of music into the voice of weeping."

SCHISM WITHIN SCHISM

But the Karaites themselves were splintered into one group after another, and for good reason. They truly followed the basic edict of Anan, their original teacher, which was: "Search the Torah yourself and do not rely upon anybody else's opinion." Thus everybody came up with his own opinion as to how things should be done in accordance with *his* particular reading of the Torah. Kirkisani, an outstanding Karaite teacher of the tenth century, gave examples of the confusion that reigned in the midst of the Karaites. He said: "Some forbid washing oneself on Shabbos, others say it is all right; some do not allow the table to be moved on Shabbos, but they allow you to make the bed on Shabbos; other Karaites allow the bed to be made on Shabbos, but they don't allow the table to be moved on Shabbos; some Karaites allow a cleanup after the meal on Shabbos, others do not allow that."

This is what must happen when there is no central authority and where everybody becomes his own interpreter. It is fine with respect to freedom of thought; it is not with respect to that discipline required in the practice of a faith without which that faith cannot survive.

Some Karaites believed in life after death, others did not; some Karaites spoke consistently of angels, while others denied the existence of angels. The result was that the Karaites began to realize after a short time that the tradition of the rabbis that they had rejected was necessary for survival.

Karaism had begun by a rejection of the ritual that had been developed by the tradition of the rabbis. It was not long before Karaites realized that without ritual, they themselves could under no circumstances survive. So they began to develop their own laws and rituals. Only because of that were they able to survive for almost a thousand years. The prognosis for their continued survival is not bright, but the fact that they have survived a thousand years is not *because* of the rejection of tradition, but despite the fact that though they rejected a tradition, they soon realized that no religion will survive without tradition. Traditions may undergo modifications, but they remain essential to the survival of any religion.

KARAISM AND ZION

The Karaites made a tremendous contribution to the Jewish people as a whole through their immense love for Zion. They were among the first to champion the idea that all Jews should leave the diaspora and go back to Palestine. There are some magnificent passages in the literature of the Karaites expressive of their passionate desire to live and to die in Palestine. The Karaites composed the following prayer in the tenth century:

> My King and my God, how long am I to be lovesick? How long wilt Thou have no mercy upon me? How long wilt Thou forget me? How long wilt Thou forsake me? How long will zeal for Thy house consume me? How long am I to be like a woman in mourning while in my heart burns a fierce fire? How long will mine eyes shed tears as I observe graves in the very gates of the capital city of Jerusalem? How long will I cry bitterly as I observe all manner of uncleanness in the Court of the Temple? Instead of a priest burning incense, how long will enemies stand up against me? They exercise their hatred upon me, they twice demolished my city, they twice burned my

Temple, they slew my sons, did Babylon's lion, Medea-Persia the evil-doer, Greece and Macedon the malefactor, Ishmael and Edom the witless. My God, pray have pity, pray have mercy, pray have compassion upon Thy poor congregation who wait assiduously at Thy gates, who knock on Thy doors, whose souls go out with longing for Thy salvation, whose eyes are eagerly searching for Thy word. Pray hearken to them and be pleased with them and have compassion upon the sheep of Thy flock and return them to Thy faithful city, the city of Jerusalem, the longing of our hearts, the destiny of our souls.

The Karaites made rapid strides in the first three centuries after the death of Anan ben David. They might have converted a large part of the Jewish world, and we would then have had a split Jewish world, but a colossus emerged, the *Gaon* Sa'adia, the last great *gaon* of Sura, indeed the greatest of them all. Sa'adia was a genius par excellence. He was one of the great philosophers and mathematicians of his time, one of the greatest Hebrew grammarians of his time, *the* greatest Talmudic scholar.

Sa'adia saw what was happening in Judaism, and he dedicated his career (he was born in the year 880 and he died in 940) to a relentless battle against the Karaites. He realized that if their propaganda were to prevail, Judaism as a whole would be the loser. To the Karaites, Sa'adia became the *"bete-noire,"* the black beast. They called him "blackguard," "rascal," "liar," "scoundrel," and danced upon his grave when he died. They saw in him a most dangerous adversary. Sa'adia fought vigorously and as events were to prove, successfully against the Karaite schism that had been begun by Anan ben David. He inaugurated practices designed to defy the teachings of the Karaites. One was the blessing over candles on the eve of the Sabbath, designed to demonstrate that the Karaite way of sitting out the Sabbath in darkness was benighted.

The placement of a ring on the bride's finger to solemnize marriage—this also originated as a result of Karaite recalcitrance. The Karaites, among other things, opposed the tradition of a marriage consummated by means of a monetary gift from the man to the woman. The rabbis wished to demonstrate that the Karaite opposition to the idea of marriage through a monetary gift is wrong, that marriage through a monetary gift is right. So they standardized the ring as the gift symbolizing the rite of marriage.

LASTING CONTRIBUTION

The Karaites today are a dying sect. Hitler and Stalin were the two people who did the most damage to the Karaites. The special units of Himmler shot thousands of Karaite Jews into ditches they had been forced to dig. Hitler made no fine distinction as between rabbinite Jews and Karaite Jews. The Angel of Death was to take possession of both groups. Stalin's persecutions against religion brought about the decimation of large groups of Karaites who inhabited parts of the Soviet Union.

But the Karaites left a precious legacy. By posing a challenge to the rabbinites, they stimulated the great rabbis after Anan ben David's time to a more careful study of that very same Torah that became the Bible of bibles to the Karaites. The study of the Bible from the scientific, linguistic, and grammatical points of view had been grossly neglected up until the time of Anan. Because of Anan's stress upon the Bible and because the Karaites became masters of the Bible, all of the rest of the Jews were forced to go back and study the Bible. An enormous impetus was thus given by the Karaites to biblical study. Nor can the contribution of the Karaites to Zion be overestimated. They were among the most important spiritual ancestors of Theodor Herzl and David ben Gurion. The emphasis they placed upon the Holy Land came at a time when, after centuries of diaspora life, many Jews had begun gradually to forget about their ancestral origins.

The Karaites now are virtually dead, but in the library at St. Petersburg there is the world's largest collection of Karaite writings, teachings, and history. In 1916, the about-to-be-born Hebrew University of Jerusalem negotiated with the czar's librarian for the purchase of the great Baron de Guinzberg collection of St. Petersburg. The negotiations were successfully completed. The money was given and the manuscripts were to be transferred to the Hebrew University. The Bolshevik revolution killed the deal. The Bolsheviks repudiated it and the manuscripts are still in Russia. Karaite manuscripts, along with many other precious manuscripts that could shed light on so much of Jewish history, are collecting dust in St. Petersburg. Some forty years ago, Professor Abraham Katsch of New York University went to Russia and was permitted to make microfilm copies of some of these precious manuscripts. The rest of the huge collection remained largely *terra incognita* until the breakup of the Soviet union in recent years.

With the dissolution of the Soviet Union, scholars have had greater access to the great Judaica manuscript collection in St. Petersburg (the former Leningrad). We may now look forward to the publication of materials that will surely shed much new light on Karaism and its founder, Anan ben David.

THE NINTH CENTURY

ELDAD THE DANITE

Eldad the Danite was not the most imprtant Jew of his or any other century, but his story reveals much about the unceasing longing for miraculous redemption that marked so much of the psyche of Jews living in an oppressive diaspora. The messianic hope was vital in sustaining their morale during times that could have spelled despair. Eldad's story begins in a quiet fashion. Zemach, the *gaon* of Sura, received an interesting letter about 880 from the Jewish community of Kairowan in North Africa. This letter told of the appearance in their community of a short, swarthy, dark-skinned Jew who spoke Hebrew but with an accent different than any had ever heard. He observed Jewish law but in a way that they had never seen or experienced. He professed himself a staunch Jew but seemed very odd. He claimed that he was a representative of Dan, one of the ten lost tribes, and that he had come from a far-away land to announce the imminent return of the ten lost tribes of the community of Israel for the purpose of redeeming the Jewish people from exile and suffering.

In reality there were no "ten lost tribes." When in the year 722 B.C.E. the community of the northern kingdom of Israel had been destroyed by King Sargon of Assyria, the ten tribes that were its inhabitants were exiled to various parts of the Assyrian empire. There they ultimately assimilated with natives and were never heard from again. Nevertheless, legends about their survival persisted among Jews and others. The strange visitor to Kairowan claimed that the tribes had reached a faraway land, the exact location of which remains a mystery. He told the Jews of Kairowan that these tribes are waiting for a providential opportunity to return to the community of Israel. Moreover, he described a set of laws practiced by the lost tribes that were very different from the laws practiced by the Jewish communities in the known world. The letter from Kairowan to the *Gaon* Zemach asked: "How do we react to this man? Do we accept what he says as the truth? Are his laws to be regarded as being within the parameters of Jewish law, despite differing radically from traditional *halakha*? What attitude should be adopted toward this man who calls himself Eldad of the tribe of Dan?"

The man to whom this query was addressed was one of the most respected Jews in the world of that time. He was not a romantic dabbler in fanciful tales. He was the *Gaon* Zemach. Surprisingly, he did not dismiss the story as ridiculous, nor did he discourage the Jews of Kairowan from believing that possibly this Eldad *was* a representative of the ten lost tribes. Zemach's letter, while not quite affirmative, was careful not to dismiss the possible authenticity of Eldad's story or for that matter to dismiss his version of the law as alien to Judaism.

THE ELDAD FANTASY

The narrative of Eldad has come down to us in six or seven different manuscript versions. They were collated by the late Abraham Epstein, an outstanding medievalist.

Here, then, is the substance of Eldad's narrative. One day, he said, he and a member of the tribe of Asher (also one of the ten lost tribes) had decided to visit the Jewish communities in Europe and Babylonia. They started out by ship. The ship was wrecked but by a miracle they succeeded in floating to a land of cannibals, "Romarnum." The Asherite, his companion, was fat and succulent. The cannibals first roasted then feasted on him. But beholding Eldad's scrawny and emaciated body, they decided to let him live. As their prisoner he observed their way of life and discovered that they were fire-worshipers in addition. He described an orgy that they had annually—apparently he spent several years there—in which the main feature was a naked girl dancing on a treetop. The tribe worked itself into a frenzy that led to total sexual abandon with no restrictions. Incest reigned. Taboos were broken. The first child to be born of this carnival of perversity was burned the following year as an offering to the fire god, and the ashes of the infant were smeared on the faces of all the worshipers. This was designed to protect them throughout the year from ill-winds and ill fortune.

In due course Eldad's emancipation arrived in the form of a Jew from a tribe of Jessachar (what *he* was doing there, Eldad does not explain), who ransomed Eldad from the cannibals. Then Eldad departed by sea for the land of Jessachar. From there he embarked on a mission to visit the Jewish communities of the world in order to tell them his narrative of the ten lost tribes.

THE "SONS OF MOSES"

The narrative consists of so many wild and disjointed stories that it is very difficult to summarize. We can say the following: The tribes of Jessachar, Zebulon, Reuben, Ephraim, and Manasseh dwelt in various places of Asia and Africa, but the tribes of Dan (of which he was a member), Naftali, Gad, and Asher lived in some land in Africa lying beyond the Ethiopian waters, a land that he described almost exactly in the same terms as Homer described the wonderlands of Greek mythology. These tribes managed to survive the Israelite destruction that took place in the year 722 B.C.E. because they left the land before the Assyrians arrived to destroy it. Conspicuous among these tribes were "The Sons of Moses," "The *B'nai* Moshe," apparently a branch of the Levites. In Psalm 137 we read that by the waters of Babylon, Babylonians requested that the exiles of Judah play music upon their harps. They refused, saying: "How can we sing the song of the Lord on strange land? If I forget thee, O Jerusalem, let my right hand forget its cunning, let my tongue cleave to its palate, if I remember thee not; if I raise not Jerusalem to the height of my joy." Said Eldad: Most of the tribes only refused to play the music upon the harps when they were so ordered by the Babylonians, but the Sons of Moses went farther. They chewed off their fingers. As a result of this sacrificial demonstration of courage, a miraculous cloud descended in the midst of a storm and carried the fingerless heroes to a land beyond the River Sambatyon. Sambatyon was an unusual river. Its waters throughout the week spewed out rocks and lava. No one could possibly navigate it. Thus the Sons of Moses were never in danger of enemy invasion. But on the eve of Sabbath the river's eruptions subsided. No lava, no rocks were emitted. Instead a pillar of fire rose from the depths of the Sambatyon and served as a dividing wall between the rest of the world and the Sons of Moses. When the Sabbath came to an end, the formidable barrier of missiles resumed its agitated activity.

A utopian life was enjoyed by the Sons of Moses. Insulated from the outside world, their life was idyllic. There were no classes, no rich or poor. It was a totally communal society, everybody shared everything in common. There was no crime. They ate no meat. There were no impure animals in their land. That land was filled with plenty, truly a land of milk and honey. The average life span was 120. All of them were holy and pure, with the holiness of the man whose name they bore, the holiness of Moshe *Rabaynu*, Moses our Teacher. The Sons of Moses communicated with the other "Lost Tribes" by means of carrier pigeons!

As to the other tribes, they did not live in quite the same Eden enjoyed by the Sons of Moses beyond the River Sambatyon. The tribes of Dan, Naftali, Gad, and Asher took turns regularly making war on neighboring pagans. They had armies of 120,000 cavalry and 100,000 foot soldiers.

Eldad's signature to his tale was: "And as to my name, I am Eldad the son of Machli, the son of Ezekiel, the son of Ezekiah, the son of Eylon, the son of Abner, the son of Shmayeh, Pdat, the son of . . . (fifteen more names follow)." The genealogy dates back to Dan, who was one of the twelve sons of Father Jacob.

It is remarkable that having read this incredible jabber the *Gaon* Zemach in his response to the Jews of Kairowan affirmed a tradition about the survival of the "Ten Lost Tribes" and that it was at least possible that Eldad was their emissary.

ELDAD'S LAWS

A word or two should be said about the *halakha* of Eldad and how it differed from rabbinic law. Eldad's *Book of Laws* has come down to us fragmentarily. Moreover, Rashi and Tosefot and some of the other commentators occasionally make reference to these laws. For example, Jews do not eat meat with milk. They must wait six hours after consumption of meat before they may partake of dairy food. Moreover, meat utensils and dairy utensils are kept separate. The law in the Torah actually said: "Thou shalt not boil the kid in the milk of its mother." Out of this law there developed the ramified laws of separation between meat and dairy food. According to Eldad's law, the only prohibition was cooking the kid in the milk of its mother. Otherwise milk with meat may be consumed at the same meal. His interpretation of the Mosaic law in regard to this was literal. Rashi, in the eleventh century, and Rabbi Abraham ben David, a twelfth-century scholar, quote Eldad's laws with a certain amount of respect. These laws were not of Eldad's fantasies. They were obviously practiced somewhere. There must have been a place in the Jewish world where a Jewish tribe, completely cut off from contact with the mainstream of Jewish leadership and tradition, did practice laws of their own that had not been rabbinic at all. The Karaites do not fit the bill. Eldad's people had an oral tradition of their own and did not deny the post-Toraitic law, as had the Karaites.

ELDAD'S ORIGIN

As to Eldad's origin, any Jewish community practicing rabbinic law must be excluded. That would eliminate Europe, North African, Iraq, Iran, Syria, and Palestine. The consensus of most scholars is that he came from either southeast Africa or Arabia. Both of these areas would satisfy the necessary geographical conditions. First, the vernacular of Eldad the Danite, his Hebrew language, is interspersed with Arabisms. Moreover, several ideas of Eldad's account are clearly lifted from the Koran. For instance, according to Eldad, the undoing of Adam and Eve in the Garden of Eden was the result of the serpent's passion and jealousy. He had become enamored of Eve and was consumed with rancor over her happiness with Adam. He set about destroying that bliss, inducing Eve to partake of the forbidden fruit. This story is to be found in the Koran in almost every detail.

The Judaism of Eldad is syncretistic, a potpourri of cults. Syncretism plagued Judaism in the days of the first kingdom, the days of David, Solomon, and their successors. An eighteenth-century traveler named Even-Safir, whose memoirs are extant, had met a pious Yemenite Jew in Arabia, who prayed in *tallis* and *t'fillin*, who practiced all of the laws of Judaism, but who was in the habit of employing a cameo for therapeutical purposes. The cameo was inscribed: "In the name of the Father and the Son and the Holy Ghost, Amen. Blessed be Jesus, son of Mary." That is syncretism with a vengeance.

ELDAD'S PURPOSE

Whatever Eldad's point of origin, what was the point to his visit with the rabbinic communities? Abraham Epstein believes Eldad was sent for the purpose of acquiring support for a military campaign to be waged by the southeast African and Arabian Jewish communities and to be financed by the entire Jewish diaspora. Those goals would be to free Palestine from the hands of the Moslems. It was indeed a grandiose scheme, preposterous on the face of it. But Eldad represented Jews who lived in remotest southeast Africa or Arabia, who truly thought that they had a chance to overthrow Arab power in Palestine. We know that he did much traveling. He traveled to Morocco, to Iraq, to Kairowan, and to Spain. We know that he was involved in beating the drum for Jewish self-help by creating a military infrastructure. He was vague about means and ends. Perhaps he was afraid to talk openly about such matters, but he was constantly active, trying to stir things up. It is hard to arrive at any other conclusion then that there was some political purpose to the activity of this remarkable Jew who called himself Eldad the Danite.

He must have been an attractive, magnetic personality. Jews flocked to him. They regarded him as a potential Messiah. Oppressed, harassed, massacred, separated one from another, utterly impotent politically and militarily, living only by the grace of the caliph or by the grace of the Christian prince or by the grace of the pope, Jews yearned for redemption. Eldad, who claimed to be speaking for ten lost tribes who one day would come to defeat their enemies and return Israel back to its Holy Land, was a vision of consolidation and hope. Eldad's name became a legend. His influence was so strong that Christians as late as the twelfth century were writing about the "kingdom beyond the Sambatyon," the kingdom of the ten lost tribes, the miracle kingdom, the salvation that is to come from beyond this river of fire and brimstone. There are documents dating from the twelfth century written by Christians for the purpose of ridiculing the widespread Jewish boast of a kingdom of Israel beyond Sambatyon. The nineteenth-century *Wiessenschaft des Judentums* school of serious Judaic scholarship ignored the story of Eldad the Danite as beneath the dignity of earnest scholarship. Thus very little was done then to uncover such kernels of fact as lie behind the Eldad fantasy.

FUNCTION OF FANTASY

Yet fantasy can serve vital purposes. It is often indispensable for those whose lives would otherwise be insufferable. It helps render their existence tolerable. In many instances and for so many people, life without its illusions is life without hope, without dignity, without purpose.

Eldad the Danite was an illusion. At a very difficult period in Jewish history, this impostor was a blessing in disguise for the Jewish people. Perhaps this was not his intention, but the tale of the Sambatyon that invaded the warp and woof of Jewish lore, the tale of the magic river behind which lay the promise of redemption for Jewish angst, was a blessing and a balm. "Somewhere over the rainbow" there streams a river called Sambatyon.

THE TENTH CENTURY

HASDAI IBN SHAPRUT

During the long, itinerant history of the Jews, they dwelt in many lands. Perhaps the most colorful chapter was their sojourn in Spain. The history of the Jews in Spain goes back to antiquity. Legends abound of their origins there as far back as King Solomon. The very existence of such traditions points to the longevity of Spanish Jewry.

We know that from Roman times there were Jews in Spain. We know that when the Temple was destroyed in the year 70, a significant number of Jews found their way into that part of the Roman empire of which Spain was an integral portion. We know that there was a substantial Jewish population there by the sixth century. Indeed, anti-Semitism was rife by that time. The Gothic King Sisebut has left a record of anti-Jewish edicts. But the consequential history of Spanish Jewry dates only from the Arab invasion of the Iberian Peninsula.

In the year 711 the Arabs invaded Spain and came close to overrunning all of Europe. They had been stopped at Tours by the French army in one of history's crucial battles. Had the Arabs prevailed at Tours, they might well have swept over the European continent. Had that happened, subsequent history would have been of a radically different complexion. But the Arabs did succeed in securing a foothold in Spain, particularly in the southern part known as Andalusia. The northern sector remained in Christian hands. Due to the fact that Spain was divided almost equally between Moslems and Christians, the Jews enjoyed relative peace. Professor Salo Baron theorizes that anti-Semitism in a particular country dates from the moment that a land becomes monolithic and uniform in its composition. When it became *all* Christian, Spain became untenable to the Jews. That was to happen after the fall of Granada in the year 1492. That very year the Jews were expelled from Spain by the pious Catholic rulers, Ferdinand and Isabella.

The Jews had lived among the Arabs and Christians in Spain from the beginning of the eighth century. Up to 1391 their conditions—economic, political, cultural, and social—were relatively serene. Especially in Arab Andalussia the Jews were able to scale the ladder of achievement in virtually all areas of society. The apex of Jewish success was reached under the powerful Arab Caliph Abd-ar-Rahaman III (912–961). In his capital city of Cordova, the great wealth attained by some Jews was in evidence. They wore silk clothes, rode costly carriages drawn by white horses, and sported the turbans that were a mark of affluence and prominence in society.

The Arab world of that time was divided among three caliphs. There was a decaying caliphate in Babylonia-Syria and a Fatimid dynasty of caliphs in North Africa, also in decline. The most important caliphate was that of Andalusia, and the most stunning period of its affluence and opulence was the reign of Abd-ar-Rahaman III. One of his closest advisors and ministers was the Jew named Hasdai ibn Shaprut, the central figure of this chapter.

HASDAI IBN SHAPRUT

Hasdai is one of the most colorful people in Jewish history. His career dominates the arena of Jewish life at its most important center in the tenth century. His father, Isaac, was a wealthy man, a liberal philanthropist, and a patron of the arts. Hasdai ibn Isaac ibn Shaprut was born into a family in which the tradition of supporting culture had already been well established. Hasdai received the best possible training that a Jewish lad could receive at that time. The most important profession to which Jewish students were steered by well-to-do families was that of medicine. Hasdai became a widely praised physician. He also acquired much learning and broad understanding of literature. His commercial acumen had been honed in the various business enterprises of his father. Thus Hasdai became a man of many talents, well equipped for the dominant role he was to play in Spanish Jewish history. Abd-ar-Rahaman appointed Hasadi as an interpreter at the Christian courts with which he had diplomatic relations. Hasdai's first achievement in this role was quite significant, considering the fact that it involved a Jew as the mediator between Moslems and Christians. Among the Christian states in Northern Spain were Leon and Navarre. Leon had a king and Navarre had a queen, both hostile to Abd-ar-Rahaman, the sovereign of Andalusia. Hasdai made a trip to Leon and Navarre during which he succeeded in pulling off an amazing diplomatic coup. He brought the queen of Navarre and the king of Leon to Cordova, and there persuaded both to sign a nonaggression treaty. This led to Hasdai's appointment as minister of trade and finance without portfolio to Abd-ar-Rahamann III. He had the power of the minister of trade and finance, but he was not given the title because, in accordance with Islamic law, a Jew could not be granted office at court. The Jews, in accordance with the Koran's teaching, are not a people to be loved. On the contrary, they are a people to be subjugated. In effect, however, Hasdai had power without title. He exercised it with consummate talent.

MINISTER TO THE CALIPH

Constantine the Eighth was king of Byzantium at that time. He had sent a birthday present of a precious medical manuscript to Abd-ar-Rahaman. It had been written by Dioscorides, an outstanding Greek physician of the early Christian era. The book was written in Greek and entitled "On Simple Remedies." The caliph asked Hasdai to have it translated into Arabic. Greek was a language Hasdai did not know. Latin was a language he knew well. Undeterred, Hasdai found a Greek scholar who translated the work into Latin. Hasdai then did the Arabic translation. The caliph was delighted with the result.

At the death of Abd-ar-Rahaman III, his son Alhakim succeeded him to the throne of Cordova. Under Alhakim, Hasdai's *de facto* role as minister was dignified with an official title as well. As a result, Hasdai's palace became a veritable court. He had emerged to his full power and influence in both the Arabic and Jewish communities.

HASDAI THE PATRON

It was with Hasdai that the Golden Age of Spain may be said to have begun. On more than one occasion he proclaimed in his writings the belief that God had called him to high office so that he could be a champion and protector of his fellow Jews. Hasdai ibn Shaprut proudly bore the banner of his Judaism from the beginning of his career to its end. There were no apologetics in his posture toward the non-Jewish world. He had absolute confidence that his station in life was charged by a mission from heaven. He became the catalytic agent who spurred a tremendous surge in Jewish learning and letters in Spain, thereby initiating its Golden Age. Many a scholar and poet was indebted to Hasdai's financial and moral support. Menachem ben Saruk, who became the outstanding Jewish grammarian of his time, compiled an important Hebrew grammar as well as a Hebrew dictionary. Another was Dunash ibn Labrat, a brilliant poet whose contribution to Hebrew poetry was path-breaking.

It was ibn Labrat who was the first to compose Hebrew secular poetry. Virtually all poetry written prior to his time was devotional and liturgical. The use of the sacred Hebrew language for secular writing was apparently regarded as an act of sacrilege. Even the biblical Song of Songs which, read plainly, is clearly a secular series of love poems, had been allegorically transmuted to reflect the reciprocal love between God and His people, Israel. It was Rabbi Akiba who declared that if all of the books of the Bible are holy, the Song of Songs is the holy of holies. Dunash ibn Labrat broke a centuries-old taboo in his writing of clearly mundane poems.

The Arabs in the tenth century produced magnificent poetry about love, wine, women, dancing, carousing and sex. Arab literature of the time was restrained by few inhibitions. Dunash was strongly influenced by that literature. After his example, secular Hebrew poetry flowed freely. Interestingly, the very same people who wrote the most sublime religious poetry also composed stunningly erotic secular poetry. The greatest of them was Yedudah Halevi, who lived in the twelfth century. Halevi wrote poems of a religious spirituality hardly ever equaled. But he also composed earthy poetry of love that would never find its way into a siddur.

Like Menahem, Dunash was a master of Hebrew grammar. Both were supported at the court of ibn Shaprut. Eventually they became rivals for the role of the great man's favorite. The result was to involve much unpleasantness and acts of shameful violence that need not be recounted here. After the death of Dunash ibn Labrat and Menahem ibn Saruk, their respective followers continued a heated literary polemic that was to prove a blessing in disguise. It greatly enriched and fructified Hebraic literature. It can truly be said, as in Samson's riddle, "out of the bitter emerged the sweet."

THE RISE OF SPANISH JEWRY

Hasdai was also the "angel" of Talmudic learning. The two great centers for Jewish life for so many centuries, Sura and Pumbedita, and the men who were at their head, *gaonim* and Exilarchs, had begun to reflect the rotting of their environment. The caliphate of the East had begun to crumble. Jewish life experienced a similar decline. If the scattering of Jews over the known world had a saving grace it was that the evanescence of one community was followed by the rise of another. "The sun also rises," said Koheleth, just as surely as the sun sets. Palestine was a blazing sun in the days of Rabbi Gamaliel and, later, Rabbi Akiba. But it was beginning to set in the days of Judah the Prince. Abba Arikha in the year 219 came to Babylonia to organize the Academy of Sura. From that date follow some 800 years of spiritual power and preeminence for Babylonian Jewry. Now the sun was beginning to set upon Babylonian Jewry, just as it was rising for Spanish Jewry. Hasdai was a herald of a new focus for the sunlight of Jewry.

The tale of the "Four Captives" is first told by the twelfth-century chronicler, Abraham ibn Daud. It is also found in other sources. Its basic ingredients are as follows: About the middle of the tenth century, the Babylonian community of Sura had sent four rabbis to various parts of the Jewish world in order to collect funds for the depleted treasury of Babylonian Jewry. Each of the four had been captured at sea by pirates. Each was sold into slavery and subsequently ransomed in four different parts of the Jewish world: Egypt, Morocco,

France, and Spain. The rabbi involved in the latter instance is Moses ibn Hanoch. With Moses ibn Hanoch, a contemporary of Hasdai ibn Shaprut, begins the spiritual leadership of Spanish Jewry. It was he who organized the first Academy of Jewish Learning on Spanish soil in the city of Cordova.

Moses ibn Hanoch's story is encrusted with legend. His wife was very attractive, and while she was aboard the ship, the pirate chieftain made improper overtures to her and threatened to slay her unless she submitted to him. She came to her husband, Moses ibn Hanoch, and said: "My Rabbi, I have a problem. I know that we all believe that in the fullness of time God will resurrect the dead from the earth. Will he also resurrect them from the sea?" Her husband understood the point of the question and in response offered a verse from the Prophet Habbakuk: "Sayeth the Lord, I will return the lost ones, even from Bashan. I will extricate them even from the depths of the sea." Thereupon she plunged overboard to her death. Moses and his young son arrived at Cordova and were ransomed by Cordovan Jews. Dressed in rags, Moses made his way to the *bet hamidrash*. There, a certain Rabbi Nathan was delivering a Talmudic lecture in the midst of which a point of law eluded him. Very tentatively, the beggarly looking Jew in tattered clothing raised his hand and modestly proceeded to clarify the whole of the subject matter upon which Rabbi Nathan had been expounding. Rabbi Nathan forthwith stepped down from his lecture stand and invited the beggar to come forward, saying: "You are the new rabbi of the Jewish community of Cordova. Your scholarship surpasses mine." Thence a new era of Jewish learning was inaugurated in Spain. Scholarship flourished. So did its cost. Hasdai covered most of it.

The demand for Talmudic learning occasioned by Moses ibn Hanoch's arrival created a shortage of books in Cordova. Copies of the Talmud in great quantity were required. Hasdai sent emissaries to Sura and to Pumbedita, who bought up every copy they could acquire. Hasdai then distributed them to all the scholars free of charge. That time marks the beginning of prolific Judaic learning in Cordova. Hasdai was the tireless champion of Jewish study in every form: Talmudic learning, poetry, grammar, and art. He also helped fellow Jews establish themselves financially. His concern for the welfare of his people and its culture extended to Jews everywhere. His ear was constantly open to sounds emanating from Jewish communities around the world.

THE KHAZAR KINGDOM

Interesting and important as are Hasdai's contributions as discussed to this point, the most romantic episode of his fruitful career was his interaction with the Jewish kingdom of Khazaria. Not far from the River Dnieper there existed from the eighth through the tenth centuries a Jewish kingdom. It had an army, a legislature, and a government. It exercised power and influence in the political–diplomatic complex of the Asiatic world of that time. As best as can be reconstructed, the story of the Khazars may be summarized as follows: In 1140, Yehudah Halevi, the greatest of Jewish poets and one of the greatest of Jewish philosophers, wrote a book in Arabic called "The Khuzari," the Man from Khazar. It is an apologia for Judaism expressed in exalted terms. It is one of the great treasures of Judaic literature.

The framework for the book yields the story of a king of Khazaria, then a pagan kingdom, who had a dream in which an angel appeared to him, saying: "Your intentions are good, but your deeds are not. You must embrace the true faith." He woke up, gathered his wise men, related the dream, and was advised to call the representatives of the three major religions in the world: Islam, Christianity, and Judaism. The king summoned a priest, an imam, and a rabbi. Each of them sang the praises of his religion. "Of course, mine is the only true religion." The king then spoke with each separately. He asked the Christian, "As between Judaism and Islam, which would you choose?" The priest said, "Judaism." The king asked, "Why?" The priest replied, "Islam is only the derivative product of Judaism. I'd rather take the original." Then he asked the Moslem how he would choose between Judaism and Christianity. The answer was the same. On the basis of these interviews, so the story goes, the king of the Khazars decided to embrace Judaism. But he needed somebody to teach him about this religion, as he was a pagan. "The Khuzari" is a dialogue between the rabbi and the king, which cleverly, beautifully, and effectively demonstrates the nature and the essence of the Jewish religion.

Ibn Daud also mentioned the Jewish kingdom of Khazar. But light was shed on the subject in the person of Johannes Buxdorf the Younger, a seventeenth-century Hebrew scholar of the Christian faith. In 1660, he produced a new edition of "The Khuzari" (500 years after it was first written). To the text he appended two letters that he had found elsewhere, one of which was presumably sent by Hasdai ibn Shaprut to the king of the Khazars, Joseph, in the tenth century, the other being the answer from Joseph, the Jewish king of the Khazars. Buxdorf declared these letters to be forgeries. He was wrong, as later scholarship established this beyond reasonable doubt. In fact, Judah al Barceloni, a tenth-century scholar who was a contemporary of ibn Shaprut, mentioned these very same letters six centuries before Buxdorf published them.

The gist of Hasdai's letter to Joseph is as follows: I have heard from reliable sources that there is a Jewish kingdom in Khazaria. This is amazing to me. Is it indeed true that there are remnants of the ten lost tribes who maintain their own strength and their own power and their own governmental apparatus? Tell me that it is true, so that I can say to the Christian abusers and to the Moslem deriders of Judaism that the statement in Genesis, chapter 39, "the scepter shall never depart from Judah" is true! If you say that it is so, though my rank is high and my position is good and my social relationships are excellent here in Cordova, I would still cast everything behind. I would rather serve the master than the slave. I would drop everything and would come and kiss your feet, O Joseph, if you be indeed the King of a Jewish nation.

Joseph responded that he was indeed sovereign over a Jewish kingdom. However, it is not composed of descendants of the ten lost tribes. But 200 years before, his grandfather, Bolan, decided to forsake paganism. He interviewed delegations from the major faiths and decided to become a Jew. (That is the kernel of truth in the legend that serves as the framework of the "The Khuzazri.") [I am very honored] said Joseph that you, so powerful and prominent a man, for your fame has reached me, would come to serve me. If you would come here, I would gladly share my throne with you, for I can make use of your wisdom. Our eyes are looking forward to the city of Jerusalem, to the restoration of the Holy Temple. Not all of my people are Jews. Only the nobility are." (Because what happened was that the aristocracy and not the masses had converted in Khazaria to Judaism. The majority remained the pagans they had always been.)

Two quotations from the letter of Joseph: "We set our eyes upon Jerusalem, also upon the Babylonian academies. May God speedily bring about the redemption. . . . You write that you long to see me. I have the same longing to make the acquaintance of yourself and your wisdom. If this wish could be fulfilled, I might speak to you face to face, you should be my father and I your son, and I would entrust the government of my state into yours hands." Thus from Joseph in the year 961, in answer to a letter written by Hasdai ibn Shaprut from Cordova in the year 960. It took a long time in those days for letters to be received and in turn to be answered. Now the essence of these letters is confirmed by Arab sources. Professor Dunlop of Princeton has written a definitive study entitled "A History of the Jewish Khazars." He cites the Arab sources that confirm the truth in the correspondence between Joseph, the Jewish king of the Khazars, and Hasdai ibn Shaprut.

Nothing came of the epistolary interchange. The Khazar kingdom shortly thereafter was invaded by the same elements that now constitute the Slavic population of Russia. That population originated in Scandinavia. The Slav invasion took place at about that time. Russia was conquered, and the Khazar kingdom was destroyed.

Among the Geniza fragments Solomon Schechter discovered what he called "an unknown Khazar document," which Professor Dunlop calls the Cambridge papers. This document fully confirms the authenticity of the Hasdai–Joseph correspondence.

It is appropriate, in summary, to conclude with these words of Dunash ibn Labrat on Hasdai ibn Shaprut:

> From off his people's neck he struck the heavy yoke; To them his soul was given, he drew them to his heart; God vouchsafe through him such crumbs of salvation to which we have fallen heir.

This is a just appraisal of a towering figure in the long and often lugubrious history of our people. Hasdai was a proud Jew, one who bore the shield of David with dignity, courage, and effectiveness.

Ibn Shaprut's life stands as monumental testimony to the efficacy of the union between temporal power and timeless spirit.

The Eleventh Century

GAON HAI

The *Gaon* Hai is the Jew of the eleventh century. Babylonian Jewry has dominated half of the chapters of the book to this point. Abbaye and Rava, Ashi and Rabbina, Bustenai and Anan ben David, all were Babylonian Jews. Without question it was Babylonian Jewry that was the most creative of Jewish communities for some 800 years. The years 250 to 450 represent the era of glory for Babylonian Jewry. It was during that time that the Babylonian Talmud took shape. It was there that the Jews achieved an economic status that was unusually high for Jews in that period. It was there also that the Jewish people enjoyed the highest degree of internal autonomy of any community in the diaspora.

FLUCTUATING FORTUNES

The next two hundred years, from 450 to 650, represent a period of decline. The last Parsee kings, Yazdegurd III and Peruz II, were harsh on the Jewish people. The status of the Jews fell markedly. So much so that an Exilarch of that time was so little regarded by the authorities that they executed his sons. Huna Mari was the Exilarch, and his sons, Amaymar and Misharshia, were executed by the Parsee power. The chief reason for this low in the fortunes of Babylonian Jewry was a national craze that intoxicated these Parsee kings, Yazdegurd and Peruz. They inaugurated a policy that all property should be shared in common and that wives, too, should be shared. The Jewish people of that era certainly were not ready to capitulate to such a sociological order. Because of their resistence, they suffered exceedingly. We hear of a member of the rabbinical family that was leading the Academy in Sura, A Mar Zutra by name, leading a Jewish rebellion for seven years, holding out with an army of Jews in the city of Mechoza, a small Jewish town not far from Pumbedita in Babylonia. Only after seven years of dogged resistance was Mar Zutra finally overcome. He was executed on the bridge of Mechoza. His wife, who was pregnant and only a week away from giving birth to her child, was also sentenced to death, but the Jewish underground spirited her away and brought her to Palestine. On the way to Palestine, the child was born. When he reached maturity, he became the head of the Jewish Academy in Palestine.

During this sad period in the history of Babylonian Jewry, there were waves of emigration involving thousands which left Babylonia. One of the interesting sidelights of this emigration is the fact that a Jewish community in China survived into the twentieth century. William C. White, a Canadian scholar, published a history of the Jews of Kai-Feng in 1942. These Jews were there from approximately the year 500, when they emigrated from Babylonia because of the persecution of the last Parsee kings. In all probability, the Jewish community of India, the Jews of Cochin—the *B'nai* Israel—owe their origin to this same emigration. That was the era of the decline of Babylonian Jewry.

RESURGENCE

The third period was one of resurgence. It came with the sweep of Arabic culture across the fertile crescent. As we have seen, Bustenai, who became a shining light of the patriarchate, had been confirmed in office by Omar, one of Islam's greatest rulers. It was during this period that the institution of the gaonate rose to pre-eminence. The *gaon* was addressed as "The splendor, the glory, the spiritual leader of the *Yeshivah* of Sura or Pumbedita." They were the legitimate successors of the great Talmudic scholars like Abba Arikha, Abbaye and Rava, Rabba and Rav Joseph, Rabbina and Rav Ashi. The *gaonim* were the mainstays of Jewish life in Babylonia from the year 550 until the death of the *Gaon* Hai, the Jew of the eleventh century, in the year 1038. The spiritual reign of the *gaonim* covered 500 uninterrupted years of fertile Judaic leadership.

Their influence extended far beyond the territorial precincts of Babylonia itself. It was with the emergence of the Gaonim as the normative religious authority that Jewish practice became solidified and standardized. Jews the world over sent questions to the *gaonim* in Sura and in Pumbedita on procedural matters in Jewish life: How to pray, when to eat, when are weddings prohibited, what should a proper document of divorce contain, how did the Mishnah come to be written? Questions by the thousands were addressed to the *gaonim*, all pertaining to the life of the Jews from womb to tomb.

The *gaonim* responded to these questions, and because of their authority, uniform Jewish practice began to prevail through most of the Jewish world. Instead of Jews praying one way in Iraq, and in another way in Germany, and still another way in Spain or France, the responsa of the *gaonim* and the authority that they carried succeeded in bringing about a standardization in the form and content of the Jewish prayer book (the siddur). So, too, with other areas of religious practice. The *gaonim* succeeded in cementing the religious unity of Jewry. The era of the *gaonim* represents the third stage in Babylonian Jewish history.

DECLINE

The fourth stage was one of decline. When the Arab empire began to crumble, when Arab culture began to deteriorate, and when Arab dynastic rivalries were exacerbated, Jewish life in Babylonia began to deteriorate, too. Rivalries among various Arab dynasties developed among the Abbasid caliphs of Iraq, the Omyyads of Spain, and the Fatimids of Egypt. This internecine Arab rivalry brought about the deterioration of life in the Middle East under Arab rulership. The result was a narrowing of the Jewish economic sphere as well as a lessening of Jewish authority and discipline.

The urbanization of the Jewish community of Babylonia occurred in one of the oldest cities in the world—Baghdad. The Pumbedita Academy had to move there. Pumbedita had been rural for many centuries. But bit by bit Jews moved away from the soil because of the increasing danger to them of life in the open, unprotected spaces. The glory of Babylonian Jewry began to evanesce almost simultaneously with the evanescence of Arab power and culture in the Middle East. The handwriting on the wall became increasingly legible, and it became clear that Babylonian Jewry had seen its best days and was headed for a sad denouement. In fact, by the tenth century, any observer who would have come to Babylonian Jewry as a visitor would have arrived at the conclusion that Judaism in Babylonia was dying. Still, before the candle was to burn itself out, it was to flare forth in a short but intense blaze of magnificence. Two of the most brilliant figures of the gaonate, which had started in 550, were the last important *gaonim* of Babylonia Jewry— the *Gaon* Sherira, who lived to be over one hundred years old and his son, Hai, who died just short of his one hundredth birthday.

SHERIRA

The *Gaon* Sherira became the *gaon* of the Academy of Pumbedita when he was 40 years old. When Sherira was about eighty years old, he received the permission of the scholars of Pumbedita to appoint his son as co-*gaon* with him. They worked together until Sherira died in 1004. Hai reigned as the *gaon* alone for the last thirty-four years of his life. We know more about Hai and Sheria than we do about the dozens of the other *gaonim* who lived from 550 until the very end of the gaonate.

The Cairo Geniza, rediscovered by Solomon Schechter about a century ago, was in his words "a hoard of Jewish manuscripts." Among them were copies of thousands of letters addressed to the *gaonim* from all parts of the Jewish world. As we have seen earlier, they were questions regarding correct *halakhic* procedures for virtually every aspect of a Jew's life. These letters had gone to Cairo first, because of its centralized location. The Jewish authorities of Cairo made copies of them for their own possible use before sending them on to Sura or Pumbedita as the case might be. When months later the responsa arrived at Cairo, they too, were copied before being sent on to their destination. When, many years later, the copies were too worn to be used, they were consigned to the *geniza*. Neither these letters nor any other writing containing the name of God could be destroyed. Virtually all writing including deeds and bills of sale contained a reference to the deity. Thus modern scholarship has been afforded the golden opportunity to learn much about the *gaonim* and the "Mediterranean society" (as it is designated in the majestic five volumes of S. D. Goitein, the definitive opus of *geniza* scholarship).

THE GAONIM

Among distinguished *gaonim* we may include the blind Yehudai. He was never able to see. This blind man had so persisted in his search for Jewish knowledge that he was to become the greatest Jewish scholar in his day and the head of the Academy of Sura. He dictated the first *gaonic* code of laws, known as the *Hilkhot Pesukot*. The *geniza* responsa include some of the *Gaon* Yehudai's contributions.

During the ninth century, the *Gaon* Amram was head of the Sura Academy. The Jewish community of Barcelona addressed a letter to the *Gaon* Amran, seeking to know the precise order and wording of the daily prayers. In response, *Gaon* Amram wrote out what is the first complete siddur (prayer book) that has come down to us. It remains basically the siddur of traditional Jewry to this day. The giant of all the *gaonim* was Sa'adia ben Joseph of Sura (880–940). He has been preempted in this book by the Spanish Hasdai ibn Shaprut because of the exigencies of our narrative. To do a measure of justice to Sa'adia, even a very lengthy chapter would barely suffice. He made immense contributions to *halakha*, to philosophy, to biblical exegesis, and to Hebrew grammar and lexicography, to name but a few areas to which his genius was applied. As we have seen, he waged a relentless and successful campaign against the Karaite movement.

GAONIC RESPONSA

We have thousands of gaonic responsa. There are some 4,000 responsa from the *Gaon* Hai addressed to communities in Spain, Italy, France, Germany, Palestine, Iraq, and India. When word got around that a new letter had arrived from Pumbedita, the synagogues were crowded with people who craved to hear the words of the *gaon*. Today, some one thousand years later, it seems almost unbelievable that this is what would fetch a large audience. The thirst for Torah, the passion for Jewish knowledge, and above all, the almost divine respect that was offered to the spiritual center and to the spiritual leader—all of these motivations were magnates for even the unlearned.

The *Gaon* Hai's influence was enormous. He was clearly the supreme *halakhic* authority for world Jewry. That is what momentarily halted the steep decline of Babylonia Jewry. It must be noted that every letter addressed to the *gaon* from afar included a monetary contribution for the support of his academy. These contributions constituted the largest part of the academy's income.

When Sherira died, there was great mourning throughout the Jewish world. It so happened that on the Sabbath following his death the biblical reading (*haftara*) concluded with the words "King Solomon sat upon the throne of his father, David, and his rule was firmly established." That day, Babylonian Jewry added to these words: "Hai sat on the throne of his father, Sherira, and his rule became firmly established."

Hai was a man of liberal inclinations, an outstanding student of the Bible text itself as well as a student of the Talmudic text. One time he was studying with one of his pupils. They reached a passage in the Bible that neither of them could satisfactorily explain. Hai turned to his pupil and said: "Here in Baghdad we have a very learned Catholic bishop. Go consult the bishop because he is a good biblical scholar."

One of the tragedies wrought by the ravages of time is the loss of precious works. It is known from remaining fragments that the *Gaon* Hai had composed a comprehensive codification of *halakhic* civil law. Indeed, Moses Maimonides was inspired by it to compose his *magnum opus* summarizing the total corpus of Jewish law (see following chapter).

When the *Gaon* Hai died, the glory of Babylonian Jewry died, too. It was a tragedy that he left no child after him. It is conceivable that had Hai left a son, the fortress known as Babylonian Jewry might have continued to stand. Samuel Hanagid lived approximately at the same time as did Hai. He wrote a dirge upon the death of Hai in which he said: "And if he died and he left no child of his own, let us be consoled by the fact that wherever Jewish children walk, they are his children."

The great poet, Solomon ibn Gabirol, wrote no less than four dirges over the death of the *Gaon* Hai. Nachmanides, the Jew of the thirteenth century, called Hai "the father of all the children of Israel." And yet, enormous as this man's work, genius, spirit, devotion, and love for his people was, he had in the course of his lifetime some bitter enemies. At one time these enemies even went to the extreme of accusing both Sherira and Hai of subversive activities designed to overthrow the Arab rulers in Baghdad. Hai and his father, Sherira, were both thrown into a dungeon cell in which they spent many months. Hai epitomizes the spirit of learning and teaching that enabled the Jewish people to negotiate the often treacherous shoals of diaspora waters.

THE TWELFTH CENTURY

MAIMONIDES

Moses ben Maimon, who was born in 1135 and died in 1204, is *the* titanic figure of the last thousand years in Jewish history. His role is ramified and variegated. He was the great codifier of Jewish law. His comprehensive knowledge of *halakha*, his unparalled acuity, and his synoptic genius enabled him to organize and summarize the vast legal material of the Talmud and the *gaonim*. His great *Code*, the *Mishneh Torah*, has served as the basis of all subsequent codifications of Judaic law. It remains indispensable to this day.

Maimonides was the great Jewish philosopher of the Middle Ages. He was the first to attempt to formulate Jewish creed systematically. To this day it defies understanding that one person, however gifted, could have accomplished what Maimonides did in a lifetime of barely seventy years. Maimonides' knowledge of Jewish and secular learning was nothing short of encyclopedic.

One of his younger contemporaries summarized in somewhat exaggerated form his sense of awe and wonder over the achievement of Maimonides: "He knew in philosophy all that Aristotle knew; he knew in mathematics all that Euclid knew; he knew in astronomy all that

Ptolemy knew; he knew in medicine all that Galen and Hipprocrates knew; and he knew of the Torah all that was ever known to his own day." Maimondies' mastery of all the fields mentioned—philosophy, mathematics, astronomy, medicine, and the vast realm of all Jewish learning—remains unquestioned.

Maimonides had an over-all reason for learning. Why should anyone study at all, and what is the purpose of study? To quote Maimonides: *"Man should try to absorb the maximum possible of all areas of knowledge, for this helps in the great objective of life, which is getting ever closer to God."* Unlike many of his contemporaries, Maimonides did not perceive the study of science as dangerous to faith. He did not think that "whys" and "wherefores" were threats to well-grounded religious faith. Many fundamentalists among his people and within Islam and Christianity, as well, were averse to scientific or philosophical inquiry, which they regarded as the antithesis of faith. Maimonides went counter to this trend. It was his contention that religious faith can only benefit from a quest for knowledge, even though he conceded that the end purpose of such a quest is to demonstrate our ultimate ignorance of God and His universe.

BIOGRAPHICAL

Moses, son of Maimon, was born Saturday the fourteenth day of Nissan, 1135, at twenty minutes past one o'clock in the city of Cordova, Spain. He died on the twentieth day of Tevet, 1204, in the city of Cairo. Some years later his body was taken to Palestine and buried in Tiberias, where his grave and monument remain on view. There are no other figures in Jewish history whose time of birth can so precisely be delineated. He was a prodigy at the age of five. He and his father were students at the same time of the renowned Joseph ibn Migash in Lucena, Spain.

In 1148, when Maimonides was thirteen years old, the Almohades, an Arab sect from Northern Africa, invaded Spain and forced their Islamic fundamentalism with tools of terror. The family of Maimon fled Cordova and traveled to Fez in Morocco. There Maimonides studied with his brother David under Rabbi Judah Hacohen, until the latter was murdered. The rabbi had refused to accept conversion to Islam and was killed for that reason. Later Maimonides was denounced to the authorities by one of his fellow medical students. As a result, the family had to leave North Africa. Their next stop was Palestine. Maimon died in Palestine. For one reason or another, Maimonides could not find his anchorage there. Finally, he and his brother David arrived at Fostat, which is a suburb of Cairo, in the year 1166, and there Moses Maimonides, who was then thirty-one years old, remained until the day of his death in the year 1204.

PHYSICIAN IN CAIRO

The early part of Maimonides' life in Cairo was pleasant. He did not have to worry about his livelihood. His brother David was a gem merchant who was only too happy to support the study of his brilliant brother. David's business took him to distant places. Tragedy struck when he was drowned at sea. An inconsolable Maimonides writes later of his brother: "My mainstaff, my boon companion, the joy of my life, is gone." Now, in addition to pursuing his scholarly work, he had to be concerned with his livelihood as well. He entered into the practice of medicine. He was one of the great physicians of his day. An Arab contemporary writes of him: "He was the greatest of all the physicians of his day, both in medical knowledge and medical practice." His fame reached the ears of the vizier (the prime minister) of the Sultan Saladin, who had crushed the Christian armies led against Islam by Richard the Lionhearted during the second Crusade. Maimonides was called to the court of the vizier to be his personal physician. Ultimately, Maimonides was appointed to join the medical staff that attended to all members of the royal family.

Maimonides carried an immense, burdened schedule. Being a physician full-time for Saladin's court was in itself extremely taxing of both time and energy. A letter from Maimonides to one of his star students offers a description of a typical day.

> God knows that in order to write this to you, I have had to escape to a secluded spot where people would not think to find me, sometimes leaning against the wall for support, sometimes lying down on account of my excessive weakness, for I have grown old and feeble. But with respect to your wish to come here to me, I cannot but say how greatly your visit would delight me, for I truly long to commune with you, and would anticipate our meeting with even greater joy than you. Yet I must advise you not to expose yourself to the perils of the voyage, for beyond seeing me, and my doing all

I could to honor you, you would not derive any advantage of your visit. Do not expect to be able to confer with me on any scientific subject for even one hour, either by day or by night, for the following is my daily schedule: I dwell at Fostat and the sultan resides at Cairo. These two places are two Sabbath days' journey distant from each other. My duties to the sultan are very heavy. I am obliged to visit him every day early in the morning, and when he or any of his children or any of the inmates of his harem are indisposed, I dare not quit Cairo, but must stay the greater part of the day in the palace. It also frequently happens that one or two of the royal officers fall sick, and I must attend to their healing. Hence, as a rule, I repair to Cairo very early in the day and even if nothing unusual happens, I do not return to Fostat until the afternoon. When I am almost dying from hunger, I find the antechambers filled with people. Both Jews and Gentiles, nobles and common people, judges and bailiffs, friends and foes, and a mixed multitude await the time of my return. I dismount from my animal, wash my hands, go forth to my patients and entreat them to bear with me while I partake of some slight refreshment, the only meal I take in the 24 hours. Then I go forth to attend to my patients and write prescriptions and directions for their various ailments. Patients go in and out until nightfall, sometimes, I solemnly assure you, until two hours or more in the night. I converse with them and prescribe for them while lying down from sheer exhaustion, but when night falls I am so exhausted that I can scarcely speak. In consequence of this, no Israelite can have any private interview with me except on the Sabbath. On that day, the whole congregation, or at least a majority of the members, come to me after the morning service when I instruct them as to their proceedings during the whole week. We study together a little until noon, when they depart. Some of them return and read with me after the afternoon service until the evening prayer. In this manner, I spend the day. I have here related to you only a part of what you would see if you were to visit me.

This, however, did not prevent him from writing a "best-seller" entitled "The Book of Medication." It offered some sound medical advice. "Don't stuff yourself." "Always leave the meal feeling a bit hungry." "Every organ needs to be exercised; one must exercise in such a way as to encompass every organ of the body." "Certain foods are bad for certain people. I have discovered that some people have negative reactions to particular kinds of food." "Sea air is very healthy."

He was the spiritual leader as well as physician to his congregation, receiving no salary. He established a public kitchen in order to feed the many visitors who came to study Torah at his feet. He was personally a significant contributor to its budget.

THE WORK OF MAIMONIDES

At the age of twenty-three, he had begun his great Commentary on the Mishnah. Much of it was written aboard rickety ships tossed upon stormy waters while Maimonides was still a wandering Jew. It is a pioneering work that remains a classic introduction to the Mishnah. In this work are enunciated the Thirteen Articles of Faith. To this day they remain the credo of Orthodox Jews. The Articles are as follows:

1. I firmly believe that the Creator, blessed be His name, is the Creator and Ruler of all created things, and that He alone has made, does make, and ever will make all things.
2. I firmly believe that the Creator, blessed be His name, is One, and that there is no oneness in any form like His, and that He alone was, is, and ever will be Our God.

(This was a very pointed but nevertheless subtle denunciation of the Christian concept of the Trinity. He would not abide by a notion that three is one under any circumstances. The Father, the Son, and the Holy Ghost as aspects of one deity was something that Maimonides categorically rejected.)

3. I firmly believe that the Creator, blessed be His name, is not corporeal, He cannot be described in terms of the body, that no bodily adjectives apply to Him, and that there exists nothing whatever to resemble Him.
4. I firmly believe that the Creator, blessed be His name, was the first and will be the last.

(This was an emphatic rejection of Aristotle's theory that matter always existed and that what God did was to shape pre-existent matter in the work of the Creation. Maimonides denied the eternity of matter.

He believed in the principle of "Creatio ex nihilo," which means that God created the world out of nothing.)

    5. I firmly believe that the Creator, blessed be His name, is the only one to whom it is proper to address our prayers and that we must not pray to anyone else.

(That was a pointed denunciation of all those among the Christian sects who prayed to Jesus, the Virgin Mary, and the saints.)

    6. I firmly believe that all the words of the Prophets are true.

    7. I firmly believe that the prophecy of Moses, our teacher, may he rest in peace, was true and that he was the chief of the prophets, both of those who preceded and those who followed him.

(A pointed renunciation of the Moslem idea that, while Moses was a prophet and Jesus was a prophet, Mohammed was *the* prophet.)

    8. I firmly believe that the whole Torah we now possess is the same that was given to Moses our teacher, may he rest in peace.

    9. I firmly believe that this Torah will not be changed, and that there will be no other Torah given by the Creator, blessed be His name.

(This, too, was a pointed renunciation of the notion that there was a new dispensation, or a New Testament.)

    10. I firmly believe that the Creator, blessed be His name, knows all the actions and thoughts of human beings; As it is said, "It is He who fashions the hearts of them all, He who knows all their deeds."

    11. I firmly believe that the Creator, blessed be His name, rewards those who keep His commandments and punishes those who transgress His commandments.

    12. I firmly believe in the coming of the Messiah and although He may be late, I will wait daily for His coming.

(This is a renunciation of the Christian doctrine that the Messiah had already come and a warning of the danger posed by Messianic pretenders.)

13. I firmly believe that there will be a revival of the dead at a time that will please the Creator, blessed and exalted be His name, for ever and ever.

The Commentary on the Mishnah was Maimonides' first major work. The second major work was to concretize the tradition that there are 613 commandments in the Torah. Moses Maimonides compiled the *Book of the Commandments* (*Sefer ha-Mitzvot*). It became the authoritative enumeration of the 613 commandments.

The most important work of Maimonides is the great *Code of Jewish Law*. He called it by two names: *Mishneh Torah*, a summary of the Law; and *Yad ha-zakah* (the Mighty Hand). Therein lies a pun. The last sentence in the Torah reads: "And for all the mighty hand . . . which Moses wrought in the sight of Israel." *Yad* in Hebrew is "hand." The two Hebrew letters of *yad* have the numerical equivalence of fourteen. *Mishneh Torah* is in fourteen parts, and therefore he called it "The Mighty Hand." The work, which appeared in 1189, had taken ten years to complete.

Following are the fourteen categories of the *Mishneh Torah*. The first is on the principles of Judaism; the second is on the rituals, designed as ever-present reminders of said principles; the third is on the holidays and seasons; the fourth is about women, including marriage and divorce; the fifth is about forbidden foods; the sixth deals with vows and promises; the seventh, the laws of agriculture as applied to the Holy Land; the eighth treats temple ritual; the ninth pertains to the sacrificial rites of the Holy Temple; the tenth involves the laws of ritual purity; the eleventh deals with the body of civil law; the twelfth, with buying and selling, contracts, and real estate; the thirteenth is on laws pertaining to the functions of the judiciary; and the fourteenth encompasses capital cases.

Maimonides wrote his great *Code* in magnificent Hebrew, a masterpiece of style and vocabulary. His Hebrew was punctilious and precise. The *Mishneh Torah* became definitive and authoritative. It was accessible to all and, of course, was encyclopedic. Nevertheless, even in his day it encountered much opposition, so rancorous at times as to lead to dire consequences. There was merit in some of the criticism. The very introduction of Maimonides to his work invited it. The author boasted that his code would render it unnecessary to spend time and energy in the quest for authoritative *halakhic* decisions. In truth, these words smack of arrogance. Moreover, opposition to the *Code of Maimonides* was expressed by those who feared that the development of Jewish law would be stultified by that work. Not that Maimonides intended that to happen. He compiled the work because he realized that unless he did so, ultimately people would not know what the law is. Moreover, not too many are competent to delve into the mighty ocean of the Talmud and to extract from its meandering and labyrinthine discussions a specific law. The Talmud is not well organized. The Talmud had laws pertaining to the same category scattered through its sixty-three tractates. It took nothing less than an encyclopedic genius to extricate the core of the entire Talmudic and gaonic corpus so as to render his *Code* "user friendly."

But the chief opposition to the work of Maimonides was on the grounds that it included an attempt to supply a philosophic basis for both the beliefs and practices of Judaism. This was regarded by the ultraconservatives as terribly dangerous, pregnant with the possibility of destruction for Judaism. They felt that once one begins to ask questions, the structure of religious *faith* would crumble. So bitter did this opposition to Maimonides become that in the year 1238, as the result of vengeful denunciation to the Church authorities, the French Inquisition carried off the books of Maimonides to a bonfire in Paris and burned them. This was one of the first and most painful examples of the treachery of witch hunting in the history of the Jews. Shortly thereafter, the stake began to take its brutal toll of *human* life with the emergence of Inquisitions in other lands.

THE GUIDE FOR THE PERPLEXED

The fourth major work of Maimonides is perhaps the most famous universally. It was written in Arabic, because he wrote it for scholars rather than for the masses. He called it *Daladet al Hairin*, which means *The Guide for the Perplexed*. This *magnum opus* of medieval Jewish philosophy begins with the following words: "A principle of principles and the pillar of all wisdom is to know that there is a primal Being Who called into existence all that is." The chief aim of the *Guide to the Perplexed* was, in the words of Israel Friedlander, "To establish by direct proof the principal truth of the Jewish religion, that is, the existence of

God, the unity of God, the eternity of God, the creation of the world by God, and Divine Revelation." The *Guide* is a taxing work, requiring intensive study. Four principle themes emerge from the work:

First is the idea that God is incorporeal. One cannot speak of God as feeling, or stretching out His hand, or becoming angry. One cannot attribute to God anything descriptive of humans, because God is not a function of any aspect of human thought, since a human being's thinking is qualified by his limitations. God, by definition, is unlimited and infinite. Maimonides spends a great deal of time in the attempt to explain away those references to God in the Bible that describe God with human attributes. "The Lord *spoke* unto Moses" is an anthropomorphism, talking of the Deity in human terms. God does not *speak*, as we comprehend that verb. The Bible is full of anthropomorphisms. Maimonides spends a great deal of his time and energy in attempting to explain them.

Secondly, Maimonides discusses at length the concept of *Creatio ex Nihilo*, that God created the world of nothing at all. This is difficult to understand. How does one create something out of nothing? Aristotle saw no other alternative but to come to the conclusion that there had to be something in the beginning, that matter was eternal, that the one hundred-odd elements always existed, and that the work of the Creator, the Prime Mover, the Prime Being, as Aristotle called him, was simply to take the elements and combine them in such a way as to create a world. Maimonides denies this idea without qualification.

Third, emphatically and clearly, albeit tactfully, Maimonides denied that Jesus was the Messiah. Maimonides said: Christians used the Hebrew Bible as a "proof text" for the advent and mission of Jesus. Does not the very same Bible predict (asks Maimonides) that when the Messiah comes, the *Jewish people* will be redeemed from their suffering? Since the advent of Jesus, Jews have had nothing but suffering. Their misery has indeed been intensified. By this circumstance, the notion that Jesus was the Messiah must be dismissed as preposterous.

RITUAL RATIONALE

A fourth category of major discussion in *The Guide for the Perplexed* is supplying the rationale for some of the laws in the Torah. Why kosher food? Why put a mezuzah on the door? Why the prohibition on wearing garments compounded of wool and cotton? The "why's" of Jewish ritual law are expatiated consistently in Maimonides. He was among the first to attempt to present the reasons that undergird ritual law, the *ta'amei ha-Mitzvot.*

Here is a remarkable example. There is a law that reads as follows: "Thou shalt bring the first fruit of your land to the house of the Lord your God; thou shalt not seethe a kid in the milk of its mother." This is all in one verse. Maimonides in his *Guide* asks two questions: First, what is the connection between the first part of the verse and the second part of the verse? The first part of the verse reads: "Thou shalt bring the first fruit of your land to the house of the Lord your God." The second reads: "Thou shalt not seethe a kid in the milk of its mother." There seems to be no logical sequence there. His second questions is: What is wrong with cooking a kid in the milk of its mother? The kid is dead, presumably. He has already been slaughtered according to Jewish law. What is wrong with taking the milk from the mother and boiling the kid in that milk? Maimonides offered the following opinion: I don't really *know* the reason, but I would speculate that among the ancient pagans there was a fertility rite wherein the mother's udder was squeezed for milk and then its first-born child would be boiled in that milk and the whole of it poured on the ground, with a fertility prayer offered to the deity that the soil should be blessed. Therefore both questions are answered, says he. If the theory is correct, then the two passages *are* linked logically. Thou shalt offer to God only those things that are proper. Offer Him the first fruit of your land, but do not offer Him a first born kid boiled in the milk of its mother because that is the magic and superstition of the Canaanites, which you must abhor. Maimonides has been vindicated by archaeology. About seventy years ago, in Ras Shamra in Northern Syria, the Ugaritic Epics were excavated. They pertain to the cult of the Canaanites in the fifteenth century before the Christian era. There we find that the ancient Canaanites practiced the very rite that Maimonides imaginatively reconstructed. They boiled a newborn kid in the milk of its mother and poured the contents on the ground while invoking a prayer to Baal that the earth might be rendered fertile through this act of pious devotion.

144

CORRESPONDENT

Maimonides conducted a correspondence with Jews all over the world. One of his famous letters, written to the Jews of Morocco, concerns apostasy. The Jews of Morocco had asked Maimonides: Inasmuch as so many Jews were forced by the sword to accept Islam, but continued to practice their Judaism in secret, may they be counted as part of the minyan in the synagogue? Maimonides answered in the affirmative. He said: It is the heart that counts in matters of faith. If by force of the sword a Jew is constrained to practice that which is foreign to his inner conviction, as long as you know that his faith has abided you must admit him to the minyan.

In the year 1172 he wrote his letter to the Jews of Yemen. The Jews of Yemen had written to him about a self-proclaimed Messiah who was preaching in their midst. Are they to believe him? Maimonides' answer: No, no, no. He is not the Messiah. The Messiah is not a "miracle worker." The Messiah is not a rabble-rouser. The Messiah would arrive quietly and by the force of his own spiritual personality would convince the people whom he addresses of the ultimate truth. Two years later, this false Messiah was brought before the ruler of Morocco. The ruler of Morocco had asked: "Are you the Messiah?" (The question is very reminiscent, is it not, of something that Pontius Pilate asked back in the year 30 or 31?) The man said: "Yes, I am the Messiah." The ruler said: "How do you propose to prove it?" He said (trying to bluff his way through): "Order your men to decapitate me. I shall still be alive." The experiment was carried out.

Maimonides was able to conduct a remarkably prolific correspondence with many people. This was a measure of the love he had for all Jews who were interested in the pursuit of their faith. One of his pupils, Joseph ibn Aknin, had written a letter to his master. "Master, you are so busy. Why do you write letters to everyone? I know of a Jew who wrote you a letter only to get an answer from you, so that he could boast to people: 'I have an answer from the great Maimonides.' He didn't write you the letter because he really wanted to know a particular point of the law. Spare yourself, Master." Maimonides wrote in response: "I have no right to withhold Torah from anyone who seeks it, be his motives what they may. I do not care what the reason is for someone's desire to study Torah, as long as it is there." He wrote a letter to a convert, Obadiah the Ger, (Obadiah the proselyte). Obadiah had written that he felt uncomfortable when he prayed in the synagogue, because of the benediction that begins: "Blessed art Thou, O Lord our God, God of Abraham, Isaac and Jacob, our Fathers . . ." "Abraham, Isaac and Jacob were not *my* Fathers," said this new proselyte to Maimonides. "I feel uncomfortable when I read that prayer for it is not true of me."

Maimonides' answer in a beautiful letter has come down to us: Obadiah, my beloved (and I am paraphrasing), a son of Abraham, Isaac, and Jacob is not a biological son of Abraham, Isaac, and Jacob. A son of the Jewish people is not a biological son of the Jewish people. A son of the Jewish people is one who wishes *now* to share their destiny, who wishes *now* to be involved in their trials and in their tribulations, who wishes *now* to be associated with what the future holds for them, and to struggle through the prelude to that future.

Maimonides also wrote a prayer for physicians: "Implant within my heart a love for my art and for Thy creatures. Permit not the love of monetary gain and the lust for praise and glory to interfere with my work as a physician. Harness my body and my spirit to be ever ready to help and to save the rich and the poor alike, the enemy and the friend. May I see in every patient only a human being."

When Maimonides died in 1204, on the twentieth day of Tevet, the Jews of Yemen who had been in correspondence with him, and for whose morale he had done so much, changed the format of their Kaddish for an entire year. They actually introduced his name into the recitation of the Kaddish, not just for one occasion but whenever that Kaddish was recited for the eleven months of the mourning period. The great poet Alharizi, who was one of the several translators of Maimonides' Arabic works into Hebrew, writes this as his eulogy: "From you, Master, derives all our praise; from you, all our greatness; your ways were profound and supreme, and your work towers high above ours; you were born to be a messenger of God, and if you and we were made in the same likeness, it is because of *you* that God had said: 'Let us make man in our image.'"

"And if you and we were made in the same likeness, it is only because of you that God had said: 'Let us make man in our image.'"

THE THIRTEENTH CENTURY

Moses ben Nachman

It is perhaps more than coincidence that the Moses of this chapter is situated between Moses Maimonides and Moses de Leon, who will be featured in the chapter that follows. If Moses Maimonides is the epitome of rationalism, and if Moses de Leon represents the locus of mysticism in Jewish history, then Moses Nachmanides serves as a bridge between the two. In a sense, he was a dual personality, because in him were combined strong rational elements with a deeply ingrained mysticism. One might say that the Golden Age of the Jews in Spain begins to fade with the disappearance from the scene of this giant, the Jew of the thirteenth century, Moses Nachmanides.

He was born in Gerona, Spain, in 1194 and died in 1270. When he was twenty years old, a Christian Ecumenical Council was held, which was to spell Jewish misery for centuries to come. It was the Fourth Lateran Council. It took place under the leadership of Pope Innocent III in the year 1215. The Princes of the Church discussed many other matters beside the Jewish people, but they gave the latter considerable attention. Their decisions were unfavorable to the position of the Jew

149

in European life. The Council made it mandatory for Jews in all Christian countries to wear the yellow badge of shame. Jews were expelled from many areas of economic enterprise. In general, Jews were to be subjected to a systematic policy of persecution and humiliation. The Pope assiduously championed the cause of anti-Jewishness in the Spanish countries where for so many centuries the Jews had enjoyed relative well being. Moses Nachmanides lived at a time when the fortunes of Spanish Jewry had begun a sharp decline.

BIBLE EXEGETE

Nachmanides was to end his life in Palestine. His was one of the fullest, richest, and most significant Jewish lives of the mediaeval era. His work embraced many fields. Like his illustrious forerunner, Moses Maimonides, he was prolific in a variety of branches of Jewish learning. Moses Nachmanides was, to begin with, an outstanding interpreter of the Bible, one of the great Bible exegetes of the medieval period. His commentaries on the Five Books of Moses are to this day a vital contribution to the understanding of the Torah. His style is terse, but withal lucid. His words are few, but his meaning is deep and thought provoking. His commentary is a repository of suggestive ideas. To cite an example, the Book of Genesis narrates the story of Jacob, reunited after twenty years with his twin, Esau. They walk together for some distance, engaged in conversation. Nachmanides observes that the moment Jacob began to walk with Esau was the beginning of Jewish tragedy. Esau's way and Jacob's simply did not and could not coalesce. Nachmanides asks: Did not a similar situation occur when Judas Maccabeus decided to walk with the modern Esau in seeking Roman help for his revolt against the Syrian Greeks? Jerusalem and Rome were not meant to venture upon a common journey. The result of that journey was tragedy for the Jewish people. Esau must walk one way and Jacob must walk another. This is one of many examples of Nachmanides' talent for drawing out of a biblical text abiding insights and enduring truths in respect to his vision of Jewish destiny.

THEOLOGIAN–PHILOSOPHER

His second area of activity was that of theologian and philosopher of Judaism. He did much thinking about the eternal problems of all religions and applied them to Judaism. As an example, one of the perplexing problems of religion is this: If God is good, why do the righteous so often suffer, and why do the evil so often prosper? This dilemma is centered in theodicy, the consideration of God's *justice*. Many responses have been offered, none of them fully satisfactory. Nachmanides advanced what was for his time a rather original answer. There is not a human being who is so good that no evil at all is to be found in him. Nor is there a human being who is so evil that he is totally lacking in goodness. So that the suffering of a good man is God's punishment for the evil within him. In that way he enters the paradisal world to come with a clean slate, there to enjoy unmitigated bliss. On the other hand, the evil man prospering in this world is being rewarded for the little good he does possess, thus clearing the way for eternal punishment in the world to come. To Nachmanides this was a satisfactory answer, though, perhaps it will not do for most of us today.

The third category of his interest and activity was the Cabala. Cabala is the generic term for Jewish mysticism. It will be treated more fully in the next chapter. Nachmanides' life corresponded precisely with the great resurgence of Jewish mystic thought. He was a vital contributor to the comprehension and appreciation of Cabalistic thought and certainly the greatest *halakhic* authority to be engaged in Cabala until the advent of Joseph Karo four centuries later.

SAVANT OF THE LAW

The fourth major area of Nachmanides' activity was *halakha*. Jews from all over the world sent letters of inquiry to him regarding procedural matters in Jewish law. He conducted a correspondence much as did the *gaonim*. A very substantial responsa of Nachmanides is available to us. One example: There is a principle in the Talmud originating with Rabbi Samuel of the third century. Rabbi Samuel proclaimed that the law of the land must be practiced by the Jews wherever they live, provided that it did not conflict with Jewish law. There was a Jewish community in Spain to whom a prince of the realm owed 100,000 dinar. The prince did not have the 100,000 dinar to pay back to his Jewish creditors, namely the whole of the Jewish community. To pay his debt he recalled the dinarim of his domain, had them cut in half and declared each half to be worth the full dinar. This was simply a crude act of currency devaluation. The prince then offered the truncated coin in payment of his debt. The Jewish community questioned Nachmanides as to whether the principle of "the law of the land is the law" applies here and that therefore they should accept what they were offered as full payment of their debt. Nachmanides answered that by no means did the principle apply to their case. The unscrupulous prince was wantonly violating the commandment: "Thou shalt not steal." You must, advised the rabbi, oppose chicanery, more as champions of divine justice than as cheated creditors.

Nachmanides' knowledge of Jewish law was both immense and intensive. To almost every tractate of the Talmud he offered illuminating interpretation and elucidation.

Nachmanides was a titan in defense of the Judaic faith. He was a powerful and courageous fighter in the ranks, a man who was a Jewish knight in shining armor fighting with dignity and fortitude against the many attacks leveled in his day against both his people and his religion. Of this, more later. Before concluding this general description of Nachmanides' versatility, it should be noted that in addition to his mastery of Hebrew and Spanish, he also had a good working knowledge of Arabic, Syriac, Accadian, Greek, and Latin. He was conversant with classical philosophy, though not to the extent attained by Moses Maimonides.

TWO MEN NAMED MOSES

A physician of eminence, Nachmanides derived his livelihood from medical practice, as did Moses Maimonides. It would be well at this point to venture a comparison between the two. Maimonides was the rationalist; Nachmanides combined rationalism with mysticism. A Jewish mystic of the sixteenth century, Hayyim Vital, wrote that both Maimonides and Nachmanides sprang from the soul of Adam, the first man, but that Maimonides sprang from Adam's left curl, which stands for judgment and severity, whereas Nachmanides sprang from Adam's right curl, which stands for tenderness and compassion. Solomon Schechter offered a beautiful parable that he applied to Nachmanides in comparison with Maimonides. Once upon a time, said Solomon Schechter (*Studies in Judaism*), there was a man who was in love with a girl. After he had been separated from her for some time, he came knocking at her door. "Oh, lover, let me in, oh lover, let me in. I am dying for you; let me in!" And the voice of the female from inside responded as follows: "Who is it?" And the lover said: "It is I." She said: "I'm sorry, I cannot let you in. There is no room for both you and me in this room. Go away. Come back next year if you still love me." A year of seclusion, misery, tears, and self–recrimination followed in which the man asked himself: "Where did I go wrong? Did I give the wrong answer?" Subsequently he knocked at her door: "Lover, let me in." She said: "Who is it?" He said, "Why, 'tis yourself!" And she opened the door. The point was that when he identified himself with her, there was room for both of them within the confines of the same chamber. Said Schechter: Maimonides, the rationalist, believed that the soul comes from God, but that it is not a part of God. Nachmanides, the mystic, held that the soul comes from God, and it is a part of God Himself. That, said Schechter, is a way of explaining the difference in theological orientation between Moses Maimonides and Moses Nachmanides.

They had differences as well in the interpretation of Judaism. Maimonides was not enamored of the idea of ritual sacrifice. He expressed quite clearly the expectation that when the Temple is restored, as he expected it would be in the fullness of time, the ritual of animal sacrifices would not be resumed. Nachmanides, on the other hand, had a positive feeling about the value of ritual sacrifice. He believed that the evil part of the human being is expressed through the sensual organs— through the drive for sex, the drive for food, the drive for drink, the drive for amassing wealth, and so on. Animal sacrifice, as he saw it, was a symbolic conquest of man's animalistic instincts. Nachmanides asked himself the question: By what right do we take a creature of God and slaughter it to eat its flesh? In his own mystic way he answered that we are doing well by the animal. By eating its flesh, we are incorporating its body into a higher form of life that is closer to God. Advocates of vegetarianism and animal rights are not likely to be impressed.

Nachmanides' mysticism is not to be taken lightly. He devoted much of his time and his energy to an analysis of the mystic quality of his religion. An illustration: The seven days of creation represent seven millennia. On the first (thousand-year) day all was chaos. The second day, all was water, an improvement on chaos because life was bred within the water. The third day, which the Bible describes as the day in which the fruit grew from the trees, represents Abraham's discovery of God and his performance of good deeds in the spirit of God—that is, the good fruit that sprang from the trees that God had planted. The fourth day, which speaks of God creating the two lights—the great light that is the sun and the lesser light that is the moon—represents the first Temple and the second Temple, which were both built and destroyed during the fourth millennium. The fifth day relates the creation of the *haya*, all animal life, and reflects the pagan and Gentile worlds, which during the fifth millennium, ruled with savagery and imposed great suffering upon the children of Abraham, who had first advanced the idea of God. The sixth day places the world on the brink of the Sabbath, when the Messiah will arrive to bring peace, harmony, and joy to God's world. It would truly be the "Day of the Lord."

Nachmanides approached the study of Torah on two levels: the literal or the plain sense of the text, and the mystic, the allegorical, which is not evident on the surface but which—when discovered—affords a much deeper comprehension of eternal verities.

THE BARCELONA DISPUTATION

On July 20, 1263, Nachmanides became involved in the great disputation at Barcelona. Official Christianity was forever anxious to persuade Jewry of the Messianic role of Jesus. From the days of the Church Fathers Origen, Chrysostom, Tertullian, and on through Jerome, Augustine, Anthony, and Ambrose, there were constant attempts to prove that the Jewish Bible—the Old Testament as they called it—foretold the advent of Jesus. Many texts of the New Testament to this day carry marginal notes designed to adduce Christological "evidence" from the Jewish Bible. When papal authority assumed formidable proportions, particularly after the Fourth Lateran Council in the year 1215, rabbis were often forced into public debate with Christian clergy, which degenerated into mass "brainwashing" exercises. The Middle Ages witnessed many such disputations.

Nachmanides was forced into the Barcelona Disputation through the machinations of an apostate Jew who assumed the name Pablo Christiani. He was anxious to tackle the most revered rabbi of the age in public debate, flattering himself that he could best his rabbinic adversary and thereby achieve some spectacular mass conversions. Christiani prevailed upon the authorities, both lay and temporal, in Barcelona to force Nachmanides into the fray.

Accounts of the debate have come down to us both from Pablo Christiani and from Nachmanides. The debate lasted for many weeks in the enforced presence of large Jewish audiences. To summarize the major arguments, Pablo Christiani began by declaring that there are three issues to be settled and only three: First, has the Messiah already come as Christians claim, or has he not come as yet, as Jews claim? Second, was the Messiah God or man or a combination of both? Third, which is the true faith, Judaism or Christianity?

> Pablo Christiani: Why can you not accept the idea that the Virgin Mary, without benefit of physical intercourse with a male, was impregnated by the Holy Ghost? Even by your definition, God is omnipotent. Why then could He not have wrought this miracle? Do you not lend credence to equally amazing demonstrations of the power of God, such as the division of the Red Sea, the manna descending from heaven, and the sun standing still at Joshua's behest in the battle at Gibeon?
>
> Nachmanides' answer was short and to the point. I cannot conceive, said he, of a God who would so demean Himself as to creep into a woman's stomach for nine months of occupation, finally emerge from her womb, walk the earth in human guise for some years and then permit himself to be nailed to a cross in abject humiliation. Our concept of the sanctity and utter Otherness of the Deity leaves no room whatever for such inglorious conception of Him.
>
> Pablo Christiani: Don't you agree that the Prophet Isaiah was a true prophet? (Nachmanides: Yes, I do.) In Chapter 11 of the Prophet Isaiah (said Pablo Christiani) we read: "And a shoot shall come forth out of the stock of Jesse, and a branch shall come out of that line, and upon him will be set the spirit of the Lord." Is not this a clear cut reference to the advent of Jesus?

Nachmanides: That sounds like a good description of the Messiah. But why do Christian propagandists always stop short of completing the passage? The chapter goes on the say that when this Messiah arrives, there shall be a transformation in the world. "And the wolf shall dwell with the lamb . . . and a little child shall lead them . . . they shall not hurt nor destroy in all my holy mountain for the earth shall be filled with the knowledge of the Lord, as the waters cover the sea." Has this part of the prophecy been fulfilled since the advent of your Messiah? Has not the earth been shaking with violence and terror these past 1300 years? Has not the wolf become even hungrier for the lamb, and are you not proving it this very moment? The lion has become more ravenous than ever. There is far less peace on earth since your so-called messiah has arrived.

Pablo Christiani: Why can't you accept the idea that God is three?

Nachmanides: Hear, O Israel, the Lord our God, the Lord is One.

Pablo Christiani: Why can't you understand, for heaven's sake, that one *can* be three?

How so, asked Nachmanides.

Christiani: Well, now look—take wine. Wine has the quality of taste, the quality of color and the quality of smell. Yet you do not speak of three items in this case. There is just one: the wine. However, it possesses three different aspects. And so it is that the Unity can be a Trinity, that one can be three.

Nachmanides: You are describing three qualities in your example, not one. None of these three qualities is the wine itself. Is the *taste* of the wine synonymous with the wine itself? Is the color of the wine identical with the wine proper? Is the aroma of the wine the same as the very wine? These are *accidents* of the wine, meaning adjectives pertaining to the wine, but not the wine itself. There is only one wine! There is only one God!

The argument raged for days on end. Pablo became more disconsolate every day because Jews were not rushing forward in droves to accept the blessings of the baptismal font. On the other hand the king was much impressed with the dignity of Nachmanides and the logic of his argumentation. The king tendered the rabbi the expenses of his trip plus a safe conduct back to his city of Gerona.

EXILE TO THE HOMELAND

Pablo Christiani was enraged and a few months thereafter, he published a document distorting the whole argument. Nachmanides had been content to let sleeping dogs lie, but when he saw the account of Pablo Christiani, his normal desire to avoid useless debate was overcome by his passion for justice. Thanks to Pablo Christiani, we possess Nachmanides' own account of the disputation. Nachmanides was a man of unimpeachable honesty. What he had to say about the progress of the argument is true. When one studies carefully and critically the document of Pablo Christiani, one can see the patent bias within it, with contradictions within the text itself. When Christiani saw the publication of Nachmanides' account, his fury mounted to such proportions that the rabbi was forced to flee his native Spain. In the year 1267, the aged rabbi migrated to Palestine. He was to spend only three more years of life on earth, but those last three years were dedicated to the preservation of Judaism in the Holy Land. The accounts that we have of letters written by Nachmanides to his son are mournful. He found Jerusalem in ruins. But in the ruins of an old mosque in Jerusalem he gathered people around him and superintended the erection of a serviceable synagogue. Two months after his arrival, Rosh Hashanah and Yom Kippur services were held in it. By Succoth time he had an academy of several hundred students, a *yeshivah*, in which he taught Torah in Jerusalem. The letters of Nachmanides from Jerusalem deserve full treatment in themselves. Three years of life were left to the man in what was for him a strange environment. But his spiritual adjustment to it was almost instantaneous. One might speak of Nachmanides as a passionate lover of Zion, a man who did more than any one in his time to encourage settlement in the land of Israel. His own arrival in Palestine marks a turning point in the history of its Jewish community. From that time on, there was never a year in which an active Jewish community, however small, did not function and labor, live and create in Palestine.

Moses, the son of Nachman, died on the ninth day of Elul in the year 1270. A legend: When he had left his own town of Gerona, on his way to Palestine, his pupils had wept: "Father, father, chariot of the Jewish people, how can you leave us? We shall be orphaned by your departure." "No, my children," he had responded, "I must go back to the Holy Land for whatever years of life are left to me. I want to be able to live out usefully the few years yet remaining. My life in Spain would be virtually forfeit." They queried: "Rabbi, communication from Palestine to Spain is so difficult. How shall we know when your time has come? We should want to weep for you." He answered, "My sons, in the cemetery of Gerona is the tombstone of my mother. When I die, her tombstone will reveal it." And so he left. His pupils established a 365-day watch over the tombstone of the mother of Nachmanides in the city of Gerona. On the ninth day of Elul, 1270, when Nachmanides died, the pupil who was standing guard observed a crack in the stone. It was not an ordinary fissure, for it was shaped in the form of the seven branched candelabra, the menorah. Immediately the pupil recited the Kaddish, for he knew that the master was gone.

A legend is the spirit of truth clothed in allegorical raiment. It would seem to say that when men like Nachmanides die, their light survives, that the body of Nachmanides interred in the soil of Jerusalem and its environs in the year 1270 was not accompanied by the soul of Nachmanides. *"Ner adonai nishmat adam"*—"The light of the Lord is in the soul of Man." The light shed by the life and teaching of the Geronese titan has continued to illuminate Jewry down to our day. On a dark and dismal day some two centuries later, expelled Spanish Jewry moved from the Iberian Peninsula to other climes—undefeated, undaunted, unbowed—despite their utter despoliation by Ferdinand and Isabella. The monarchs of Aragon and Castille could not deprive the exiles of the luminous legacy of Moses Nachmanides.

The Fourteenth Century

MOSES DE LEON

The word "Cabala" derives from the Hebrew root *cabail*, which means "to receive." It refers to the esoteric teaching transmitted by the initiate from one generation to the next. Perhaps the adjective "occult" in English would describe our subject more precisely. The occult is the mysterious, that which is known to the few, and perhaps that which is knowable only to the few. Cabala, or Jewish mysticism, by its very nature was an esoteric, occult, "exclusive" lore. Indeed, part of its teaching was that Cabala should never be expounded in public. Its lore may be transmitted only to those deemed spiritually qualified to absorb it.

Cabala is associated chiefly with Moses de Leon, who died in 1305. Mysticism has been a significant current in the history of the Jews. Moses de Leon is the best point of departure for a discussion of this current.

THE ZOHAR

Who was Moses de Leon? He was a Spanish Jew who, about the year 1286, broadcast the news that he had discovered a precious manuscript called the Zohar (which in English means the Book of Radiance), which was written in the second century. It had been written, he claimed, by one of the great rabbis of the second century, a pupil of the great Rabbi Akiba, and whose name was Simon ben Yohai. Simon ben Yohai is a famed figure of the Tannaitic era. He is involved in some mysterious events related in the Talmud, but he is not known to have written any book of mysticism. As a matter of fact, the book was written by Moses de Leon himself. The work was a forgery, the most significant forgery in the history of Jewish religious writing.

But was Moses de Leon therefore a charlatan? Was Moses de Leon an underhanded liar? Was Moses de Leon a despicable man? The answer to all three questions is: No. He was not a charlatan; he was not a liar; he was not an underhanded man, although what he did was technically underhanded. Literary forgeries were an old tradition, going back to the Bible itself. If a man believed deeply in the truth of his message, he would often attribute its authorship to some venerated figure from the distant past. In that way he felt confident that people would read and take note of it. The biblical Book of Daniel is, technically, a forgery, inasmuch as it was ascribed by its second pre-Christian century author to a legendary hero who actually lived in the sixth century B.C.E. Nor were the Canticles and the Book of Ecclesiastes written by King Solomon. Such literature is described as pseudepigraphic, that is, writing by one person falsely attributed to someone else, usually to a personage of long standing historic eminence. The Zohar, then, is a pseudepigraphic work.

The influence of the Zohar in Jewish life is eclipsed only by the Bible and the Talmud. There is not a book, except the two mentioned, which has had a more far-reaching influence on the life of the Jewish people for a longer period of time down to and including the twentieth century. Were it not for the Zohar, the vital Jewish community of Safed in the sixteenth century could not have come into being. Nor could the cataclysmic appearance of the false Messiah, Sabbetai Zvi in the seventeenth century have taken place. Nor would the revolutionary religious movement known as Hassidism have materialized in the eighteenth century.

THE WRITINGS OF DE LEON

Moses de Leon was born in the middle of the thirteenth century in the province of Castile, in the town of Guadalajara. His was a life of wandering, the last years of which were spent in the city of Avila. He died in 1305 in the town of Arevalo while he was on his way back to Avila from Valladolid. The Zohar is not the only work composed by Moses de Leon. He wrote extensively under his own name. Scant attention had been paid to these writings until it was established beyond doubt that *he* was the author of the Zohar. He wrote *Shoshan Edut* in 1286; *Sefer Harimon* in 1287; and *Mishkan Ha'Edut* in 1293.

The Zohar was not written in Hebrew, but in Aramaic. Aramaic had been a dead language for hundreds of years, but because it was de Leon's claim that Simon ben Yohai was the Zohar's author, he employed the language spoken in the Palestine of that time. Aramaic, a sister language of Hebrew, *was* the vernacular of Palestinian Jewry in the second century. For a Jew in thirteenth century Spain to write a major work in Aramaic was, indeed, a *tour de force*. Moses de Leon composed his work in the language he imagined to be representative of the speech of a people and a society one thousand years dead!

We cannot here describe the prodigious investigative work that was done in order to ascertain that Moses de Leon was the author of the Zohar. The late Gershom Scholem devoted some sixty years of his life to the study of Cabala and Jewish mysticism. He remains the chief authority on the subject. His now classic work *Major Trends in Jewish Mysticism* is the best book extant on the subject. It is a work that any intelligent person can read and understand. It was Scholem who established conclusively through the study of the Zohar's syntax and vocabulary and through textual comparisons with de Leon's known Hebrew works, that de Leon was the author of the Zohar. One illustration of Scholem's methodology might be useful. He discovered that often in the Zohar Moses de Leon quotes himself! That is to say, he quotes in Aramaic whole chunks of passages that he had previously set down in Hebrew in works whose authorship he had *not* disguised. Never expecting to be found out, de Leon had no hesitancy in quoting himself in Aramaic translation.

MYSTICISM

That the Zohar, which was to become the bible of mysticism, was composed when it was is no accident. During the high-tide of Spanish–Jewish culture, science, philosophy, and the spirit of rationalism received a

Judaic emphasis they had not previously enjoyed. Moses Maimonides embodied this emphasis. He tried to explain Judaism in terms that would recommend themselves to the learned. In fact, Maimonides even tried to reconcile some basic teaching of Judaism with the philosophy of Aristotle. As a result of this rationalist emphasis, some saw a danger that Judaism would be undermined. Chief among these were the Cabalists. There is meaning in the Torah, they claimed, which lies beyond the obvious. This is the secret teaching imparted only to the chosen. The time had come, some Cabalists thought, to come forward with the *sisrai Torah*, the meaning that cannot be seen on the surface.

The performance of a commandment of the Torah transcends its meaning. When one puts on *t'fillin*, for example, or affixes a mezuzah or utters a prayer or performs the rite of circumcision or betroths a wife or executes any of the hundreds of minutiae in which Jewish rite abounds, one is involved in a mystic operation. One may not understand it, but by doing what he does he is assisting in some way in the execution of God's purpose. Put another way, mystic thought about ritual laws may be explained as follows: every ritual act, every *mitzvah* performed by the Jew, is part of God's purpose in running the universe. One is helping God to make the universe function through the performance of ritual acts of which only the initiate understands the complexities.

Every *mitzvah* is regarded as a *tikkun*. The Hebrew word *tikkun* means "reparation." The world is in a shattered state because of the sin of Adam and Eve in the Garden of Eden. The original design of God had almost been destroyed by man. In order for the world to be fully mended and for mankind to achieve salvation, man is required by God to help repair the mechanism. Every *mitzvah* that one performs is an act of *tikkun*, an act of repairing the mechanism that had been shattered.

The purpose of mystic tradition is to bridge the gulf that exists between God and the world, to bring about a union with God even in this life, through mystic practices and mystic knowledge. There are several problems about God. We know what we are made of, we know that each one of us can be chemically analyzed. Can God be chemically analyzed? By definition, no, certainly not. Because, as Maimonides said in his very first Article of Faith: "I believe with a perfect faith that God is not a body and that therefore no adjective pertaining to the body can pertain to God." God is, if you will, Spirit, but there is no physical element in God Himself. Now if this is the case, the first question must be that if God is not corporeal, then how could the material world have derived from an Original Being who is *not* material?

CAN GOD CHANGE?

A second problem is this: Since it is maintained that God created the world out of nothing—in other words, that nothing whatever preceded God, *then some change in God had to have taken place in the process of the creation*. But by definition, God Himself is unchangeable. Only the physical and the imperfect can change, and God is neither. If something is perfect, change can only be for the worse. Indeed, perfection is utterly inconsistent with the notion of change. Change to what? To something better? Impossible! To something worse? Unthinkable! But if God does not change, then how did He bring about a change from a state of "nothingness" to a state of "somethingness?" Moreover, Creation must imply a change in the Divine Mind. How is that conceivable in a Perfect Being?

Another theological dilemma: If God is perfection and absolute unity, how could this absolute unity have given rise to variegated, differentiated matter? How could differentiated things have developed from something that is a complete unity, that is to say God.

Another question: If God is all-good, how can we account for evil in the world? How can we account for the abundance of rottenness, mendacity, and perversity in an environment that *God created?*

These are vexing questions. Cabala offers its answers. At the beginning and at the end, says the Cabalist, was the *Ein Sof* (in Hebrew, that which has neither beginning nor end)—God the Unknowable, Unlimited, Infinite, Indescribable. No adjectives pertain to the *Ein Sof* because an adjective modifies, and if the *Ein Sof* means the Unlimited then it cannot be modified.

Originally, there was and there still is the Primal Will of the *Ein Sof*. The Primal Will was always the same. God from the very beginning intended certain things to happen in the course of time. This is the answer to the question: How does it happen that that which is perfect should change its mind? There was no changing of the mind. The Primal Will always, from the very outset, said that It Is My Will that at a certain instant in time or eternity the universe should come into being. So that when the universe was created, and when things were differentiated, it did not represent a change of mind on the part of the Eternal. It was the Primal Will that this or that should take place at a designated time. Thus was it intended from the very beginning. Each successive stage in history represents the realization of another phase of that Primal Will that has *never* changed.

Still another staggering problem must be dealt with: If God is infinite, then He must take up all of space. Were there some space that He does not fill, then He would not be infinite. Therefore, if there were no space, where was the room for the universe to be created? How did the world come into being? How does God make room?

To this puzzle the later Cabalists offered a one-word answer: *tsimtsum*. It means "contraction." God, says the Cabala, has infinite power, which means He can do anything. He could contract Himself if He wished, in order to make it possible for the world to come into being in the new space afforded by God's self-contraction. This theory has significant moral implication. It means that if there were only perfection in the world, there would be no human beings. If there were only perfection, there would be no room for the universe. God, Who wanted to *create* man and the universe, neither of which is perfect, had to leave some room for the less-than perfect, the less-than superlative. Therefore, He contracted Himself.

THE SEFIROT

The *Ein Sof* is the *Infinite*, is God. The *Ein Sof* cannot be in the picture. He is Unknowable. We cannot even talk about the *Ein Sof*. But, says Cabala, from God there emanated ten different stages, ten different aspects of the Deity. These are called the *sefirot*, or the emanations. At the top is the *sefira* known as crown (*keter*); then descending to the left, is the *sefira* known as *binah* or understanding, which is parallel to *hochma* or wisdom. Underneath *binah* is *din* or Justice, and underneath *hochma* is *hesed*, or compassion. All of these *sefirot* lead to *tiferet*, or glory. Beneath glory and on the left is *hod*, or praise. To the right is *nezach*, or eternity. Below them is *yesod*, or foundation. Finally, at the bottom of the chart is *malchut*, or the kingdom. When we pray to God, we are not praying to the *Ein Sof*, to the Infinite, because it is beyond us. The *sefirot* are the way-stations God that make possible the relationship between God and man. The first three *sefirot*—*keter*, *hochma*, and *bina*—

constitute the world of thinking and being. The next three—*hesed*, *gevura*, and *tiferet*—represent the world of feeling, the physical world, the world that can be described by the five senses. The final four emanations—*nezach*, *hod*, *yesod*, and *malchut*—represent the world we know, the natural world. So when we pray, "Praised are You, O God, King of the Universe," we are addressing to the last of the emanation, *malchut*, or kingdom.

THE PLACE OF EVIL

Evil is necessary. Evil is necessary for the good, according to the Cabala. If there were no evil in the world, say the Cabalists, man would not have a ladder on which he could climb toward God. By overcoming evil we rise ever higher to God. Evil must be faced and vanquished if the human race and its universe are to be in harmony with the Creator.

ADAM'S FRAGMENTS

The Cabala of Isaac Luria (sixteenth century) introduces a remarkable concept. Adam, the original man, incorporated the world of humanity within himself. When he fell, it was with such devastating impact that his body was fragmentized and strewn over the universe. The world was filled with "shards of the broken vessel." But since Adam was created in the image of God, every bit of that vessel, every fragment contains a spark of God's spirit. The shards, or *klippot*, would not survive without that life-giving spark of God. In order to rid the world of the *klippot*, the divine sparks must be extracted from each of them. When all that is accomplished, all the *klippot*, representing evil as they do, will perish and the world will have been restored to its pristine beauty and glory, the glory of the *Ein Sof*. The world will be restored to its wholeness. There will be no room for evil within. Humanity shall have scaled great heights and will have come to a closeness with the Creator that it has not known since the days of Eden. Thus, Cabala charges man to dedicate his life over to the collection of divine sparks out of the morass and ugliness and evil that prevails in the world.

Moses de Leon died in 1305, but his spirit abides. The Zohar's teachings were to inspire Isaac Luria, Hayyim Vital and Joseph Karo in Safed of the sixteenth century. They were to be turned on their head by Sabbetai Zvi, the false messiah of the seventeenth century. They were deeply inhaled and exhaled by Israel Ba'al Shem Tov, the founder of Hasidism in the eighteenth century, and spread by his disciples into every section of the European Jewish world in the nineteenth century. Now in our own century, the last of this millennium, the Zohar has become the source of a Jewish neomysticism whose effects are yet to be assessed.

The Fifteenth Century

DON ISAAC ABRAVANEL

For well over one thousand years, Jewish people lived, died, loved, and worked usefully and creatively on the Iberian Peninsula. For one thousand years they were intimately associated with everything constructive that took place in that country. For the last four hundred years of their residence in Spain, they were among the chief contributors to its culture, politics, and finance. The Jews of Spain would have been completely justified had they claimed about 1350 that Spain was the panacea of diaspora and that the persecutions and terrors that Jews experienced elsewhere could not befall them.

Yet it happened that in the year 1492, two hundred thousand Jews were forced to leave Spain, spewed out to other destinations that half of them never reached because they perished in transit. How had this come about? The answer to this question is of continuing importance because the Spanish experience is abundantly relevant to a proper understanding of the nature of Jewish history.

What were the factors involved in the expulsion of the Jews from Spain after a millennium of relative security there? The factors fall under the categories of economics, religion, and nationality. For many years, the Jews had led a normal economic life. They were engaged in all of the economic activities of the non-Jewish population. They owned and cultivated land. They practiced handicrafts. They engaged in unrestricted trade. During the Middle Ages, Jews had been deprived of the privilege of owning land. Church law and state law combined to make that virtually impossible. A Jew could not employ a Christian. This policy began in the time of Justinian during the sixth century. As the eleventh, twelfth, and thirteenth centuries unfolded, the Jew and the soil had become almost totally divorced.

At the same time, Jews were excluded from most of the crafts. A Jew could not be a shoemaker, a carpenter, a blacksmith, a draper, a candlestick maker, or a baker. To practice a craft, one had to belong to the appropriate guild. The guild was more than an economic organization; it was a cultural-religious organization as well. A member of the guild was required to perform certain religious rites and to take an oath as a Christian before joining. The guilds were Christian organizations, and the Jew was effectively barred from their membership.

ECONOMIC STRAITJACKET

Having gradually been ousted both from working the soil and serving as an artisan, the only economic area in which the Jew could operate involved money. Expelled from the soil, Jews moved to the cities in ever-increasing numbers. Here, rather than in specific legislation, may be found the true beginning of the ghetto. The money industry in which the Jew was involved was the result, ironically enough, of the Torah injunction against lending on interest. The Church stringently upheld this prohibition. It barred Christians from lending money on interest. However, its ruling did not apply to Jews. The Jew, on the other hand, was not prohibited by his Torah from lending money on interest to a non-Jew. Neither was a Christian prohibited from lending money to a Jew by Church law. In this situation the Jew held an advantage. He had a much larger potential clientele in the Christian community. Jews became money lenders in increasing numbers during the late Middle Ages. Jews even became a major source of credit for the Churches themselves.

The Jew as money lender was also protected by the feudal lords. The nobility borrowed heavily from Jews. High interest rates were justified by the very high risk incurred by Jewish lenders. Much of his lending ended in disaster. What was to prevent the feudal lord from borrowing 100,000 ducats from a syndicate of Jewish lenders and then defaulting on the loan? Jews were most often not in position to sue high and mighty Christians in court. The persistence of the charge that the Jew was a blood-sucking usurer is in part attributable to the high interest rates he was obliged to charge if he was to stay in business. The Jew was disproportionately involved in the money trades, which in addition to lending included minting, currency exchange, and tax farming. Such an economic imbalance was an important cause in the developing precariousness of the position of the Jew in Spain and elsewhere.

THE CHURCH AND THE JEWS

The Church and the Jews have had a defined relationship throughout the Middle ages. It was not a happy one for the Jews. The Church and its Popes engaged in anti-Jewish policies. We need remind ourselves of 1215, the date of the Fourth Lateran Council, at which Pope Innocent III and his cardinals had legislated some very serious anti-Jewish measures including the wearing of the yellow badge and further restricting the Jew in agricultural and other economic endeavors. There is something else to be considered. The Church had trouble on its hands in the form of mushrooming heresies with which it had indeed been plagued from its very inception. The person of Jesus was involved in most of these heresies. As far back as the second century, disagreements were rife among church theologians with regard to the nature of Jesus. Was he human? Was he God? Was he God and man combined? If the latter, was the God element stronger than the human or was it the reverse? This led to a proliferation of sects that caused Christianity from its outset to experience serious trouble with regard to its quest for catholicity, which means universal subscription to its official thinking by all who deemed themselves Christians. During the twelfth and the thirteenth centuries, the heresies in Christianity proliferated. Henry C. Lea's classic work *The History of the Inquisition* relates much of the conflict within the Church that these heresies engendered. The Inquisition was initially designed to ferret out Christian heretics. In France, the little town of Albi gave birth to the Albigensian heresy. The Inquisition began primarily as a measure against the Albigensian and other heresies of the twelfth and thirteenth centuries.

At the same time the Church was engaged in a battle to the finish with its mighty rival, the religion of Islam. The Mohammedan world was very powerful at this time. Christianity and Islam were vying for the souls of those who were outside their respective folds. The Church thus fought heresy from both within and without. The Jew was inevitably caught in the squeeze.

THE NATIONAL STATE

The third major factor in the deterioration of the Spanish Jew's condition was the evolution of the national states. Today every one of us is nation-conscious. The terms "national" and "international" are integral to the modern vocabulary. It was not always so. The concept of a national state is barely a thousand years old. England, that tight little island, was made up of many different political entities. Feudal lords reigned over them. There was no central government. The state emerged as a result of the struggle between the king and the feudal lords—barons, counts, or grafs, depending upon the language of the country. The national state was the outcome of the victory of the king over feudal lords. In England, this victory took place toward the end of the thirteenth century, when England became the first European national state. At precisely that time—1290—the Jews were expelled from England. In France, a national state emerged at the beginning of the fourteenth century, about 1300. In the year 1306, the Jews were expelled from France. In 1492, Spain became a national state when it succeeded finally in conquering the last outpost of Islam in Spain with the fall of Granada. In 1492, the Jews were expelled from Spain. We seem to see a cause and effect relationship between the emergence of a national state and the expulsion of the Jews.

How can we account for this seemingly strange phenomenon? The reason seems to be that the Jew is best served by the diversity of the realm he inhabits. Whenever a country becomes monolithic, when it assumes the character of one corporate unit, that is when the Jew sticks out like the proverbial sore thumb, resulting in his eviction. An enforced uniformity allows no room for dissent. The Jew has been the perennial dissenter from the days of the Patriarch Abraham.

174

ABRAVANEL

The tragic fate of Spanish Jewry is symbolized in the person of Don Isaac Abravanel, one of the most attractive figures to be encountered in the gallery of Jewry's great men. Don Isaac Abravanel was a deeply committed Jew. His dogged courage in the face of repeated calamities reflects glory upon the indomitable spirit that separates giants from ordinary mortals.

His father had been expelled from Spain for political reasons and had migrated to Portugal. From early youth Isaac demonstrated unusual financial acumen, a quality that was recognized by Alphonso V, King of Portugal, who appointed him royal treasurer. Alphonso was succeeded by his son John II in 1481. John began a battle against the feudal lords of Portugal in hopes of becoming undisputed master of all of the country. His chief adversary was the duke of Braganza. As it happened the duke of Braganza was a friend of Isaac Abravanel. When, in 1483, the duke was beheaded by John II, Isaac Abravanel had to flee for his life because of malicious rumors that he had been plotting against his royal master. He fled to Spain. Shortly thereafter he was taken into the inner circle of Ferdinand and Isabella. Isabella was the ruler of Castile. Ferdinand was the ruler of Aragon. It was Don Abraham Senior, rabbi and financier, who had been instrumental, so the story goes, in arranging the match between Ferdinand and Isabella. The two most powerful Christian kingdoms in Spain were thus united under the joint sovereignty of Ferdinand and Isabella. To this royal couple, Don Isaac Abravanel became the financial minister.

Ferdinand and Isabella had been in a lamentable financial estate prior to their nexus with Abravanel, but he managed to render their treasury solvent despite the constant wars they were waging against the Moslem enclaves in Spain. Indeed, Abravanel helped make possible the final battle, which ended in the complete unification of Spain, thus crowning with total triumph the several centuries designated in Spanish history as the *Reconquista*, the Christian reconquest of Spain from the hands of the Moslems. It is not too much to state that Abravanel's financial wizardry helped make this victory possible. Shortly thereafter, Spanish Jewry was dealt a devastating blow by the edict of expulsion. It came like a bolt from the blue. No one had expected it. The edict gave the Jews three months to be baptized or to leave the land. Monolithic political unity entailed a drive for an equally monolithic religious unity. Islam out of the way, it was now the turn of the Jews to go.

MARRANOS

We have no precise figures on the Jewish population of Spain at that time, but it may safely be said that a high proportion converted to Christianity rather than leave their ancestral land behind. Many tens of thousands went into exile. Over one hundred thousand left for nearby Portugal. Tens, if not hundreds of thousands of others became Christians. Most of them, to be sure, did so with unwilling minds and broken hearts. Still the record should be kept honest. It is the consensus of most historians that most of these Jews remained secretly loyal to their faith and practiced its traditions covertly. That many did so is an indisputable fact. Our data does demonstrate that there were Conversos or Marranos who for generations practiced their Judaism underground, while superficially leading the life of Christians. They went to Mass on Sunday but they lit candles Friday evening behind drawn curtains. They ate only kosher food. They circumcised their children at grave personal risk. Still there are revisionist historians like B. Netanyahu who argue that within a generation or two the Marranos became sincere Christians, some of them even avid and fanatic about their new faith. They rose to high stations economically and socially. They married into the Christian nobility, so much so that many of the eminent Spanish families of today carry Marrano blood in their veins. Rabbi Abraham Senior, eighty years old at the time of the edict of expulsion, could not bring himself to leave the land in which he and his family had been living for so many generations. He converted to Christianity.

When Don Isaac Abravanel first heard about the edict of expulsion, he and Abraham Senior ran to Isabella. They pleaded with her to rescind it. They recounted the immense contributions made over the centuries by Spanish Jewry to their land. They advanced logical arguments. They invoked moral appeals. They appealed to religious scruples. On the practical plane, they offered a huge sum to the royal treasury if the Jews were permitted to stay.

Ferdinand and Isabella were ready to accept the financial offer. Legend has it that at this point Tomàs de Torquemada, the grand inquisitor, entered into the palace of the queen (to whom he was Father

Confessor), held up a crucifix in his hand, gazed sternly at her, eyes gleaming with wild hatred. He said: "Judas Iscariot sold our Lord for thirty pieces of silver. Are you about to sell him all over again for three hundred thousand ducats?" Thereupon he threw the crucifix at the feet of his queen. That act, the legend concludes, doomed Spanish Jewry and sealed its melancholy fate.

THE ROAD TO EVERYWHERE

The long and bitter trail to a variety of destinations began for some two hundred thousand Spanish Jews. Yet a very large number reached no destination at all. Greedy ship captains took all they could from helpless Jewish passengers for trips in dilapidated vessels. Many of them unloaded their human cargo into the deep waters or dumped them on desert islands. The survivors, broken in heart, found homes in different lands. Don Isaac Abravanel arrived in Naples. There he became the financial advisor to its ruler, Ferdinand I. Shortly after Abravanel's arrival, Ferdinand I was defeated in a war with Charles VIII of France. Ferdinand was exiled to Corfu, and Isaac Abravanel went with him to Corfu and thence to Monopoli.

In Corfu and in Monopoli begins another phase in the career of Isaac Abravanel. One does not usually associate a man of affairs with the life of the spirit. Most men of affairs are not spiritual, and most spiritual figures are inept at mundane matters. Isaac Abravanel was a unique combination of both. He was a man of affairs, financial genius, political activist, diplomat extraordinary—but withal, a deeply spiritual personality.

THE SOUL OF ABRAVANEL

All of his life he had worked on a commentary to the Bible. Isaac Abravanel has justly been called the last of the great medieval commentators of the Bible. To this day, a study of the Bible without Isaac Abravanel's commentaries would be ill advised. It is hard to imagine a man who was so overwhelmed with earthly matters finding the time to write commentaries on the Bible. They took him decades to complete. Sometimes years elapsed between one spurt of exegetical work and the next, but he always stayed with it. Whenever there was a pause in his political activity, there was a resumption of his feverish literary activity.

He knew the New Testament thoroughly. He often quotes the Christian Bible scholars. Despite what he and his people suffered at Christian hands, he did not write unkindly about Christianity. There is no rancor toward it in his writings. The mood is occasionally sad, rarely vindictive. Staunch and proud champion of Judaism that he was, his writing is free of invidious comparisons with the faith that produced Torquemadas. It is for this reason that Abravanel is a favorite with Christian Bible scholars, although they could not have been happy with his commentary on Isaiah. Abravanel's Isaiah commentary was nevertheless included in the Catholic Index of Forbidden Books. In it are listed convincing arguments against the cumulative Christian propaganda that purported to see in the Book of Isaiah a foreshadowing of the arrival of Jesus Christ.

MESSIANIC WRITING

Another important area of his work was his Messianic writings. Isaac Abravanel realized that what the Jews needed was a spiritual uplift. They were crestfallen and despondent as a result of their 1492 calamity. Some even became disillusioned with their faith. Some began to question whether it was worthwhile to live as a Jew at all. Was Judaism worth the price of so much suffering when a few drops from the baptismal font could solve all problems? Apostasy was rife; many took the road out of Mosaic faith, and a good many others were wavering. It would have taken very little to push them into the Christian camp.

As with other calamities in their history, the Jews overcame. They clung to their traditions and, doing so, were nourished by them.

Isaac Abravanel contributed to the strength and the spirit of his people by authoring pious works in which he promised the Jews that the days of the Messiah were not far off. He even predicted 1509 at first as the date for the arrival of the Messiah. Then he pushed it into the 1530s. Fortunately for him, death prevented his disappointment. Yet messianic aspirations are a deep need in an era of despair and apostasy, as shall be demonstrated in the chapters to follow.

KING LEAR AND DON ISAAC

Don Isaac Abravanel was a glaring symbol of the Jews' insecurity. There is no land in the world, the experience of Spanish Jewry seems to say, that is a safe harbor for a people that is not anchored in its own land. Over a thousand years of residence in Spain had been wiped away from the mind of the persecutor. The example of Don Isaac Abravanel teaches that the lesson of his life is the ultimate triumph of the spirit.

Thinking of Don Isaac Abravanel, the image of King Lear emerges in the imagination. Abravanel was evicted by his daughter Goneril (if you would substitute Portugal). He was evicted by his daughter Regan (if you would substitute Spain). Both lands were terribly ungrateful. He had given them his all, and they recompensed him with exile. Still, when he went out into the cold, cold world, he did not curse and rant as did Shakespeare's tragic Lear. He was a towering moral figure. In the fullest sense of the word, we are justified in saying that Don Isaac Abravanel, who died in exile on the island of Monopoli, was the Jew of the fifteenth century.

THE SIXTEENTH CENTURY

DON JOSEPH NASI

Two people dominate this chapter. One is a woman, one of the most remarkable in Jewish history. She bore two lovely names: Beatrice De Luna, when she was a Christian, and Dona Gracia Nasi, when she was a Jewess. She went through the cycle from Judaism to enforced baptism and back to the Judaism that in her heart she had never left. Certainly, she was "the Jewess of the sixteenth century." The other was her nephew Don Joseph Nasi, the Duke of Naxos.

Dona Gracia was the wife of Francisco Mendes, a Jew of Portugal who was forced during the intense persecutions of that land to become a Christian. Francisco Mendes remained a staunch Jew throughout his life. He practiced the rules of his faith behind the closed doors of his palatial home, as did all of the members of his family. He and they went through Christian motions when in public. He had a bank and was also engaged in international trade in precious stones. He was one of the wealthiest Jews of the sixteenth century.

Not the least of his gems was his wife, Dona Gracia. Some portraits of her that have come down to us reveal a beautiful, stately woman of aristocratic bearing. True beauty emanates from the soul of a person. The life of Dona Gracia, filled as it was with drama and trauma, reflected beauty of soul as well.

THE WANDERING MENDESES

Dona Gracia and her husband, Francisco, had decided that they were not going to remain secret Jews indefinitely. Francisco opened a branch of his banking business in Antwerp in the year 1512. Antwerp was one of the largest commercial centers of Europe at the time, and there he sent his brother, Diego, as manager. His idea was to move his family to Antwerp as soon as most of his fortune could be moved out of Portugal without attracting the attention of the Inquisitorial sleuths. This was accomplished. In the year 1536, Dona Gracia (whose husband had meanwhile died), her nephew, and her daughter, Reyna, left for Antwerp where they established the headquarters for all their business interests. Now Antwerp was still under Spanish control, but the Spaniards were lenient toward the Marranos of Antwerp as long as they remained officially Christian. They did not interfere with their covert Judaic practices. To have done so would have destroyed the commercial center of Antwerp, which was dominated by Marranos.

Dona Gracia, through her charm, intelligence, and social elegance, became a favorite at the court of the queen regent of the Netherlands. The queen took a fancy to Reyna, who was a beautiful seventeen-year-old girl at the time. One day, the queen regent approached Dona Gracia and said: "I have a marvelous match for you. One of the finest and richest dukes in my kingdom has been captivated by your lovely daughter. This is a God-sent opportunity for you to rise to the highest echelon of our society." Beatrice de Luna, or Dona Gracia, fixed her eyes upon the queen regent of the Netherlands and said: "I would rather see Reyna dead. She will not marry out of our faith." "But you are a Christian," said the queen. "I am not any more, in fact," was the answer. The queen was incensed, and pressure was exerted upon the Mendes family to give up its secret practice of Judaism. It became necessary for them to leave again. Here, Joseph, her nephew, enters the scene. He was a budding young financial genius, well-formed, tactful, and gracious. With the death of his uncle he had become the senior man of the family. Most of its financial undertakings now rested on his shoulders. The family had one major objective: to return to Judaism unconditionally. They were sick of visiting church services for appearance sake, when everybody knew that they were practicing Jews in their home. The problem therefore was to get all their wealth out of Spanish Inquisitorial lands into a new home in which they might be Jews freely and openly. A banking business was quietly established in Lyons, France. From Lyons their funds were moved to Venice, then to Ferrara, then to Constantinople, the most powerful stronghold of Islam in the sixteenth century, and eventually out of the Christian domain entirely. The Mendes family finished its journey to uninhibited Judaism.

ARRIVAL IN CONSTANTINOPLE

Between their moving from Antwerp and their arrival at Constantinople, several incidents transpired that are worthy of mention. In 1544 or 1545, the family had settled in Venice, and because there had been a falling out between Beatrice de Luna (Dona Gracia) and her sister, the latter went to the authorities in Venice to condemn Dona Gracia as a false Christian. When Dona Gracia realized that the Inquisitorial power of the Church was after her because of her sister's denunciation, she left for Ferrara. In Ferrara, where a liberal duke ruled, she returned to the official fold of Judaism. The year was 1550. Still that was not good enough for the Mendes family because Ferrara was still a Christian domain. In the year 1553, exactly one hundred years after the Turks had conquered Constantinople and had destroyed the last vestige of the Byzantine empire, Dona Gracia, Joseph, and her daughter, Reyna, arrived in Constantinople.

From that point on, a phenomenal career began for Joseph. The family reassumed its original name, Nasi. Joseph Mendes was now Don Joseph Nasi; Beatrice de Luna was now Dona Gracia Nasi. They were Jewish, and Reyna, who had been secretly in love with her cousin for many years, was married to him in Constantinople in the year 1554 in a synagogue and under a *huppah* "according to the law of Moses and Israel."

Don Joseph Nasi rose in the hierarchy of the sultan. The sultan was one of the most famed personages of the history of the Turkish empire. He was Suleiman the Magnificent, a great warrior king under whose regime the Turkish empire had achieved its zenith. Into the court of Suleiman arrived Don Joseph Nasi, who became in the course of time one of the most powerful men. Suleiman needed him for various reasons. First, he was an invaluable contact with the Christian world. Second, he had connections with financial institutions all over the world as a banker of many years' standing. Third, and not the least important, he had the ability to supply the palace with all of its desired luxuries, especially in the area of food and drink. In those days, fancy and exotic foods were available only to the tables of sultans and caliphs and the very wealthy. Someone had to know where to get these special foods and how to bring them into the country. Don Joseph had branched out into the food trade and had become a connoisseur of fine foods. He knew when and where they were available and saw to it that the tastes of his sovereign were served. He had a special influence with the sultan's son, Selim, dubbed the Sot.

THE POWER OF DON JOSEPH

Selim needed Don Joseph Nasi desperately. He was an alcoholic, despite the Koranic ban on all intoxicating consumption. Selim had a bountiful harem but no official wine cellar. Selim made it known to Joseph that what he desired above all were the finest wines available. Joseph Nasi found a way of supplying him with such wines by placing them at the bottom of barrels of herring imported for the sultan's table.

Selim became a champion of Don Joseph. Unlike his illustrious father, Selim was mediocre, even during his very rare moments of sobriety. He came to rely heavily upon Don Joseph. Thus Joseph acquired enormous influence at the Turkish court. Three facts may be adduced in illustration. When Maximilian, the holy Roman emperor, had ascended the throne, he had wanted to establish good relations with Suleiman the Magnificent. We have a letter on record from Emperor Maximilian to the Jew Don Joseph Nasi, asking him to put in a good word with Suleiman before Maximilian's diplomats arrived to negotiate. Turkey was a Mohammedan state. Arabs were in its majority. There were two minorities in Turkey: a growing community of Jews and Marranos who had escaped from the lands of Spanish domination and had come to Turkey to return to their faith, and a substantial community of Christians who were not members of the Catholic Church, but of the Eastern Orthodox wing of the church. As soon as Selim ascended the throne, the archbishop of the Greek Orthodox Church in Constantinople wanted to make sure that the special privileges granted to minority groups, to wit, the Christians, would not be taken away by Selim. They had been granted, after all, by his father, Suleiman, and it was now up to Selim either to retain or to renounce them. The archbishop came and pleaded his case with the Jew, Don Joseph Naoi. He begged for his good offices and great influence with Selim to ensure a continuation of Christian privileges. Thus a Marrano who had escaped Christian persecution so that he might resume his Jewish identity was solicited to help the Christians retain their own. In Poland, Jews were regularly persecuted. That did not prevent the Polish ambassador from reporting to Don Joseph Nasi before he presented his credentials to either Suleiman or Selim.

Don Joseph Nasi branched out into textiles, tax farming, and shipping. He held a near monopoly on the wine business in Turkey, profitable despite its official illegality. To state that Don Joseph Nasi became one of the wealthiest men in the Turkish realm would not be an exaggeration.

JOSEPH AND HIS PEOPLE

Joseph was a man who knew how to take good care of himself and his family. But for him, the Jewish people were integral to the concept of family. The Spanish Inquisition was tightening its tentacles about Jews and especially pseudo-Jews, Marranos, throughout the world. Even *genuine* Christians who had once been Jews were forced to flee from the hands of the Inquisition because the Inquisition tortured them for no reason at all. The Inquisition claimed that they were not genuine Christians when, in fact, they were. The Inquisition put them to the rack and to the screw and inflicted upon them the most fearful sorts of tortures. Thousands of Marranos were subjected to this horror, and in sheer self-defense many began to flee Spanish territory. In the 1800s, when black slaves fled from their masters in the United States, a system developed called the Underground Railroad. An underground railroad of sorts developed among the Marranos, who were escaping or trying to escape the long arm of the Inquisition. Joseph Nasi was a supporter of a vast network of "underground railroad" stations for Marranos running for their lives. He spent a good part of his fortune in financing this expensive and complex project for the saving of the lives of his coreligionists.

POPE PAUL IV

In 1555, Pope Paul IV, the former Cardinal Caraffa, established what is known as the Counter-Reformation in Italy. Martin Luther had shattered the unity of the Catholic Church during the first decades of the sixteenth century by inaugurating the Reformation, which rejected the authority of the pope and discarded many Catholic doctrines and practices. The Christian world, which had been a monolithic entity for over a thousand years, was suddenly marked by schism. The papal Counter-Reformation was the response to the Protestant Reformation. It was led by Pope Paul IV, a tough-visaged citizen. He instituted for the first time in the history of Italian Jewry an Inquisition directed at heretics and Marranos. It was carried to such extremes that for the first time in the history of Italian Jewry, in the city of Ancona in the year 1555, some thirty Marranos were burned at the stake by order of Pope Paul IV.

Don Joseph Nasi went into action. He embarked upon a project so grandiose as to stagger the imagination. It was no fault of his that the project failed. Don Joseph Nasi and Dona Gracia devised a plan to boycott Ancona which was one of the important commercial ports in Italy. The Nasis had scores of merchant ships and were strong enough to influence others in the shipping industry to join in the boycott. The Jewish merchants of Ancona protested. "We do not wish to leave Ancona," said they in effect. "If you boycott Ancona, we starve." "Our lives are as important as the interests of world Jewry." The Anconese Jews sent *strong* protestations to leading rabbis around the world. The responsa literature of the time shows that rabbinic opinion was divided. Some favored the boycott. Others were opposed. The bold-souled rabbis said: "Boycott them to the limit! Show them for a change that you can fight back! And if a few Jews have to suffer in the process, it is a small price to pay." On the other hand, there were prominent rabbis who said: "You have no right to penalize even a handful of Jews in the interests of world Jewry."

It is an interesting moral problem: Is it right to sacrifice the few in the interests of the many?

In the end, Don Joseph was thwarted in his grand counterattack by his fellow Jews of Ancona. The boycott failed. But Don Joseph's ambitious plan was a stunning demonstration of courageous leadership. The Nasi family was courageous and forceful in the ongoing battle to defend its coreligionists and to uphold its ancestral pride.

THE TIBERIAS EXPERIMENT

The persecutions of Jews and Marranos created many thousands of refugees looking for anchorage wherever they might find it. Some crowded into Turkey and resorted to beggary. Many were ill; and many were crushed in spirit. Joseph Nasi was a man of ideas and action. He induced Selim the Sot to cede to him the city of Tiberias in Palestine. Four hundred years before Theodor Herzl, in 1561, Joseph Nasi sent hundreds of workers at his own expense to try to establish a colony for Jews that would ultimately become self-sufficient and self-supporting in Palestine. But the Tiberias Experiment failed. The Jews were not ready to start from scratch in an unpromising land. And the Arabs in Palestine were not ready for it either.

DUKE OF NAXOS

Shortly thereafter, Joseph Nasi was given the title Duke of Naxos. Naxos was called "the Premier Duchy of Christendom." Joseph Nasi, ex-"Christian," became the duke of that island. In the back of his mind was the idea that perhaps in Naxos he might be able to create a Jewish state. All of his life was directed toward the goal of finding salvation for his harassed people. One of the crucial battles in history was a sea engagement at Lepanto in 1572. It was between the Turkish Empire and the Venetian Republic. Joseph Nasi had encouraged this war because he thought that if Venice could be brought to heel, the tight ring of anti-Jewish, anti-Marrano violence would begin to crumble since Venice was a strategic commercial area for all of Europe. But he had miscalculated. In the Battle of Lepanto, the Turks suffered a disastrous defeat, and from that time Turkish power began to wane and, with it, the influence of Don Joseph.

But Don Joseph did not die defeated, poor, or disillusioned. Although still in the prime of his life when death took him in his late fifties, he and his wife, Reyna, dedicated the years after Lepanto toward the amelioration of the lot of their suffering fellow Jews. In his own lifetime, Don Joseph Nasi, Duke of Naxos, became a legend. It has been said that Don Joseph was the model of Christopher Marlowe's drama *The Jew of Malta*. Anti-Semitism pervades the work, but the playwright cannot withhold his admiration of his subject.

Joseph died a duke, the title being his for the last decade of his life. But for all of his life he was a prince of his people. The saga of Don Joseph Nasi and his splendid aunt, Dona Gracia, is one of the highlights of the history of a people that during the sixteenth century seemed to have reached a low point. After the passage from the scene of Joseph Nasi and Dona Gracia, the lot of the Jews in Turkey, in Spain, in Europe everywhere, even in South America, began to deteriorate. Despair once again gripped the hearts of Jews. Many turned their eyes to heaven and began in haunting, plaintive tones to invoke the prayer: "Send us the Messiah, O Lord, send us the Messiah." In that same Turkey in which the Duke of Naxos had flourished, there was born in the year 1624, barely half a century after his death, a visionary young man who heard the plaint of his fellow Jews and their call for the Messiah. One day he rose in the synagogue and proclaimed himself that Messiah. Many a demented person throughout history had done precisely that, but the wonder of it all is that this man succeeded in persuading much of world Jewry that he was, indeed, the Messiah. His name was Sabbetai Zvi.

THE SEVENTEENTH CENTURY

SABBETAI ZVI

In the painful history of the Jews, there were two notable Messiahs. One of them is to this day a vital influence in the lives of many millions. However, he was never regarded as a Messiah by the Jews—although he and his disciples were Jewish. Otherwise is the case with the other Messiah. At one time, indeed, a large proportion of Jewry believed in him. His impact was almost catastrophic.

His name was Sabbetai Zvi. He was born on Tisha B'Av of the year 1626 in the city of Smyrna, Turkey. The trenchant fact to bear in mind is that, unlike the first Messiah, who had been rejected by most of his people about the year 30, the second was acknowledged as the Messiah. From present-day perspective it is baffling that normally rational folk—rabbis included—were actually led to believe that Sabbetai was the long-awaited redeemer. Sabbetai Zvi proclaimed himself the Messiah in 1648 at age twenty-two.

Some ten years later, millions of Jews were convinced that marvelous things were on the point of happening. The poor and the starving believed that their horn of plenty would magically materialize at any moment. Many others were convinced that the Jews would go to

193

war against their enemies, led by Sabbetai Zvi, and that having thoroughly disposed of them, they would return to Zion, there to establish a Jewish homeland. Privation and sickness and misery would then vanish from the earth.

SABBETAI AND HIS ENTOURAGE

How could all these expectations have come about? How could sober people become so intoxicated? How could down-to-earth people begin to believe so passionately in fantasies? How could they have behaved like lemmings willingly heading for perdition? An understanding of the Sabbatian phenomenon must begin with the man himself.

Sabbetai Zvi was physically attractive with a commanding presence. He was tall, well formed, possessed piercing, mesmerizing eyes, and was gifted with a voice of siren-like magnetism. All of the accounts that have come down to us from that time, including accounts from Christians and Moslems, attest that when Sabbetai Zvi began to sing, people were spellbound.

He had very effective "press-agentry." The right "build-up" can make a bony ass seem like a sleek panther. Moreover it helps considerably if the prophet for a cause—however misbegotten—sincerely believes in himself. Such a publicist, for example, was Paul, who fervently believed in the deity of Jesus and in his own mission. It was Paul's indefatigable work that established the Christian faith. Sabbetai Zvi had his own Paul in the person of twenty-two-year-old Nathan of Gaza in Palestine. Curiously, Nathan was, like Paul, an epileptic. This brilliant young man truly believed that Sabbetai Zvi was the Messiah. Through his worldwide propaganda he was able to make believers of thousands. To the work of Nathan must be added that of a charlatan named Samuel Primo, who was always close to the ear of Sabbetai.

That Sabbetai Zvi believed in himself cannot for a moment be doubted. That Nathan was a true believer is self-evident from the whole sad chronicle. Samuel Primo, who was in a sense Sabbetai's secretary, presents another story. For him, Sabbetai was a gold mine and a source of glory and lucre. It was he who "ghosted" Sabbetai's messages and who with uncanny intuition stage managed most of the scenes in the developing farce.

THE AGONY OF ISRAEL

The Sabbatian episode unfolded against a background of Jewish suffering that in 1648 was climaxed by the Chmielnicki massacre of an estimated 150,000 Jews in the Ukraine. The history of the Middle Ages is awash in Jewish blood. The Crusades, the expulsions, the Inquisition, the blood libels, the Black Plague butcheries, and assorted outbreaks of mob violence against defenseless Jewish communities punctuated the life of the Jew through the many centuries of the Medieval era. An example of the latter category is offered by the aftermath of the so-called Black Plague. It had broken out in 1348 all over Europe. One out of every three Europeans perished. The proportion of Jewish victims was much smaller. The hygiene involved in the observance of the dietary laws was doubtless a partial explanation. The Jews washed their hands and salted and rinsed their meats prior to partaking of a meal. These measures certainly had antiseptic effects. But the somewhat smaller proportion of Jewish dead led the masses to the belief that the Black Plague was the result of the poisoning of the wells by the Jews. (Presumably the Jews had access to caches of untainted waters.) Wild pogroms followed in which thousands of Jews were killed.

The later Middle Ages saw the expulsion of the Jews from several European countries. They were expelled from England in 1290, from France in 1394, from Spain in 1492, and through the early part of the sixteenth century they were expelled from many cities and regions in Western Europe. Then in 1648, the year in which Sabbetai Zvi proclaimed himself the Messiah, the bloody pogroms took place. They were the Chmielnicki massacres. Chmielnicki led his Cossacks in revolt against the feudal lords. The story has some complex economic and sociological ramifications involving Polish Jewry into which we cannot now enter. For the purpose of our present chronicle, it must be recorded that some 150,000 Jews were put to the sword by the Chmielnicki hordes in 1648 and 1649. It was the most devastating disaster the Jews had known to that time in the diaspora.

Unbearable agony breeds unspeakable visions. Suffering so often affects the mind. That the mind of an individual can be thus affected we well know. But an entire people can also lose its balance under the sledgehammer blows of persistent adversity.

CHRISTIAN ASPIRATIONS

In trying to understand the Sabbatian episode, Christianity, too, must be placed in the picture. The Book of Daniel narrates the tale of the Four Kingdoms. The prophet foretells of the rise and fall of these Four Kingdoms and speaks of the ultimate advent of a Fifth Kingdom: the Kingdom of God. Now some Christians had taken the Fifth Kingdom of Daniel to mean the Second Coming of Christ. According to their calculations that was to be in 1648, which was the beginning of the fifth millennium. The time period we are discussing corresponds to the Puritan Revolution in England. The Puritans placed a great deal of stress upon the Old Testament. They believed that before the Second Coming of Jesus, the Jews had first to be brought into the fold. Puritan thought in this regard was somewhat as follows: a Messiah will come to the Jews, who will show them the truth, and who will lead them to the acceptance of Jesus as the son of God. Only then will Jesus be ready to return to earth, for that return is conditioned upon his own people's acceptance of him. Some Christians deliberately encouraged the idea of a Jewish Messiah whom they expected to reveal the light of Christianity to his people.

Sabbetai Zvi's father, Mordecai Zvi, was a merchant who traveled to England and returned with some such stories. His growing boy was a dreamer and a stargazer. He heard these stories. They sank into his mind. According to Gershom Scholem, Sabbetai was manic-depressive. In his monumental study *Sabbetai Zvi the Mystical Messiah*, Scholem persuasively documents Sabbetai's psychosis. The manic stages find the victim in a highly excitable, ecstatic, exalted mood as though injected with narcotic stimulants. By contrast, the depressive state finds the subject enveloped in a brooding, silent, introverted, stark, and forbidding withdrawal. That Sabbetai's conviction that he was God's chosen Messiah was influenced to an important extent by his psychic affliction can hardly be doubted.

THE "MESSIAH"

In the year 1648, when Sabbetai Zvi declared himself the Messiah, he had risen in the synagogue at Smyrna. He pronounced the ineffable name of God, the Tetragrammaton. The twenty-two-year-old Sabbetai did in the synagogue what only the High Priest had been permitted in the inner sanctum of the Holy Temple on Yom Kippur, the holiest day in the Jewish year. The congregation was so shocked that Sabbetai was excommunicated on the spot. That did not, however, stop him or the small circle of devoted followers he had managed to attract. They went on to conquer new worlds in Constantinople, the sultan's capital.

At Constantinople two things became characteristic of Sabbetai Zvi. He did not preach to people; he was a singing Messiah. Up and down the streets of Constantinople, he sang the Psalms. His voice was enough to charm listeners into his orbit. He was a Pied Piper whose melodies captivated the souls of the masses. One of the men he attracted was an expert forger named Abraham Yachini. Yachini was brilliant at what he did. He forged a document that was supposed to have originated in the second century before the Christian era that "prophesied" the advent of Sabbetai Zvi as the Messiah to Jewry. Yachini swore that he "discovered" this document. A true believer in Sabbetai, he justified his chicanery as a sacred measure in winning over skeptics to the cause of the truth.

From Constantinople, Sabbetai traveled to Salonika, where he ascended the pulpit of the synagogue, opened the Ark, took out a Torah and ceremoniously performed a marriage between the Torah and himself, invoking some mystic and unintelligible formula in the process. Some people were shocked at this behavior. Others felt that only the messiah of God could act so brazenly.

At this point, something should be said about the sexuality of Sabbetai. He was, to be blunt, sexually impotent. He had been married at the age of twenty. Three days later his wife had come to the Jewish court in Smyrna to testify that her husband was incapable of coming near her. She was granted a divorce. Two years later, the same thing happened. Within three days, his second wife had come to the Bet Din and—on the same grounds—was also granted a bill of divorcement. The irony of the matter is that this impotent man was later to be married to a chronic nymphomaniac.

THE WEIRD SARAH

The year 1648 was, as indicated, the year of the Chmielnicki atrocities. One Jewish family in Poland nearly was wiped out, with the exception of an eight-year-old girl named Sarah. She was crazed by seeing her father and mother killed and by witnessing brutalities designed to sear the soul of a child. She was never to regain the full use of her mental facilities. She had run off to hide in a cemetery, where she lived like a wild animal for a period of time until found by compassionate nuns who brought her into a convent. Some years later, a surviving brother sought her out and took her to live with him. She somehow found her way into a brothel. Her constant fixation was that she was destined to marry the Messiah. This, far before she had ever heard the name of Sabbetai Zvi. The weird manner and attitudes of the strange Sarah achieved a high degree of notoriety. In due course, it reached the ears of Sabbetai. He made a snap decision: If she is to be the wife of the Messiah, then it is I who am to marry her. Somehow, Sarah was brought from Poland to Turkey, and in a ceremony surfeited with pomp and glitter, she was married to Sabbetai. He was never to touch her. But it is certain that she was not to remain untouched. She was indeed touched by many hands. Moreover, her husband encouraged it! From his demented perspective, there was a purpose to this. An interesting teaching of Cabbala was that salvation would come to the world only after it had sunk to an abyss of absolute evil. Man, according to this notion, would have to sink to the lowest depths before the advent of the Messiah. Therefore, Sabbetai thought to himself, it behooves the Messiah to accelerate the pace of man's moral deterioration. What could be better for this purpose than to encourage others to commit adultery with one's own wife, especially since jealousy was no factor?

SABBETAI'S "MACHINE"

Money came from Sabbetai's family, which was affluent. The money came also from an Egyptian Jew named Raphael Halebi, one of that land's richest Jews. Funds poured in from far and wide as soon as people were convinced that there lived in Turkey a man who would redeem them from all of their suffering. Nathan of Gaza sent hundreds of letters filled with propaganda all over the Jewish world. He first met Sabbetai Zvi in Palestine after Sabbetai arrived there from Salonika. Although the "Messiah" did not stay there very long, he managed to inspire a coterie of followers as well as to acquire his prophet, Nathan. Here is a typical letter written by Nathan:

Hear, ye brethren of Israel! Our Messiah has come to life in the city of Ismir, and his name is Sabbetai Zvi. Soon he will show his kingdom to all and will take the royal crown from the head of the sultan and place it on his own. Like a Canaanite slave shall the king of the Turks walk behind him, for in Sabbetai is the power and the glory. When nine months have passed, our Messiah shall vanish from before the eyes of Israel, and no man shall be able to say whether he is alive or dead. But he will cross the River Sambatyon, which as all men know no mortal has ever crossed. There he will marry the daughter of Moses, and our Messiah shall ride forth to Jerusalem with Moses and all the Jews of old mounted on horses. He himself shall ride on a dragon whose bridle reins shall be a snake with seven heads. On his way, he will be attacked by Gog and Magog, the enemies of Israel, with a mighty army. But the Messiah shall not conquer his enemies with ordinary weapons made by men. Nay, with the breath of his nostrils shall he rout them, and by his word alone shall he utterly destroy them. When he has entered into Jerusalem, God shall send down a temple of gold and precious stones from heaven. It shall fill the city with its brilliance. In it shall the Messiah offer up sacrifices, and in that day shall the dead throughout the world rise from their graves. I hasten to tell you these things.

Letters of this kind were sent by Nathan of Gaza to Jewish communities far and wide. It is a commentary on the state of the collective mind of the Jewry of the time that so many were persuaded.

With lightning speed the idea of Sabbetai Zvi as the Messiah spread through the Jewish world. To his native Smyrna he returned a conquering hero. He had been, as we will recall, excommunicated by its spiritual authorities. Now he came back to it in a chariot drawn by twelve white horses, with Sarah in a flowing white gown by his side. He swept through its streets singing Psalms in his haunting voice and leaving a trail of ecstatic and prostrate people behind. His eerie repertoire of songs included a guttural Spanish song about one Dulicena, a woman of ill repute. To queries about the aptness of such a song on the lips of a Messiah, he responded that it possessed a certain mystic significance bearing upon redemption and salvation that could only be comprehended by those initiated into the occult realm of Cabbalistic lore.

COLLECTIVE MANIA

The Jewish world was in a frenzy. Special prayers were offered up in hundreds of synagogues for the Messiah Sabbetai Zvi. Here is an example:

> May he who gives succor to kings, potentates, and princes, whose kingdom is the kingdom of every world, the great just and terrible God, the Holy King whom we adore, and who has not his like in heaven and on earth, who ruleth in the sky and sitteth on the throne; who hath made a covenant with his servant David. May He bless, protect, strengthen, uphold, and exalt ever higher and higher our Lord our King, the wise, holy, pious and supreme Sultan, Sabbetai Zvi, the divine Messiah, the Messiah of the God of Jacob, the Heavenly Lion, the King of Justice, the King of Kings, Sabbetai Zvi. O King of Kings, God, keep him, we implore Thee through Thy mercy. Let him live and protect him in all his troubles and trials. Lift up the stars of his kingdom and bow the hearts of all princes and rulers that they may please him and us and all Israel, Amen.

The Sabbatian obsession was a holiday for lunatics. In the streets of Constantinople and Ismir—as in the streets of Jerusalem and Amsterdam—men, women, and even children were seized with self-induced frenzy and indulged in "prophetic" babbling and prattling that was as frightening as it was senseless. Here is one example from the many spontaneous, manic and oracular pronouncements that have come down to us from that mad era:

> Oh God, I heard Thy call. The king of kings shall rule unto all eternity. Hear, O Israel, the Lord our God, the Lord is One. The king has been crowned with a crown, he is our king, Sabbetai Zvi. God protect Israel. Our prayers have been heard from the depths of our plight. A great joy, let him now live and be praised. Bring forth the crown of our king. Woe to him who believeth not. He is chosen. Blessed be he that hath the good fortune to live in this age of divine song and blessing to every man who believeth in God. Hear us, O God, and deliver us. We have already given him the crown. His kingdom shall endure. Thank God for the truthful Messiah, Sabbetai Zvi. May great joy reign among ye. Open thy hands, God his Master, as God returns us from captivity of Zion. May great joy reign among the Jews. Thank the Lord of Heaven, for He has given us a king. Woe to him who believeth not in him! The divine star of our kingdom has

risen. God, I in my life stand before Thee, like an angel I implore unto Thee! Glory be unto him that cometh unto His name. God will repay ye in the day of sorrow. Truth, truth, truth, help us, O God! In Thy mercy, there is no evil. God has heard my prayer, O God has heard my prayer.

Does this have a faintly familiar ring to it? Indeed it is the rabid evangelistic talk that may still be heard on gospel-sponsored radio and television stations around the country.

ECONOMIC CHAOS

The messianic delusion was so strong for thousands of believers that they began to divest themselves of their worldly possessions by selling them haphazardly and often at ridiculously low prices. They were so certain that the return to Zion under the banner of Sabbetai was imminent that they did not wish to be encumbered with possessions, especially of the immovable variety.

Many closed their stores in Ismir and in Constantinople. Jewish artisans and businessmen, buyers and sellers, merchants and professionals by the thousands simply stopped their economic pursuits. "Why bother if tomorrow we shall sail on to glory?" seemed to be their rationale. Many Jews awaited the miraculous manifestation from the rooftops of their homes, seemingly in confident expectation of a miraculous shuttle-service to Jerusalem. Chaos and pandemonium reigned supreme. It was at this point that the governmental authority saw fit to intervene.

The sultan had by then heard enough about the ample Sabbatian hints at governmental upheavals. As may well be imagined, such talk did not appeal to him. Too, the stoppage of productive Jewish enterprise was seriously damaging the Turkish economy. Sabbetai Zvi was arrested by the vizier on the charge of sedition. A substantial monetary bribe was instrumental in sweetening the Messiah's imprisonment, which hardly proved to be that at all. He was shipped off to Galipoli. Ostensibly, he was under arrest. It did not take long however, before Galipoli became one massive royal court for the "Messiah." The governor of Galipoli saw the economic advantages in permitting this. Jews from all over the world made pilgrimages to Galipoli. They considered that the "Messiah's" imprisonment was a necessary prelude to the final Redemption. They dubbed the fortress to which Sabbetai was confined *Migdal Oz*, meaning the Tower of Strength. Galipoli became a boom town, and its star resident was the recipient of a torrent of expensive tributes. The diabolically cunning Samuel Primo gleefully managed the three-ring circus that the entire affair had become. The feverish apostolic messages from Nathan, the "Prophet" of Gaza, continued apace. The balloon was fully inflated. It fairly screamed to be punctured.

THE BUBBLE BURSTS

It was a Polish Jew who applied the initial pin-prick to the Sabbatian dirigible. His name was Nehemiah Cohen. He was a mystic who had predicted that the Messiah would arrive in 1656. It was in this very year that reports reached him about this man who claimed to be the Messiah. He determined to check him out, so he made the long trip from Poland to Galipoli and asked for an interview with Sabbetai. They were closeted for three days. At the end of that time, Nehemiah burst out of Sabbetai's presence, declaring him an impostor and announcing his intention of denouncing Sabbetai to the sultan as a dangerous political revolutionary. This he promptly did. The sultan, Mohammed IV, had by now had enough. He summoned Sabbetai Zvi to him and gave him an ultimatum: Accept Islam or die. There was a very simple procedure in those days for accepting Islam. The Jew's headgear had to be discarded and the Turkish turban donned in its stead. Sabbetai Zvi put the turban on his head. That was the beginning of the end for the wild saga.

The overwhelming majority of the Jews, when they heard that the "Messiah" had converted to Islam, were brought back to their senses as if ice water had been poured over their fuzzy heads. Still there were many hundreds who so passionately believed that Sabbetai Zvi was the Messiah that they followed him into Islam on the theory that he knew what he was doing. If salvation meant sinking down to the lowest level before rising to the highest pinnacle, then this must be part of the process. Sabbetai Zvi had the best of two worlds for a few short years. He preached at both synagogue and mosque. He took off one hat and put on another, depending upon where he was. If it were a mosque, he wore the turban and preached from the Koran. If it were a synagogue, he wore what was the equivalent of the yarmulke in those days and preached the Jewish tradition. Soon he was regarded as too dangerous to be allowed free movement. The sultan ordered him into solitary exile and confinement on the small island of Dulcinio in the Mediterranean. There Sabbetai died a lonely, painful death. He probably succumbed to cancer. He died quite alone, with no one at his side.

But Sabbetai's influence did not die out for over a hundred years. Sabbatian sects continued in underground activity almost to the end of the eighteenth century. The most infamous offshoot of the Sabbatian psychosis were the Frankists who followed a Polish Jew named Jacob Frank. Their practices involved sexual orgies that were incestual and ugly—a *reductio ad absurdum* of the Cabbalistic idea that in order to achieve salvation, the depths must first be plumbed.

THE EIGHTEENTH CENTURY

ISRAEL BA'AL SHEM TOV

About 250 years ago, Judaism experienced a revolutionary phenomenon: the birth and growth of the Hasidic movement. The movement was initiated by Israel Ba'al Shem Tov, our Jew of the eighteenth century. This was not merely a religious revolution; it involved social and cultural upheaval as well. Sociologically, the relationships between Jew and Jew as a result of Hasidism were to change drastically. In cultural terms, Hasidism effected a significant change in Jewish literary output for decades to follow. The spirit of the writing was different. The content of the writing was different. Hasidism represented a tripartite revolutionary trend in Judaism. The man who started it all was Israel, called the Ba'al Shem Tov, or Master of the Good Name.

He was born in 1700 in a small village of Podolia near the Carpathians in Poland. As a child, he had been orphaned of both father and mother. He was brought up as a charity case. Of formal learning, he never had much. Nor was his a mind of notably intellectual character. His greatness was manifest in his prodigious capacities for sympathy and understanding and in a heart vibrating with religious sensitivity. He loved people with heart, soul, and mind.

EARLY YOUTH

Israel's early youth was spent as a virtual nonentity. As mentioned, he was a charity ward of the Jews in the area. They took pity upon this poor, destitute orphan who exhibited oddness and otherness. He did not play with the other children. He did not attend classes regularly, more often playing the truant. He would leave the stifling atmosphere of the *heder* for the invigorating mountain air. What he did in the mountains, nobody knew. Occasionally he was found wandering there with his eyes constantly fixed at some point in far off space. He preferred the outdoors to the indoors and seemed to have no desire for intellectual achievements, for the *Humash*, for the *Gemarah*, for the *Mishnayot*. He was a poor student. Disenchanted by his seeming mediocrity, the local guardians assigned him at the age of fifteen to the lowly station of a *behelfer*. This was a sort of male babysitter whose chores included taking children to and from the *heder* and tending to their needs while at study. Great talent for this kind of work was not a requisite. It was the job of a ne'er-do-well. Yet Israel loved it because he loved children. His work was a source of deep delight for him.

Very little is known to us of his early years. Legends abound upon which we need not expatiate. We know that he was a woodchopper early in his life, that he was married at the age of twenty to the sister of a scholarly rabbi who was much ashamed of the match. The rabbi was Gershon of Kutov. His sister loved the man she married despite his seeming ignorance, despite his falling so far short of the scholarly standards of her brother. For the first half of the Ba'al Shem Tov's career, his brother-in-law would hardly speak to him or about him. But it is a measure of the Ba'al Shem Tov's magnetic personality that in the course of time, Rabbi Gershon of Kutov became one of his most loyal followers.

EMERGENCE FROM OBSCURITY

The year 1736 marks the beginning of his active career. And here a word must be offered on the subject of a *ba'al shem*. This was a calling that might best be described as soothsaying. The period under discussion is still one of superstition. Physicians were not usually summoned to the sickbed. There were instead itinerant mystics known as *ba'al shems* who invoked some holy formulae and incantations for the purpose of effecting cures. Cameos and Cabbalistic lore served as substitutes for medicine and physical therapy. The *ba'al shem* who applied them was regarded as an initiate in the occult knowledge that was indispensable to healing. Many such spiritual practitioners plied their way along the countryside, stopping off where they were needed and practicing their special art.

That is the way our Israel began his career. This, of course, is very reminiscent of the career of another man who lived about 1800 years before, who also achieved great popularity through his vaunted healing powers. But Israel's career as a *ba'al shem* did not last long. However, the title remained with him through the rest of his life. He was called the Ba'al Shem Tov, the Master of the Good Name. His career was given to the teaching of a revolutionary concept regarding both the matter and the manner of religious worship.

Let it be said that the doctrine of the Ba'al Shem Tov is one of the most inspirational in religious history. He himself wrote next to nothing, but like Martin Luther, the great reformer of the sixteenth century, he had many people around his table. There was much spiritual table talk that has been transmitted to us by outstanding disciples of the Ba'al Shem Tov in much the manner that the teachings of Socrates have come down to us via the quill of his great pupil, Plato.

BASIC DOCTRINES

There are several basic doctrines in the teaching that ultimately came to be known as Hasidism. The first and most important is that God is *here*, not *there*; that God is *near*, not *far*. The question is not Where is God? The question is rather Where is He not? Now this was not new. It had been taught—among many other things—by the prophet Isaiah in the eighth century B.C.E. "Holy, holy, holy is the Lord of Hosts, the whole earth is filled with His glory." But the constant *emphasis* upon the fact that God is everywhere was an essential element in the teaching of Israel Ba'al Shem Tov and of Hasidism. It is well expressed in a Yiddish folk song whose words are "Master of the Universe, I wish to sing to you a 'You, you, you' song: Wherever I go, You; Wherever I stand, You; Are things good for Me? You! Are things ill for me? You! Wherever I turn, You, You, You. East? You! West? You! North? You! South? You! Heaven? You! Earth? You!"

A second vital Hasidic doctrine is that the heart, rather than the mind, is the fountainhead of piety. This does not mean that the mind is to be dismissed. The Ba'al Shem Tov never asked for that. But he reacted against the intellectualization of Judaism that had resulted in the denigration of the masses of Jews who were not necessarily conversant with the complexities of Talmudic law. For centuries, these Jews were second-class citizens of the community. A Jew with neither wealth nor learning was a virtual pariah. It is to such that Hasidism appealed most. Hasidism taught that the purity of the human heart is the most heavily weighted factor in God's assessment of man. Thus the masses of the people were re-enfranchised and reintroduced to their place in the sun.

The heart, said the Ba'al Shem Tov, is the true determinant of one's religious worth. A faulty heart is one that is envious, hateful, and ungenerous. A worthy heart is loving, compassionate, and charitable. Such a heart is the invaluable vehicle of communication with the deity. And such communication is the essence of prayer. Therefore, asked Israel Ba'al Shem Tov, why do you learned rabbis make sport of poor, slovenly *am ha'aretz*? It is unfair. Not everybody is equipped to escape the condition of being an *am ha'aretz*, but everybody is equipped to escape hardness of heart. One moment of communion with God via the heart, the Ba'al Shem Tov said, is worth a lifetime of arid scholarship.

It was here that his doctrine of *devaykut* entered into the picture. In Hebrew, the word *devek* means "glue," the word *devaykut* being "the condition of being glued together." The whole purpose of religion and prayer, said the Ba'al Shem Tov, was for man to achieve *devaykut* with God—not to feel that God is someone other, but rather that God is part of one's self. To achieve unity, a clinging with and to God—that is the objective of all prayer. In this connection, Israel Ba'al Shem Tov told the following parable:

> Once there was a rich and learned man who was punctilious about attendance at all services. His servants awakened him early each morning so that he would never be late for the minyan. In the afternoon he arrived promptly for the *mincha* prayer and then returned for the *Ma'ariv* service without undue strain. He was quite pleased with his religious self. It so happens that his neighbor was a very poor *ba'al agala* (coachman). He had to get up very early in the morning to provide bare subsistence for his family. He never had money left over from the previous day. He always regretted that

he could not attend regular services in the synagogue. Still he ran breathlessly to the synagogue whenever he could, if only to catch the end of the service. One day, our comfortable friend was leaving just at the end of the service at the very moment our ignorant coachman was rushing in. They collided. The poor one asked: "Are they still praying in there?" His voice was so pained, it was like a groan from the heart. The rich one smugly answered: "They have finished," grinning superciliously. In due course both died. A decision as to their ultimate celestial destination was pending. When the sins and merits of each were weighed on the scales a rare thing happened—they were balanced! What to do? The Archangel Gabriel sent a heavenly messenger earthward for the purpose of finding some overlooked merit that might decide the issue. Or perhaps the reverse. The messenger came back with two angelic portfolios. One contained the groan of the coachman as he rushed in for prayer and collided with his comfortable friend. The groan was placed on the merit side of the scales with the result that he was admitted to heaven. The other bag contained the superior smirk of the comfortable worshiper. It was placed on the debit side of the scale.

The story makes the point that the road to hell may be paved with smugness and self-satisfaction and the road to heaven may be paved with anxiety and pain for one's failure to achieve something noble.

In prayer, then, it is not formal correctness that counts. It is rather the complete identification of the soul with its Creator. *Devaykut*—clinging unto God—is a quintessential Hasidic doctrine.

THE MANDATE TO BE HAPPY

The worship of God must be a joyous experience, the Ba'al Shem Tov taught. He was very fond of quoting the passage from the Psalms: "Worship the Lord with glee." When one comes to the synagogue to pray, said the Ba'al Shem, or when one stays in his home to pray, his prayer should be joyous. Religion is not morbid, devotion is not to be associated with anxiety and terror. On the contrary, to achieve *devaykut*, oneness with God that is the height of religious quest, melancholy must be eschewed. Melancholy is sinful in the adoration of God. The lugubrious nature is untouched by true religious feeling. To the Ba'al Shem Tov, sadness was a grave sin! Certainly one should be sober in confessing one's errors in the course of prayer. But one should be simulta-

211

neously optimistic that the good Lord will forgive and redeem. Thus the spirit of prayer should be informed by an irresistible exaltation. It should not consist of self-flagellation. He decried Jews who thought that they would get closer to God by afflicting their souls. They would fast on Monday, they would fast on Thursday or whenever else they could devise a reason for it. He did not approve of this practice at all. God does not require affliction, he said. God loves his children. God does not desire their pain. Whenever he saw sadness in the face of a man, he would say: "Satan has established residence in that man's soul."

THE PARABOLIC METHOD

Above all, the Ba'al Shem Tov was a spiritual emancipator. The slaves that Israel Ba'al Shem Tov freed were the disenfranchised and disinherited Jews who were scorned by the rich because they were poor and by the wise because they were ignorant. They felt like outcasts. Israel Ba'al Shem Tov affirmed most emphatically that they were not. He told stories through which he communicated his philosophy. Two examples:

Once upon a time there was a Jew who was an ignoramus. He could barely read the siddur. He could not attend the synagogue because he lived many miles from it. He was poor and had to struggle to earn the barest of livelihoods. Once a year, *erev* Yom Kippur, early in the morning, he started his long trip to the synagogue so that at least on that holy and solemn day he could pray in the midst of his people. On one such occasion a violent storm broke out. The wheels of his wagon sank in the mud. He was stranded with no help in sight. The sun was setting. His heart ached. He knew none of the prayers by heart. He had no prayer book with him. He sat and wept. Suddenly he was struck by an idea. All is not lost! He stood in front of a tall oak and looked towards its top. Beyond that he could not see. He prayed, "Master of the Universe, You know what an ignoramus I am. You know that I can hardly read. You know that I do not know any of the prayers by heart. Would it not be tragic that I should not be able to pray to You on the holiest day of the year? Do not let it happen. Is not every prayer in the prayer book composed of the aleph-bet? That aleph-bet I do remember. Let me recite for You, and You in your wisdom will combine the letters so as to form the words: 'I love You, God'." Then he began to recite: "Aleph, bet, gimel, etc." The Ba'al Shem Tov concluded his story by saying that a voice descended from heaven: "Know, my son, that you have offered me the most beautiful prayer I have every heard."

A rugged, brawny farmer brought his 14-year old boy for the first time to the synagogue. Ignorance was the hallmark of that family. The husky farm boy knew nothing about prayer, but in the synagogue he heard everyone praying. Again it was Yom Kippur. Jews were wrapped in their *taleisim*, filled with piety, voices mounting tremulously: "May our pleas ascend to You, O God, from eventide unto the morn." A spirit of exultation began to envelop our lad. But he was frustrated because he could not express it. He turned to his father: "Father, I do not know how to pray. But I *can* whistle. You know, when I call the sheep together, I put my two fingers into my mouth and whistle." The father said: "In the synagogue, one does not whistle." Ten, fifteen minutes go by "Father, I must whistle! If I cannot pray, I must at least whistle! All I can do is whistle!" The prayers reached a pitch of excitement; the son tore his hands out of his father's tight grip, put his two fingers in his mouth and the synagogue was shattered by a piercing whistle. Worshipers were about to pounce upon the boy in anger over what was deemed an act of desecration. Israel Ba'al Shem Tov strode to the pulpit saying: "Children, you must not lay a hand on this boy. He is a *tzaddik*, a saint. His whistle was the most heartfelt prayer that has been sounded in this synagogue tonight. It was his way of communicating with God, his way of achieving *devaykut*." For (and this was one of the great arguments of the Ba'al Shem Tov) so many people think that prayer is the function of the vocal chords. He believed that the truest of prayers is a function of silence, for silence implies a complete absence of any physical distractions, even the physical distraction of sound. One who can communicate with God wordlessly is the most likely to achieve *devaykut*.

THE GROWTH OF HASIDISM

To Israel Ba'al Shem Tov, this was the essence of prayer. Thus he was the great leveler of the ranks of Jewry. The poor and the rich, the wise and the ignorant were all equal in the eyes of God. Hasidism placed Judaism on a renewed plateau of enthusiastic spirituality. It was the work of Israel Ba'al Shem Tov that instilled this new life into the belief and practice of Judaism. The movement grew slowly during his lifetime, but as he was approaching his last years (he died at the age of sixty) his fame began to spread. His disciples were many. After his death they spread the teachings of Hasidism through the Jewish world. For 150 years, from 1750 to 1900, the Hasidic movement was the most vital force in Judaism. It has had a renaissance since the "Tremendum," Arthur Cohen's word for the Holocaust. It is too early to predict what the juices of its re-invigoration might do for the foreseeable future. On his deathbed, as thousands of people waited outside his chambers, shattered by the imminent death of their great champion, his last words were: "May the foot of pride never stamp upon me." He did not wish to be carried away by the adulation of the masses. He died as he had lived, a humble man who tried to impart the true feeling of Judaism and Jewishness to the hearts of so many thousands. One of the most important aspects of religion through exultation that Israel Ba'al Shem Tov first introduced, and which his disciples later developed was the heavy emphasis upon music in prayer. In Hebrew and in Yiddish, the word for "melody" is *nigun*. The Bal'al Shem Tov was a master of *nigunim*, and so were his disciples. The Hasidic movement has had so much to do with the introduction of the *nigun* into Jewish life. The Hasidic motif is prevalent in synagogue music and in life-cycle rituals.

I remember the rebbe and the Hasidism sitting around the table late Shabbos afternoon as the shadows were beginning to fall. The rebbe was "saying" Torah, preaching about the portion of the week. He inevitably finished his Torah with a little "bim-bom." What is "bim-bom"? It is not a nonsense syllable. Hasidism is wrapped up in "bim-bom." It is the eternal song without words—without words because it doesn't need any, because the very soul of a Hasid is expressed in it. They danced and swayed to the cadences of a *nigun*. The Hasid places his hand on the shoulder of his fellow. They trot about the room, singing "bim-bom, bim-bom." They can do this for hours at a time with undiminished exultation.

Every wordless *nigun* sends this essential message: God, you are there, and I am here. I know that You are concerned about me, and I want You to know that I appreciate the fact that You are. Be with me always!

"But where is God?" a Hasid once asked his master.

The answer: "Wherever people let Him enter."

THE NINETEENTH CENTURY

Samuel David Luzzatto

The French Revolution of 1789 redirected Jewish history from a road traveled for some two thousand years to one it travels still, one whose ultimate destination is clouded with uncertainty. Jews have been wrestling with the problem of Jewish survival as a result of the cataclysmic changes that have taken place in their lives, changes that have affected religion, politics, society, and ideology. The Jewish psyche has not been the same since 1789.

For hundreds of years Jews lived in the ghetto. During this time they were the pariahs of society, its outcasts and its scapegoats. For all this time the Jew lived in relative isolation from the non-Jewish world. The question then was not spiritual survival; it was physical safety. Since the Jew was isolated, he conducted his life with little interference from the outside world. He was contained within his four ells, he had his own spheres of activity, his own religious life, his own communal organization. Indeed the political authority encouraged Jewish communal autonomy. There was, for example, no problem of the Jew keeping a kosher home, since the only food available to the Jew within his ghetto domicile was kosher. There was no problem of Sabbath observance, since Jewish communal structure was predicated upon the rule of *halakha*. There was also no need to reconcile the beliefs of the outside world with his own. Whatever the winds of change wafting outside the ghetto, they were largely irrelevant to the inner life of a religiously autonomous Jewish community.

IMPACT OF THE FRENCH REVOLUTION

The French Revolution changed all that. When the battle cry of *"Liberte, egalite, et Fraternite"* was sounded through the European world the walls of the ghetto began to crumble. The French Revolution was driven by a passion for human equality. At least theoretically, all men were created equal, "all men are endowed by their Creator with certain inalienable rights," in the words of the United States Declaration of Independence. "Among these rights are life, liberty, and the pursuit of happiness." Governments are set up for the purpose of guaranteeing these rights. When governments do not live up to that purpose, the people have the right to overthrow them by force if necessary. This is the premise that effected the overthrow of Louis XVI and his regime in 1789. Then came Napoleon, who exported the ideas of the French Revolution throughout Europe by force of arms. Napoleon was himself a tyrant, but the net effect of his activity was to inculcate the Revolution's ideals of liberty and equality in the lands his military campaigns succeeded in conquering.

Napoleon awakened the spirit of nationalism. Where in Italy, for example, there were a dozen different states and petty principalities, and where in Germany as late as the eighteenth century there were no less than three hundred mini-states, the spirit of nationalism, the desire of all people speaking the same language and living within certain defined geographical areas to be unified was accelerated by the Napoleonic sweep through Europe. The result not long thereafter was to be the consolidation of many small states into such national units as are represented in modern Italy and Germany.

A vital factor associated with the French Revolution is summarized in one word: Enlightenment. The French Revolution brought to a head the notion that all of the preconceived ideas of men with respect to God and with regard to relations with each other were to be subjected to renewed scrutiny; that the time had come to banish superstition and idle beliefs from the minds of the masses and to inaugurate a new era of Enlightenment. The last part of the eighteenth century produced first-rate minds who advanced the ideas of Enlightenment. Among them were Voltaire, a Frenchman of keen political insights and considerable literary talent; Diderot, the author of the first great encyclopedia of the modern era; Montesquieu, the author of the *Spirit of the Laws*, who made a notable contribution to political philosophy; Rousseau, the stalwart champion of human rights; Goethe, a superb poet and thinker; Lessing, who wrote the powerful philo-Semitic play *Nathan the Wise* in which his model was Moses Mendelssohn; and John Stuart Mill in England, whose essay "On Liberty," remains a classic of its kind.

IMPACT UPON EUROPEAN JEWRY

Such were the currents that both inspired the French Revolution and set a new tone for the modern era. For the first time in many centuries, the Jew was swept up in these currents. When the walls of the ghetto were broken down, a Jew found that he had Christians as his neighbors and that he had to come to terms with them and their new way of thinking about society. No longer was the Jew insulated from the winds of change. He found himself right in the middle of them. He was forced to re-evaluate his position, perhaps even re-orient it, if his entry into general society were to be successfully achieved. How to do so without sacrifice of his ancestral identity is a challenge with which Jews are dealing to this day. The French Revolution affected much more than the political status of the Jew. It posed acute challenges to the theory and practice of his religion.

Moses Mendelssohn was a pioneer in the attempt to face the challenge of the Enlightenment. He had made his way from the ghetto in Dessau, Germany, into the highest echelons of the cultural world of Berlin. The story of Mendelssohn deserves much more space than is afforded by this chapter. Suffice it for our purposes to say that he is justly regarded as the father of *haskalah* (Jewish Enlightenment). Mendelssohn was himself a pious Jew. In his time he was a highly respected philosopher. He and his disciples translated the Bible into German and brought the ideas of the Enlightenment into the Jewish world. It is ironic that Moses Mendelssohn, a loyal Jew who prayed thrice daily, was the father of children and grandchildren who left the fold of Judaism to become Christians. The most famous of them is his grand-son Felix Mendelssohn Bertholdi, the renowned composer.

BREAKDOWN OF THE GHETTO

With the shattering of the walls of the ghetto there was a breakdown of Jewish communal authority. It was no longer possible for an orga-nized Jewish community—a *kehilla*—to enforce Jewish practice or to impose theological belief. With the disappearance of the ghetto, Jewish autonomy came to an end. The Jew was told in effect: You are part of society now. You are now subject in every way to the laws of the State. Indeed, there were Jews who did not welcome political equality. They perceived it as a danger to the survival of their age-old religious beliefs and practices. On the other hand, there were a great many Jews who were intoxicated by their new freedom. The great dream that the day will come when all men would be equal, when swords would be bro-ken into ploughshares and spears into pruning hooks, when the lion will dwell with the lamb, with a little child leading them, the day of the Lord, that Zecharia and Obadiah and Isaiah foresaw, *that* day, they believed, *had* arrived. After two thousand years of servitude, abuse, deg-radation, and isolation, Jews seemed to be sailing the open seas of free-dom. "Our troubles are over at long last," they said, "but now we have to prove to the gentile world that we deserve this great boon bestowed upon us, that we are, after all, good people. We are under the obliga-tion of demonstrating that we are a people who have made vital con-tributions to human welfare and culture and that we shall continue to do so."

The nineteenth century was a century of revolution. Wherever one turned, revolution was in the air. There were revolutions in 1830, 1848–1849, 1852, and 1860. The revolutionary spirit swept across Italy, Germany, Austria, and Hungary. Many Jews saw these revolutions as chapters of their own redemption. They threw themselves with vigor and abandon into revolutionary movements. They felt that they, above all, had a major stake in them; they above all had to prove themselves worthy of the equality that humanity was seeking to establish. Jews whose political instincts had been frustrated by two thousand years of statelessness were suddenly running for public office. A few were actually elected. A brave and beautiful new world (as they saw it) was being unveiled in the diaspora.

WIESSENSCHAFT DES JUDENTUMS

A more important aspect that bears more directly upon our Jew of the nineteenth century is the new cultural phenomenon that in German went by the name *Wissenschaft des Judentums*. Loosely translated, it means "The Science of Judaism." Jewish scholars were out to show that Jewish culture was meritorious, that Jews are capable of producing doctoral dissertations, that the Talmud and Rashi and the Tosafists and Maimonides and ibn Ezra were worthy subjects for scholarly and scientific inquiry. In Berlin, for example, a Society for Jewish Culture was organized by three men: Zunz, Heine, and Ganz. Heinrich Heine was, of course, one of the great poets of the nineteenth century. Leopold Zunz was a giant of Jewish scholarship. Ganz was nothing special. Their purpose was to show how distinguished Jewish scholarship could be by offering original studies *in German* so that non-Jews would appreciate what Judaism had to contribute. Heinrich Heine ultimately wound up at the baptismal font and became Catholic. However, Heine remained a Jew at heart throughout his life. He said that he accepted baptism because it was the passport to the society of Germany in the nineteenth century. Zunz remained to his last day a devoted and dedicated (though, in many respects, a saddened) Jew. He is regarded as the father of the *Wissenschaft des Judentums*.

Importantly included in this coterie of the Science of Judaism were Marcus Jost, who wrote the first modern, scholarly history of the Jews; Ludwig Phillipson; Abraham Geiger, one of the leading spirits of the Reform movement and a formidable Jewish scholar; Michael Sachs, an eloquent preacher in Berlin who translated the poetry of Yehudah Ha-Levi into German and thereby gave the world an appreciation of the magnificence of medieval Jewish poetry (in fact, it was this translation that inspired Heinrich Heine to a great love for the immortal poet Yehudan Ha-Levi); Heinrich Graetz, the greatest Jewish historian of modern times; and the remarkable Moritz Steinschneider, an incredibly erudite bibliographer of Judaica. His major work is a catalog describing the Jewish manuscript collections in the British Museum and at Oxford. Graetz wrote in German. Zunz wrote in German. Phillipson wrote in German. Geiger wrote in German. Of course, Germany was the center for the renaissance of Jewish culture, as the German nomenclature for this entire movement indicates.

The subjects and persons with which the *Wissenschaft* scholars dealt were largely steeped in the Hebrew language, but most of them regarded Hebrew as dead, never to be reborn. They did not want to waste their efforts in employing it. Also, as said, they wished to impress the gentile scholars, most of whom did not know Hebrew. Zunz honestly believed that Judaism and Jewish culture, as such, were coming to an end, and that therefore the time had come to write a definitive summary of the Jewish heritage. Many of his contemporaries thought that their work was in the nature of a monument to a Jewish world in the throes of dying.

SAMUEL DAVID LUZZATTO

Samuel David Luzzatto, our Jew of the nineteenth century, vigorously disagreed. A distinguished member of the *Wissenschaft* school, it is true to say that he was *with* them, but not *of* them. He worked alongside of them, but he did not share their psychology and their outlook. He did not share their delusions, and he did not in any way represent their spirit. Samuel David Luzzatto, the Italian Jew, was born in 1800 in Trieste and died in 1865 in Padua. He was one of the giants of Jewish scholarship of the nineteenth century. Not for a moment did he regard Jewish emancipation as utopia. He was not impressed by the French Revolution nor by Napoleon. He was not convinced that Jewry was on the verge of a new lease on life as an equal in the family of nations. He did not think that the Messiah had come, nor did he regard Jewish scholarship of his time as a summing up process, but rather as the beginning of a new era of cultural resurgence. *He wrote almost exclusively in Hebrew*, although he could write in Latin, Greek, Italian, French, and German, as well as in Aramaic and Syriac. Yet he wrote primarily in Hebrew because he believed that Hebrew was and must continue to be a living language and that it was up to the scholars of the Jewish world to give Hebrew reinforcement. He, unlike the Geigers of the Reform school, did not believe that traditional Judaism was obsolete. He did not believe that the Sabbath was outdated, and that *kashruth* should be buried. He did not believe that the *mitzvot* of the Torah were superannuated. On the contrary, he believed that Judaism was never more vital to the life of the world than it was in the nineteenth century. He developed a philosophy of his own in analyzing the difference between Atticism, by which he meant the Greek world, and Abrahamism, by which he meant the Jewish world. To him the Greek world, or Western civilization, is not concerned with morality, with human relations, with love, or with compassion. It is concerned with form, with beauty, with style, with syntax. But it is not concerned with the heart of the matter, which is the love of God and the love of Man. He said that Atticism informed the spirit of modern science. To be sure, it seeks scientific truths. But the important truth—the most important truth to the world—is "and thou shalt love thy neighbor as thyself." He said that this truth did not have to wait for the scientific revolution. In fact, already in 1800 B.C.E., Abraham had been told to walk in the way of the Lord, to "pursue the ways of justice and peace." To Luzzatto the way of the Lord consisted mostly of this one word, which in Hebrew is *rachamim* and in English may be translated as "compassion." He said that Judaism has only one great treasure to give to the world. That treasure still has not been accepted by mankind. It is the treasure of human compassion, the treasure that comes from the understanding of God as One who loves all of His creatures and through whom men must come to love each other.

Greek civilization, said Luzzatto, will not save mankind. The French Revolution will not save mankind. The Enlightenment and the quest for science will not save mankind. Certainly science will take great strides forward, but those strides are not in the direction of ennobling the human heart and purifying the human soul. They are in the direction of making it easier for the human being to destroy himself. This was said a century and a half before Hiroshima and Nagasaki! Only the spirit of Abrahamism can achieve concord within human society.

LUZZATTO ON THE EMANCIPATION

Luzzatto warned his fellow scholars: "If you think that the Messiah is coming on the wings of scientific advance and Enlightenment, you are wrong." He appeared odd and anachronistic to most of his colleagues in Judaic scholarship. He was often labeled "bigoted," "blind," and "reactionary." Still he refused to capitulate. He was a courageous spirit and a tireless fighter for his beliefs. He spoke out with utmost severity against some ideas of the men with whom he worked at the Science of Judaism. He denounced Geiger's outlook and Phillipson's notions and even Zunz's approach. He said: "If you think, Geiger, that Berlin is to be your Jerusalem, and if you think, Munk, that Paris is to be your Jerusalem, and if you think, Schorr (an Austria-Hungarian scholar), that Vienna is going to be your Jerusalem, I say to you all: there is only one Jerusalem! There always was one, and it always shall be." This was a half-century before the advent of our Jew of the twentieth century, Theodor Herzl. Samuel David Luzzatto said that Judaism without a national home for the Jewish people is inconceivable, that he could not imagine a Jewish people and the Jewish religion divorced from the ideals of the national state. This, at the very time when others were arguing that the idea of a Jewish return to their ancestral homeland posed a danger to their full acceptance by their European Fatherland.

LUZZATTO, THE SCHOLAR

It is amazing that one man, whose lifetime reads, paradoxically, like a Greek tragedy, could have accomplished so much. He was the greatest Hebrew philologist of the nineteenth century. He did more for the resurrection of the Hebrew language and its employment in the modern idiom than any other scholar of the nineteenth century. He was the outstanding Hebrew grammarian of his time. He was the outstanding Jewish interpreter of the Bible. He was one of the most eloquent apologists for the tradition of Judaism.

When in 1848 the Italian Revolution made it possible for Jews to write without censorship, Luzzatto hastened to compose four essays in a pamphlet that was called *Il Giudaismo Illustrato, Judaism Illustrated*. They were gems of Judaic propaganda. The lectures on Jewish ethics and the dogmas of Judaism that he had delivered to his students also were published in Italian. He was a Hebrew poet of merit whose lyric works were published in the two volumes entitled *Kinnor Naim*. Luzzatto once wrote a sonnet in honor of Geiger's birthday in no less than four languages: the first four lines in Hebrew; the next four lines in German; the next three in Aramaic, and the final three in Italian.

But the most important role of Luzzatto was as a midwife to scholarship. More than any other Jew of the nineteenth century, he was responsible for bringing out the best in the potential scholarly capacities of many others. When speaking of the accomplishments of Luzzatto, one must also give him a great share of the credit for the work of Rapoport, the great Galician scholar; of Geiger, the great German scholar; of Zunz; of Sachs, whom we have already mentioned; of Dukes, and of Letteris, to mention only six names out of many dozens whose scholarship was abetted and encouraged by Samuel David Luzzatto.

Luzzatto wrote over five thousand letters in his lifetime. They were not of the "having wonderful time, wish you were here" variety. Most of his letters involved scholarly treatment of an important subject, generally in response to a question asked by another scholar pertaining to the work in which he happened to be engaged. Some of his letters ran to twenty or thirty pages of tightly written Hebrew or, less often, Italian or German. Most of his letters have been collected in four volumes. He corresponded with Zunz and thereby contributed to the latter's monumental work on the history of Jewish liturgy. He corresponded with Geiger and thereby contributed to *his* magnum opus on the internal development within the Bible itself that was occasioned by changes in Jewish theology while the Scriptures were themselves in the making. Sachs wanted to write a work on Yehudah Ha-Levi. It was Luzzatto who supplied him with much of the manuscript material. Letteris published an important sixteenth-century document on Jewish history that had not been published before. It was Luzzatto who sent him the document, who sent him the notes on it, who gave him the ideas as to how to compose the introduction. He had an overwhelming influence on his pupils. From his twenty-ninth year to the day of his death, he served as the professor of Hebrew and Jewish history at the Collegio Rabbinico, the Rabbinical College that was organized in Padua in 1829 and to whose faculty of two Luzzatto had been appointed. The faculty was not understaffed. Four students a year was about par for the course. But even three or four students a year over a period of about thirty years comes to a total of some one hundred. The students of Luzzatto proved to be the salvation of Jewish life in Italy through the nineteenth century. They loved their master, and it was this love that helped to make his miserable life bearable.

THE LIFE OF JOB

Samuel David Luzzatto was born, as mentioned earlier, in 1800 in the city of Trieste. His father was a poor carpenter who knew the *Tannach* by heart and studied with his son every day as long as he was alive. Hezekiah was his name. Fervently and incessantly, the father and the son studied. Luzzatto had poor vision through most of his life. As a child he had to be taken out of the formal school he attended in Trieste and was only allowed to take private lessons. But Luzzatto was perhaps the foremost Jewish autodidact of the nineteenth century.

His family was very poor. His mother had died, and he and his father and little sister had to support themselves. As a thirteen-year-old, he was employed in the production of vermicelli, a form of pasta. Luzzatto made vermicelli this way: He stood for hours turning a contraption by hand. He was not interested in the vermicelli, he was interested in the particular book that he held in his free hand.

One of his teachers had been Raphael Segre. Luzzatto later married Raphael Segre's older daughter in 1828. By then he had become well known because of the contributions he had made to Jewish scholarly periodicals, particularly *Biccurai Ha-Ittim*. Also, he became well known through his edition of the *machzor* in use by the Jews of Italy. It was called *Machzor K'Minhag B'nai Romi*. And so in 1829, when the new school called the Rabbinical College was organized by order of the Austrian emperor (who wanted to modernize the rabbis of Italy by affording them a secular education along with their religious studies), Luzzatto was appointed at the recommendation of the noted Italian-Jewish scholar Isaac Reggio. In 1830, his first child was born. He gave him the name Filosseno, which means "love of the proselyte." In Hebrew, the name was Ohev Ger. He was working at the time on Onkelos, the second-century proselyte who had translated the Bible into Aramaic. Luzzatto expressed his own love for the proselyte by naming his son Ohev Ger, lover of the proselyte. Every time a child was born to him, the name Luzzatto gave the child was associated with the book he was working on. He had been working on a commentary of Isaiah when his second son was born. So he named him Isaiah. When he worked on the Book of Job, he named the child Job. This in itself is a psychological indication of what was important to him. His work was his life.

FILOSSENO LUZZATTO

Filosseno was a genius. At age eighteen, he made a most significant contribution to the history of the Jews in Ethiopia, the Falashas. At the age of twenty he wrote the first important monograph on Hasdai ibn Shaprut (see chapter 10). He opened up the world to scholarship on this subject. At the age of twenty-three, his father sent him to Paris to pursue his studies. There the young man developed cancer. Six months later he had to be brought home, and Samuel David Luzzatto was by his son's bedside as he rapidly faded away. Five of the most bitter months imaginable ensued for father and son. Still Filosseno worked ceaselessly and feverishly upon his agonizing deathbed to the very last day of his life.

The death of Filosseno was a shattering experience for Luzzatto. But other tragedies had come before. Between Filosseno's birth and death, Luzzatto had lost three children—Isaiah the first (another Isaiah had been born later); his daughter Malka; and his seventeen-year-old daughter, Miriam, who had been to him what the daughters of John Milton were to that blind poet. When Luzzatto could no longer read, she read for him. When he could no longer write, he dictated to her, and she wrote. Pneumonia took her away at the age of seventeen, a blooming and beautiful girl. His first wife became mentally ill after the loss of Isaiah the first. He cared for her, did the house chores, and continued his work of instruction at the Collegio Rabbinico. Out of the last penny that he could muster he bought some of the most precious manuscripts that were available in the world of Jewish scholarship at that time. Fortunately for him, after his wife died in 1841, he married her sister, Leah Segre, an angel in disguise. This was the one bright spot in his personal life. She was a loving woman who raised the surviving children of her dead sister. She bore him three children herself, two of whom died during Luzzato's lifetime. He has left us a tragic description of the death of his son Baruch Iyov. This seven-year-old child had come home from school with a terrible inflammation. He was put to bed and was dead within six days. On the last day of his life, his father brought him three apples, and some neighbor's children came into the house. Baruch Iyov, the little son of Luzzatto, turned to the neighbor children saying: "I don't think I'm going to have much use for these apples. First of all, I don't have an appetite, and second I won't live long. Won't you have them?" And then he died. His father had been witness to the conversation. He recorded it in one of his letters.

He sat *shiva* all of his life, it would seem, almost every other year. But throughout this time, he wrote and he worked and he produced. He spent what little money he had (it was precious little, because his salary was always meager) on the expensive manuscripts that served as the material with which he encouraged Jewish scholarship all over the European continent. Unceasing, sacrificial scholarly activity marked his life to within days of his death. Five days before Yom Kippur, he took sick with an illness that nobody could diagnose, not even his son Isaiah, who was a physician. On the eve of Yom Kippur 1865, he died just after reciting the *Kol Nidre* prayer.

A JEW TO REMEMBER

Samuel David Luzzatto has been terribly neglected by biographers and historians. About thirty-six years ago, the present writer was doing course work at Columbia University for his doctorate under the late Professor Salo Baron, the most eminent Jewish historian of our century. He asked: "Well, what have you chosen for your doctoral dissertation?" The answer: "I've been giving some thought to Samuel David Luzzatto." He rose from his seat to say: "God bless you! I've been looking for somebody like this for a long time. This is the most neglected Jewish scholar of our modern era. Nobody is doing any serious work on him." This writer's dissertation on Luzzatto was the very last to be supervised by Salo Baron. (It was published in 1979.)

Luzzatto, it may finally be said, was probably the most prophetic scholar of that great nineteenth century of Jewish scholarship. Everything that he predicted has come to pass. The world is still to heed Luzzatto's warning that if it is to survive, "Abrahamism" must prevail over "Atticism."

THE TWENTIETH CENTURY

THEODOR HERZL

Theodor Herzl wrought a monumental change of direction in Jewish history.

He was not a radically original thinker. He left little impact upon the religious or cultural consciousness of the Jewish people. But he was distinguished from all of his predecessors in one vital respect: *He was the man who acted; he was to translate dreams into reality*. He may justifiably be called the architect of the State of Israel today. He was not a pioneer; he was a culminator. Other people did the pioneering. Not even his masterpiece, the *Judenstaat*, was original. Herzl himself said sometime after he wrote it that had he read Leon Pinsker's *Auto-Emancipation*, written in 1881, he, Herzl, would never have written the *Judenstaat* ten years later.

The State of Israel was not conceived in 1947 when the United Nations voted for a Jewish State in Palestine. The State of Israel was not really born on May 14, 1948. It was born in August 1897 in Basle, Switzerland, at the First Zionist Congress, convened by Herzl. Commenting upon it, Herzl made this entry in his diary: "If I were to sum up the Basle Congress in a single phrase—which I would not dare to make public—I would say: In Basle I created the Jewish State. Were I to say this aloud, I would be greeted by universal laughter. But perhaps fifty years hence, everyone will perceive it." Herzl died in 1904. The United Nations voted for a Jewish State exactly fifty years after the Basle Congress. The near-perfect accuracy of Herzl's prophecy is uncanny.

HERZL'S ENVIRONMENT

Theodor Herzl was born on May 2, 1860, in Budapest into a fairly assimilated Jewish family. His father and mother were far from being observant Jews. Herzl's Jewish education was threadbare. A few months before his bar mitzvah, a private tutor was employed to give him an accelerated course so he could recite the blessings over the Torah. He attended the public school system in Vienna, to which city the family moved in his early childhood. He entered law school when he was twenty years old and graduated with high honors at the age of twenty four. But he never practiced law. Herzl was a very pragmatic man whose illusion prior to law school was shattered shortly after he entered it. The illusion was that being Jewish need not be a problem and that in the newly "emancipated" world everybody is free, including cultured Jews who were in tune with the spirit of the times. He was disabused of this notion in law school because the students called him a "dirty Jew," along with other choice epithets. The professors did not exhibit any great kindness toward the Jewish student. He decided that inasmuch as there is anti-Semitism in the legal profession, he would rather not be a lawyer. Herzl was a young man with ambitions. He was determined to attain the top of any profession he chose to pursue. When he put his teeth into a project, he either conquered the project or the project conquered him. In the case of the Great Project that was his life's work, both things were true. He conquered the project without knowing so, for his arduous labors killed him at age forty-four, seven years after he had convened the first Zionist Congress.

It was the law school situation that had brought home to Theodor Herzl what Samuel David Luzzatto knew from the beginning: To wit, neither French Revolution nor emancipation nor the breakdown of the ghetto would bring an end to anti-Semitism. Indeed, the early promise, the "springtime of the nations," when Jews entertained such high hopes for their achievement of civic rights was rapidly sinking in a morass of virulent anti-Semitism the bitterness of which only the twentieth century was to surpass. Nineteenth-century anti-Semitism took primarily a literary-cultural form. Some very good minds were exercised in producing poisonous anti-Semitic tracts. In France, Drumont wrote a best-seller entitled *La France Juif*, in which he argued that all of France was being consumed by the cancer of organized Jewry plotting the destruction of the motherland. Drumont's book went through many editions, often liberally illustrated with ugly caricatures that anticipated the hellish drawings of Nazi literature. Richard Wagner, who was a great composer and also a great anti-Semite, had a son-in-law named Houston Stuart Chamberlain—a brilliant man who was corrosively anti-Semitic. He wrote a book that became a bible of sorts for intellectual anti-Semites. A man named Stoeckel did his part in inflaming many to Jew-hatred. A long list of literary and oratorical Jew-baiters could easily be assembled. They were contemporaries of Theodor Herzl.

DRAMATIST AND JOURNALIST

As a young man in his twenties, Herzl realized that anti-Semitism had not been cured by the French Revolution or by the Emancipation. But because he came from an assimilated home, because his Jewish affiliations and loyalties were tenuous, he was moved to write a little essay that is startling in historical retrospect. Herzl said in this essay that there is only one solution to the Jewish problem. The Jews must all baptize and intermarry. They must cease to be; otherwise, he said, there is no solution to the problem of the eternal suffering of those of whose heritage he knew very little at that stage of his life.

Herzl turned to writing, for which he had a talent. He was not a great writer, by any means, but he had popular appeal. He was a good journalist, and into this field he invested his energies. He wrote light articles called *feuillitons* a genre of semi-serious commentary on the passing political scene. He was very well known in Vienna. It was not long before he became a writer for the most prominent Viennese newspaper, the *Neue Freie Presse* (*The New Free Press*). He also had ambitions to be a playwright. He wrote a number of mediocre plays, some of which were produced and enjoyed moderate success. It is significant that one of these was a foreshadowing of the way the mind of Theodor Herzl would be headed. It was a play called *Der Neue Ghetto* (*The*

New Ghetto). In it he gave expression to the idea that though the old ghetto that had been surrounded by walls of bricks and mortar had collapsed, the Jew still found himself in a ghetto, a ghetto surrounded by the hatred and animosity of the people in whose midst he lived. So that even though the physical ghetto was destroyed, the new ghetto was just as wicked and in a sense, more depressing, since one might break down a physical wall, but it is very difficult to break down an attitude.

He was appointed foreign correspondent for the *Neue Freie Presse* early in the 1890s. He was then just about thirty years old. He filed some interesting dispatches from Paris, light matters of no earth-shaking import. Herzl was happy. He was married and the father of a child. He enjoyed a good reputation and had standing as the Parisian correspondent for a major European newspaper.

And then the bomb fell in the form of the Dreyfus Affair. In 1870 and 1871, a war had been fought between Germany and France, known to history as the Franco-Prussian war. Its result was a humiliating defeat for France and the fall of that lesser Bonaparte known as Louis Napoleon. It also resulted in the temporary occupation of Paris by German troops, as well as the looting of the Louvre, in all a terrible loss of face for the French people, especially for the vaunted French army.

The army shopped around for a scapegoat. They found him in a Jewish captain named Alfred Dreyfus.

Dreyfus was as assimilated a Jew as any in Europe. A career army man, he was loyal, competent, stolid, unimaginative, and uninspiring—not the life of any party. He was a person of rare honor. It was this very person who was accused by the French General Staff of having sold military secrets to the German enemy, which presumably had made possible as well as explained the defeat of France by Germany. Documents were produced pointing unmistakably to the alleged criminal. Dreyfus was publicly tried, stripped of his military decorations, and exiled to Devil's Island. There were a handful of thinking men who suspected foul play in the entire procedure. Emile Zola, in his famous "J'Accuse!", publicly voiced his belief that Dreyfus was the victim of diabolical mendacity. There were others who voiced strong protest. Ultimately, the real criminal was exposed on the French General Staff, when Baron Esterhazy was proved to have forged the documents that had sent Dreyfus to years of harsh suffering on Devil's Island. In the end Dreyfus was exonerated.

DREYFUS AND HERZL

Theodor Herzl covered the story for the *Neue Freie Presse*. What he saw transformed him. He saw more than a travesty of justice, more than an innocent man stripped of his honor and dignity. He looked into the hate-filled eyes of the mobs on the streets of Paris, who chanted *"A Morte les Juifs!"* (Death to the Jews!) He read the venom in their eyes and the scales fell away from his own. It was under the impact of this awakening, and at an unbearable pitch of feverish excitement, that Theodor Herzl, in the course of one night in 1895, wrote his *Der Judenstaat*. This was to become one of the most influential of pamphlets and was to shake the foundations of the Jewish world.

Some of the *Judenstaat's* salient arguments must herewith be advanced. First, the Jews are not merely a religion, they are a nation, a people, said this ex-assimilationist. Second, for too many years they had sacrificed their blood and marrow upon the altars of other peoples. It was time for them to tend to their own vineyard. Therefore, a Jewish State was called for, a State over which the Jews themselves would exercise total control, a State in which the Jews would be the subjects *initiating* action in their own behalf, rather than the docile and passive objects that they had been for two thousand years of dispersion. Third, in order to establish a State, the Jews all over the world must be organized. Herzl called for the organization of a Society of Jews, the instrumentality for bringing a Jewish State into being. Fourth, the pragmatic Herzl, who knew that without funds hardly anything could be accomplished, advocated the creation of a Jewish Company that would raise funds from Jews all over the world for the purpose of carrying the great enterprise forward. Fifth, and most important in the Herzlian scheme, was the imperative of acquiring international sanction for the establishment of a Jewish State. It was toward this end that Theodor Herzl was to dedicate the lion's share of his energies in the few years of life left to him.

JUDENSTAAT AND WORLD JEWRY

The *Judenstaat* electrified world Jewry. Suddenly, as if they had been waiting for generations for the leader to arrive upon the scene, there was a tacit agreement by large segments of world Jewry that the leader was at hand and that his name was Theodor Herzl. Zionism was nothing new, even in the days of Herzl. There *were* Zionist organizations prior to Herzl, the *Hovevei Zion* (Lovers of Zion), for example, which had been organized by men like Leon Pinsker. There was a long history through the nineteenth century of attempted colonization projects in Palestine. But most of these *Hovevei Zion* societies were of the theoretical, parlor-strategy variety. Its members were incessant debaters whose activity generally began and ended over the tea kettle. Perhaps such talk—at once fervent and futile—was a necessary overture to the advent of Herzl. In any event, the theoreticians suddenly found a man who was ready and able to move into the arena of action. The general had arrived to galvanize a waiting but hitherto immobilized army.

Men of stature flocked to his banner, men like the novelist Israel Zangwill, author of *Children of the Ghetto*. Men like Max Nordeau, brilliant French journalist, who was to serve at Herzl's right hand for the balance of the latter's life. There was mystic magnetism to Herzl. He had an imposing, majestic, and handsome bearing as familiar to every Jew as is the gaunt, lugubrious image of Lincoln to every American. Perhaps a description by Richard Gottheil, a historian of Zionism, is here in order. He wrote: "Theodor Herzl was a beautiful man . . . with none of the effeminate associations attached to that adjective. He was a perfect picture of an inspired god. He had the easy grace of one who was born to glory. He had the image of an ancient Assyrian Prince." Herzl bespoke both vigor and conviction. Truly was he the ideal figure of a leader.

FIRST ZIONIST CONGRESS

Herzl was thence seized, possessed, and bedeviled by a solitary objective: to secure international approval for the Jewish state. Toward the achievement of that end, he roamed the earth perennially. He knocked upon the doors of kings, caliphs, kaisers, and career men on the international scene, until his knuckles were bloody by abrasion and the rest of his body prostrate.

Herzl's first major act was the calling of the first Zionist Congress. It was convened in Basle in 1897. It had *almost* convened in Munich, and thereby hangs a tale that needs to be told. Herzl thought the Congress should be held in Munich, an international city. All arrangements had been made for the purpose. But when the Jews of Munich heard what Herzl had in mind for their city, they fumed. They applied negative pressure upon the authorities. They did not wish their super-patriotism to the German Fatherland to be blemished by allowing in their midst a gathering of fellow Jews who were bent on the establishment of a Jewish national homeland. Some people said to Herzl: "Fight the sycophants! Whether they like it or not, confront them with the fact that they are Jews." Herzl said: "The sycophants do not deserve the Zionist Congress in their midst. We shall take it elsewhere." They took it to Basle, Switzerland.

Two hundred and four delegates from all over the world were assembled—tall and short, bearded and unbearded, "befringed" and "unbefringed," Orthodox and Reform (though few of the latter and not too many of the former), Jews from East and West, Lithuanians and Galicians (and that's a combination!), Sephardic and Ashkenazic, capitalists and proletarians—a motley crew of drifting souls who were tired unto death of drifting and determined unto life to begin steering instead. The historic significance was that it was the first time in two thousand years that a representative body of Jews had met to discuss its own destiny. For two thousand years other bodies had met, like the Fourth Lateran Council in 1215, called by Pope Innocent III, to discuss the Jewish "problem." There had been many conferences to discuss the Jewish problem. There had been only one thing lacking for two thousand years: a *Jewish* conference to discuss the Jewish problem. This was the irony of *galut*, of diaspora life. Herzl managed to assemble 204 Jews from all over the world and put them in a position to wrestle with their own destiny and seek means of reclaiming their honor and heritage.

The Congress began with an invocation "*Baruch atoh Adonoi Eloheynu Melech Ho-olam Shehecheyonu Vekiyimonu Vehigiyonu Lazeman Hazeh.*" "Blessed art thou, O Lord our God, King of the Universe, Who has sustained us in life, and brought us into a position to see this day." Dr. Joseph Klausner, who died thirty-six years ago, professor of Hebrew literature at the Hebrew University, was a youthful delegate to that first Zionist Congress. He once delivered a speech about the Herzl etched into his memory that day. Its refrain was: "There stood the prophet."

Still all was not harmony, even at the outset of that first Congress. It had its share of heartaches. Hostility issued from Jewish quarters. Many Orthodox Jews wanted no part of a Jewish State encompassed before the arrival of the Messiah. Zion, they argued, must be restored only through divine intervention. Human labors in its behalf are heresy. On the other hand, most Reform rabbis (whom Herzl had dubbed the "Protest-Rabbiner") argued that the newly gained opportunity to secure complete emancipation will come to grief because of the "unpatriotic" implications of Zionism. Thus, Herzl had it from both sides. Still he remained undeterred and undaunted.

OPPOSITION

Herzl chaired seven Zionist Congresses from 1897 through 1903. They were surfeited with pitfalls, disappointments, rifts and drifts, recriminations, and bitterness. But the work went on. It was under the influence of Herzl that several instruments that would ultimately bring about the Jewish State were forged. One was The Jewish National Fund, whose purpose was the purchase of land in Palestine for Jewish development and cultivation. The Jewish Colonial Foundation was another of the Herzlian instruments that ultimately brought about the creation of the Jewish State. But from the very beginning, Herzl had to contend with opposition. There was a very young man born in a little Russian town of Motele. Not quite dry behind the ears, tall, vigorous, scientific, he was a "Litvak" who had pursued and gained a first rate scientific education. He was to become an outstanding chemist in later years, after acquiring his doctorate in Switzerland. His name was Chaim Weitmann. He did not agree with Herzl at all, and for very good reason. He said to Herzl: "Why are you killing yourself seeking support from princes, kings, and sultans? Why so many interviews with the kaiser and his henchmen? Why an attempt to see the flunkies of the czar? Why try to pull strings to try to get an interview with the prime minister of England? Let's get down to something that we can *do* without having to rely upon prime minister, sultan, czar, or king. Let's build Palestine. Let's buy land there now. Let's try to create as many settlements as we can. Let's go down to the Negev and see what we can do there. Let's go down to the Dead Sea and see if we can wrestle successfully with its sunken phospates. Let's do something in Palestine; let's do intensive work within Palestine itself; let's stop waiting for permission." And Herzl said: "No, what is the good of investing time and effort there when the whole project may fail because the world will be against it? Let's first get a guarantee from the world of some kind, and then we can invest our energy in building the State."

The Weizmanns disagreed with Herzl, the Asher Ginsburgs disagreed with him, and so did others. History proved Herzl wrong and them right. If they had listened to Herzl and waited for the official piece of paper from some high-ranking personage in some palace or presidential mansion, Zionism would not have gone far. There would have been no colonization in Israel, there would have been no development of a potential Jewish State. The fact of the matter is that the State of Israel was being built from the moment the first Zionist Congress was convened. All other Zionist activity was simply designed to get a *de jure* approval for that which, as a matter of fact, *was* a fact. From 1897 and forward, *de facto*, one might say that a Jewish State of sorts began to take shape in Palestine. Colonization proceeded space. Land was bought and farmed. Swamps were dried. Streams of Jews, especially after the Kishenev pogroms of 1903, migrated to Palestine and ultimately created the State of Israel. Herzl was disappointed. The czars, the kaisers, and the sultans were much impressed with him. They accorded him very lovely receptions, but in the final analysis, they let him down. No guarantee of Palestine as the Jewish State, not even a whisper of such, was forthcoming. So Herzl began to think in terms of other territories. After all, he thought, if we can establish sovereignty anywhere at all, we may be able to control our own destiny there.

The British were ready to consider the Jewish colonization of Uganda in Africa. Herzl was earnest about Uganda. At the sixth Zionist Congress in 1902 he made a strong speech in favor of accepting the offer of the British government for the colonization of Uganda by Jews. The ultimate idea was its establishment as a Jewish State. There was turmoil at that Congress, followed by outright rebellion. The issue was debated for days and then the vote was taken. The powerful voice of Theodor Herzl carried the pro-Uganda forces to a 295–177 victory. As soon as the vote was announced, the 177 delegates in opposition rose in a body, walked out, and reconvened at another hall in Basle for the purpose of organizing a new Zionist party whose goal was the eternal Zion. They walked out, weeping. Herzl left the podium, rushed after them, accosted them in the hall, and pleaded with them to come back. He said: "I will use my influence to drop the Uganda idea. I have been taught a lesson, that the land of Israel is more than a matter of geography. It is a matter of history, of psyche, of religion. There can be no substitute for the Promised Land."

"IF I FORGET THEE, O JERUSALEM"

He had the inspiring thought to end that session of the sixth Zionist Congress with the words: "If I forget thee, O Jerusalem, let my right hand forget its cunning, let my tongue cleave to its palate if I remember thee not, if I place not Jerusalem at the very height of my joy." But the grief of that Zionist Congress hastened the death of Theodor Herzl.

Shortly thereafter, he had his first heart attack. He was to have three more. The mountain town in Austria to which he repaired on Friday, July 1, 1904, was visited by his mother. He suffered an attack on July 2. On July 3 in the morning, he appeared ghostly. He was smitten with pneumonia in both lungs and began to cough up blood. On July 3, 1904, just before midnight, Herzl was dead. One hundred thousand Jews attended the funeral of Theodor Herzl. They arrived from all over the world.

Herzl's body lay in Austrian soil for forty-five years. On August 17, 1949, an Israeli Air Force plane—an *Israeli* Air Force plane—took off from Lydda on its way to Vienna. His remains had been exhumed, were placed in a coffin, flown back to Tel Aviv, where they stayed overnight. One quarter of a million Jews in the space of four hours filed past the bier. Tel Aviv's population in 1949 was barely four hundred thousand. One may imagine how many of them were children. So it is in effect correct to say that all the Jews of Tel Aviv filed past that bier. The next day, he was brought for burial on a hill renamed Mount Herzl in Jerusalem. It was a very unusual ceremony of burial.

This I know. I was lucky enough to be in Israel at that time. It was one of those moments that will stay with me forever. No eulogies. Nobody spoke. A memorial prayer was chanted. Kaddish was recited. The funeral was attended by some three hundred representatives of the three hundred-odd kibbutzim and collective settlements in Israel. Each came with a shovelful of dirt from his or her kibbutz. Thus he was buried underneath 300 shovelfuls of earth, from all over the land of Israel. There was no loud weeping or wailing. I saw only a sea of silent tears, not tears of melancholia by any means, but tears of joy.

An old Jewess wearing a babushka and shawl was talking to herself, as Jewesses with babushkas are wont to do. I heard her say in Yiddish: "*Boruch Hashem*, Herzl has come home, thank the Lord." Nobody could have said anything more appropriate. This was the point. He did come home. For if any man ever deserved finally to be united with the soil of Zion, it was Theodor Herzl, the Jew of the twentieth century.

SELECTED BIBLIOGRAPHY

Allon, G. *Studies in Jewish History in the Times of the Second Temple, the Mishna and the Talmud*. Jerusalem: Hakibutz Hameuchad Publishing House, 1958.

Altmann, A. *Moses Mendelssohn*. University of Alabama Press, 1973.

————ed. *Studies in Nineteenth Century Jewish Intellectual History*. Waltham, Mass.: Harvard University Press, 1964.

Ashtor, E. *The Jews of Moslem Spain*, 3 vols. Philadelphia: Jewish Publication Society, 1973.

Baer, Y. *A History of the Jews in Christian Spain*, 2 vols. Philadelphia: Jewish Publication Society, 1966.

Baron, S. *A Social and Religious History of the Jews*, 18 vols. New York: Jewish Publication Society, 1952–1983.

————. *The Jewish Community*, 3 vols. Philadelphia: Jewish Publication Society, 1942.

Ben-Sasson, H. H., ed. *A History of the Jewish People*. Cambridge, Mass.: Harvard University Press, 1976.

Buber, M. *Tales of the Hasidim*, 2 vols. New York: Shocken Books, 1947–1948.

Charlesworth, J. H. *The Old Testament Pseudepigrapha*, 2 vols. New York: Doubleday and Co., 1988.

Cohen, G., *The Book of Tradition*. Philadelphia: Jewish Publication Society, 1967.

Cohen, I. *The Zionist Movement*. New York: Zionist Organization of America, 1946.

Cohen, M. A. "Reflections on the Text and Context of the Disputation of Barcelona," *Hebrew Union College Annual*. (1964) 35:157–192.

Dohm, C. W. *Concerning the Amelioration of the Jews*. Cincinnati: Hebrew Union College, 1957.

Dubnow, S. *History of the Jews*, 5 vols. South Brunswick, N.J.: Thomas Yoseloff, 1968–1972.

———. *History of the Jews in Russia and Poland*, 3 vols. Philadelphia: Jewish Publication Society, 1920.

Finkelstein, L. *Jewish Self-Government in the Middle Ages*. New York: Jewish Publication Society, 1924.

——— ed. *The Jews: Their History, Culture, and Religion*, 4 vols. Philadelphia: Jewish Publication Society, 1949.

———. *The Pharisees*, 2 vols. Philadelphia: Jewish Publication Society, 1946.

Friedlander, M. *The Guide of the Perplexed of Maimonides*. New York: Hebrew Publishing Co., n.d.

Ginzberg, L. *Geonica*, 2 vols. New York: Hermon Press, 1968.

Goitein, S. D. *A Mediterranean Society*, 6 vols. Berkeley and Los Angeles: University of California Press, 1967–1993.

Graetz, H. *History of the Jews*, 6 vols. Philadelphia: Jewish Publication Society, 1967.

Grant, M. *The Jews in the Roman World*. New York: Charles Scribners' Sons, 1973.

Grayzel, S. *The Church and the Jews in the 13th Century*. Philadelphia: Jewish Publication Society, 1933.

Halkin, A. and Hartman, D. *Crisis and Leadership: Epistles of Maimonides*. Philadelphia: Jewish Publication Society, 1985.

Herford, R. T. *The Pharisees*. London: MacMillan Co., 1924.

Herzberg, A. *The French Enlightenment and the Jews*. Philadelphia: Jewish Publication Society, 1968.

Hoenig, S. *The Great Sanhedrin*. Philadelphia: Jewish Publication Society, 1953.

Katz, J. *Out of the Ghetto: The Social Background of Jewish Emancipation.* Cambridge, Mass.: Harvard University Press, 1973.

Kamen, H. *The Spanish Inquisition.* New York: New American Library, 1968.

Klausner, J. *From Jesus to Paul.* New York: Menorah Publishing Co., 1943.

Laqueur, W. *A History of Zionism.* New York: Schocken, 1976.

Lieberman, S. *Hellenism in Jewish Palestine.* New York: Jewish Theological Seminary, 1950.

Margolies, M. B. *Samuel David Luzzatto: Traditionalist Scholar.* New York: Ktav, 1979.

———. *Syllabus for the Teaching of Jewish History.* New York: United Synagogue of America, 1985.

Malter, H. *The Works of Saadia Gaon.* Philadelphia: Jewish Publication Society, 1921.

Marcus, J. R. *The Jew in the Medieval World.* Cincinnati: Sinai Press, 1938.

Moore, G. F. *Judaism in the First Centuries of the Christian Era,* 3 vols. Cambridge, Mass.: Harvard University Press, 1971.

Nemoy, L., ed. *Karaite Anthology.* New Haven, Conn.: Yale University Press, 1952.

Netanyahu, B. Z., *Don Isaac Abravanel.* Philadelphia: Jewish Publication Society, 1953.

———. *The Origins of the Inquisition.* New York: Random House, 1995.

Neusner, J. *A History of the Jews in Babylonia,* 5 vols. Leiden: E. J. Brill, 1965–1970.

———. *A Life of Rabban Yochanan Ben Zakkai.* Leiden: E. J. Brill, 1962.

Newman, L. L. *Hasidic Anthology.* New York: E. J. Brill, 1934.

Parkes, J. *The Conflict of the Church and Synagogue.* New York: Atheneum, 1934.

Patai, R., ed. *The Complete Diaries of Theodor Herzl,* 5 vols. New York and London: Thomas Yoseloff, 1960.

———. *Encycolopedia of Zionism and Israel,* 2 vols. New York: McGraw Hill, 1971.

Poliakov, L. *The History of Antisemitism,* 5 vols., New York: The Vanguard Press, 1975.

Rivkin, E. *The Shaping of Jewish History.* New York: n.p., 1971.

Roth, C. *A History of the Marranos*. Philadelphia: Jewish Publication Society, 1974.

———. *The History of the Jews of Italy*. Philadelphia: Jewish Publication Society, 1946.

———. "The Dark Ages," in *The World History of the Jewish People*. New Brunswick, N.J.: Rutgers University Press, 1966.

Sachar, H. M. *The Course of Modern Jewish History*. New York: Knopf, 1958.

Schechter, S. *Studies in Judaism*, 3 vols. Philadelphia: Jewish Publication Society, 1908.

Scholem, G. *On the Kabbalah and its Symbolism*. New York: Schocken, 1965.

———. *Major Trends in Jewish Mysticism*. New York: Schocken Press, 1965.

———. *Sabbatai Sevi*. Princeton, N.J.: Princeton University Press, 1973.

Schorsch, I. *Jewish Reactions to German Anti-Semitism, 1870–1914*. New York and Philadelphia: Jewish Publication Society, 1972.

Sperber, D. *Roman Palestine (200–400)*. Ramat-Gan, Israel: University of Haifa, 1974.

Spiegel, S. *Hebrew Reborn*. Philadelphia: Jewish Publication Society, 1962.

Starr, J. *The Jews in the Byzantine Empire, 641–1204*. New York: Columbia University Press, 1939.

Steinsaltz, A. *The Essential Talmud*. New York: Schocken, 1977.

Stern, M. *Greek and Latin Authors on Jews and Judaism*, 3 vols. Jerusalem: The Israel Academy of Science and Humanities, 1974.

Strack, H. L. *Introduction to the Talmud and Midrash*. Philadelphia: Jewish Publication Society, 1972.

Stillman, N. *The Jews of Arab Lands*. Philadelphia: Jewish Publication Society, 1979.

Synan, E. A. *The Popes and the Jews in the Middle Ages*. Oxford: Oxford University Press, 1967.

Szajkowski, Z. *Jews and the French Revolutions of 1789, 1830, and 1848*. New York: n.p., 1970.

Twersky, I. *A Maimonides Reader*. New York: Behrman House, 1972.

Wallach, L. *Liberty and Letters: The Thoughts of Leopold Zunz*. London: Institute of East and West Library, 1959.

Wiener, M., ed. *Abraham Geiger and Liberal Judaism*. Philadelphia: Jewish Publication Society, 1962.

Weinryb, B. *The Jews of Poland*. Philadelphia: Jewish Publication Society, 1973.

Yadin, Y. *Judean Desert Caves*. Jerusalem: Hebrew University Press, 1960–1961.

Zeitlin, S. *The Rise and Fall of the Judean State*, 3 vols. Philadelphia: Jewish Publication Society, 1962–1978.

INDEX

ABOUT THE AUTHOR

Morris B. Margolies is Rabbi Emeritus of Beth Shalom Congregation of Kansas City, Missouri and a former professor of Jewish history at the University of Kansas. He was ordained by Yeshiva University, has a master's degree from the University of Chicago, and also holds a doctorate in Jewish History from Columbia University. Rabbi Margolies is the author of numerous books, including *Torah Vision*, *Ten Turning Points in Jewish History*, *The Jew of the Century*, *Syllabus for the Teaching of Jewish History*, and the reissued *Gathering of Angels*. He has also contributed both scholarly and popular articles to many periodicals. His major scholarly work is *Samuel David Luzzatto*, which was published in 1979. He was the last of the pupils of the preeminent Jewish historian, Salo W. Baron, to defend his doctoral dissertation with Baron presiding. Rabbi Margolies and his wife, Ruth, reside in Leawood, Kansas. They are the parents of Daniel, Jonathan, and Malka, and have five grandchildren.